CW00933129

Eric Eve is a Senior Research Fellow and Tutor in Theology at Harris Manchester College, Oxford. He has published a number of articles and other short pieces on various aspects of the Gospels and Jesus (usually related either to miracles or to the Synoptic Problem) and is also the author of *The Jewish Context of Jesus' Miracles* (2002).

THE HEALER FROM NAZARETH

Jesus' miracles in historical context

ERIC EVE

For Christabel

First published in Great Britain in 2009

Society for Promoting Christian Knowledge
36 Causton Street
London SW1P 4ST

Copyright © Eric Eve 2009

All rights reserved. No part of this book may be reproduced or
transmitted in any form or by any means, electronic or mechanical,
including photocopying, recording, or by any information storage and
retrieval system, without permission in writing from the publisher.

SPCK does not necessarily endorse the individual views contained in its publications.

Scripture quotations are either the author's own translation or are taken from
The Revised Standard Version of the Bible, copyright © 1946, 1952, 1957 and
1971 by the Division of Christian Education of the National Council of the
Churches of Christ in the USA. Used by permission. All rights reserved.

British Library Cataloguing-in-Publication Data
A catalogue record for this book is available from the British Library

ISBN 978–0–281–06001–6

1 3 5 7 9 10 8 6 4 2

Typeset by Graphicraft Limited, Hong Kong
Printed in Great Britain by Ashford Colour Press

Produced on paper from sustainable forests

Contents

Contents

Preface

In a very real sense this book has grown out of my researches as a doctoral student, which I formally completed nearly a decade ago. The immediate fruit of those labours was my first book, *The Jewish Context of Jesus' Miracles*, which had a great deal to say about the Jewish context but very little to say about Jesus' miracles. As an expanded version of my doctoral thesis it was very much a specialist academic work for other academics. Applying my research to a book actually about Jesus' miracles aimed at a wider audience seemed an obvious next step, but it was only with a visit from SPCK's commissioning editor Rebecca Mulhearn in April 2007 that this obvious next step turned from vague aspiration to concrete plan. This present book is the result.

There has been no shortage of books on the historical Jesus of late, including several on Jesus' miracles, but I hope this one will offer something distinctive. Rather than a detailed analysis of each miracle story in the Gospels I aim to give an overall account not only of the kinds of miracle Jesus may have performed but also of what their significance may have been in the context of his ministry. In doing so, I have endeavoured to combine different kinds of evidence – historical, cultural, literary and social-scientific – to arrive at an overall view. In this endeavour my debts to a variety of scholars will be readily apparent. I have also tried to build on my earlier work in *Jewish Context*, summarizing its salient conclusions for the wider audience of this book; I am grateful to Continuum for allowing me to reuse parts of my earlier work for this purpose.

My desire to reach a wider audience than I could with my earlier book meshed very nicely with SPCK's wish for a book aimed at undergraduates, clergy and laity who are taking their study of the New Testament a little further. Although this book is primarily targeted at this audience it will hopefully contain something of interest for other readers as well, not least fellow scholars. The approach taken attempts to steer a middle course between naive credulity and dogmatic scepticism, not to arrive at some 'absolute truth' but rather at an interpretation of the Jesus miracle tradition that should make sense on the basis of presuppositions widely shared among modern Westerners, regardless of their faith stance. Only in the last few pages do I offer some tentative suggestions for the theological implications of my historical conclusions.

Preface

I should like to thank everyone who has helped make this book possible: especially Rebecca Mulhearn, who commissioned it in the first place, and who has been patiently responding to my many queries ever since, as well as offering a number of helpful comments on the draft, David Sanders, my eagle-eyed copy-editor, and Rima Devereaux, who saw the book through into production.

Eric Eve
Harris Manchester College, Oxford

Abbreviations

//	Synoptic or other parallel text
1–2 Apol.	Justin, *First & Second Apology*
2DH	Two Document Hypothesis
Abraham	Philo, *On the Life of Abraham*
Acts Pil.	*Acts of Pilate*
Ag. Ap.	Josephus, *Against Apion*
Alleg. Interp.	Philo, *Allegorical Interpretation*
ANRW	*Aufstieg und Niedergang der römischen Welt: Geschichte und Kultur Roms im Spiegel der neueren Forschung* (ed. H. Temporini and W. Haase; Berlin, 1972–)
Ant.	Josephus, *Jewish Antiquities*
Apoc. El.	*Apocalypse of Elijah*
b.	*Babylonian Talmud*
Ber.	*Berakhot*
BETL	Bibliotheca ephemeridum theologicarum lovaniensium
BJRL	*Bulletin of the John Rylands Library*
BTB	*Biblical Theology Bulletin*
BTNC	Black's New Testament Commentaries
BZNW	Beihefte zur Zeitschrift für die neutestamentliche Wissenschaft
CBQ	*Catholic Biblical Quarterly*
CD	Damascus Document
Dial.	Justin, *Dialogue with Trypho*
EG	*Egerton Gospel*
Ep. Apos.	*Epistula Apostolorum*
ExpTim	*Expository Times*
FRLANT	Forschungen zur Religion und Literatur des Alten und Neuen Testaments
Giants	Philo, *On Giants*
Gos. Thom.	*Gospel of Thomas*
H.E.	Eusebius, *Ecclesiastical History*
HTR	*Harvard Theological Review*
ICC	International Critical Commentary
IEJ	*Israel Exploration Journal*
JAAR	*Journal of the American Academy of Religion*

Jan. Jam.	*Jannes and Jambres*
JBL	*Journal of Biblical Literature*
JSHJ	*Journal for the Study of the Historical Jesus*
JSJ	*Journal for the Study of Judaism in the Persian, Hellenistic and Roman Period*
JSNTSup	Journal for the Study of the New Testament: Supplement Series
JSP	*Journal for the Study of the Pseudepigrapha*
JSPSup	Journal for the Study of the Pseudepigrapha: Supplement Series
JTS	*Journal of Theological Studies*
J.W.	Josephus, *Jewish War*
L.A.B.	Pseudo-Philo, *Liber antiquitatem biblicarum* (Book of Biblical Antiquities)
LCL	Loeb Classical Library
Life	Josephus, *Life*
LXX	Septuagint
m.	*Mishnah*
Me'il.	*Me'ilah*
Moses	Philo, *On the Life of Moses*
NCB	New Century Bible
NovTSup	Novum Testamentum Supplements
NTS	*New Testament Studies*
Num. Rab.	*Numbers Rabbah*
OTP	James H. Charlesworth (ed.), *The Old Testament Pseudepigrapha* (2 vols; New York: Doubleday, 1983–5)
QG	Philo, *Questions and Answers on Genesis*
RevQ	*Revue de Qumrân*
SBLDS	Society of Biblical Literature Dissertation Series
SBT	Studies in Biblical Theology
Sib. Or.	*Sibylline Oracles*
SNTSMS	Society for New Testament Studies Monograph Series
STDJ	Studies on the Texts of the Desert of Judah
t.	*Tosefta*
Ta'an.	*Ta'anit*
T. Levi	*Testament of Levi*
T. Naph.	*Testament of Napthtali*
WUNT	Wissenschaftliche Untersuchungen zum Neuen Testament
ZNW	*Zeitschrift für die neutestamentliche Wissenschaft*
ZPE	*Zeitschrift für Papyrologie und Epigraphik*

Dead Sea Scrolls

Dead Sea Scrolls are typically referenced with a siglum mmQnn, where Q denotes Qumran, mm (the number preceding the Q) denotes the cave in which the manuscript was discovered (the caves being numbered 1 to 11), and nn (the number following the Q) is a sequential catalogue number (each cave having its own sequence). Occasionally the sequential catalogue number is replaced with a brief abbreviation of the name, so that, for example, 1QapGen is the scroll of the *Genesis Apocryphon* discovered in Cave 1.

Introduction

All four Gospels depict Jesus as a miracle-worker. In all four Gospels he heals some people and raises others from the dead. In all four Gospels he feeds a crowd numbering five thousand with a few loaves and fishes. In three of them he walks on the sea, in three he stills a storm with a word of command, and in three he casts out demons. In one of them he even turns several gallons of water into wine. For some people such deeds are central to who Jesus is, a proof that he was the incarnate Son of God. For others, they are a stumbling-block, a clear indication that the Gospels are historically unreliable. For many they are a puzzle: did Jesus perform the marvellous deeds attributed to him? If so, what does that tell us about him? If not, why are they reported in the Gospels? Were the Evangelists (the authors of the Gospels) incapable of telling fact from fiction, or did they simply not care? Or are we to assume that they were indeed telling the unvarnished truth, however incredible it may seem to us?

Posing the questions in such stark terms may be unhelpful. It encourages us to adopt a polarized either–or mentality: either the Gospels are totally reliable and Jesus did everything they say he did, or they are totally unreliable and should be dismissed as utter fantasy. This is not how we assess most historical reports; if we read a secular historical source or a modern newspaper we expect there to be a mixture of truth and error, fact and fiction, honest reporting, polemic, propaganda, wishful thinking, rhetorical exaggeration, genuine insight and skewed perception. At least, we should expect that if we are to read at all critically, and we should also expect the proportions of those ingredients to vary considerably from text to text. What we should not do is to approach them with a predetermined attitude either of naive credulity or of dogmatic scepticism. Reading critically means reading with discernment, questioning what we read, and being open to different possibilities about both meaning and truth.[1]

For several reasons, this turns out to be particularly difficult when reading the Gospels for information about the historical Jesus. For one thing, Jesus is a figure of central religious importance for nearly everyone interested in carrying out historical research on him, in that most researchers are likely to be either broadly sympathetic or broadly hostile to Christian

---

[1] See John Barton, *The Nature of Biblical Criticism* (Louisville: Westminster John Knox, 2007).

claims about Jesus and are most unlikely to be totally neutral towards him. Doing research on the historical Jesus is different from doing research on the historical Augustus or even the historical Napoleon, since there is so much more investment in the results.

Another major difficulty is the nature of the sources. We shall be looking at the sources more closely in Chapter 4, but it is clear that our main source of information about Jesus remains the canonical Gospels. What sort of texts are these? It is a commonplace in biblical scholarship to say that they are not straightforward historical reports but rather documents of faith, designed not principally to inform people about the historical figure of Jesus of Nazareth but to proclaim the good news about him. They are documents written from particular theological perspectives in support of particular points of view. But while such observations are undoubtedly correct, they leave many questions open. No one would accuse either the ancient Roman writer Tacitus or the Jewish author Josephus (say) of writing purely unbiased history from a neutral viewpoint designed only to report facts; few if any ancient historians (or modern ones) ever did that. A work like Josephus' *Jewish Antiquities* clearly has a theological agenda. That does not prevent scholars from classifying the writings of Tacitus and Josephus as ancient historiography and reading them accordingly. There is far less agreement on how the Gospels should be classified, although there has been no shortage of suggestions, including: history, *bioi* (the ancient equivalent of biographies) and romances (the ancient equivalent of novels). But even if we were to settle, say, on the Gospels as *bioi* that would not in itself tell us how historically reliable they are. It might tell us that the Evangelists in some sense intended to talk about a real figure of the past, and not merely a religiously inspiring myth, but it does not tell us what liberties they felt justified in taking with the facts in the interests of their message, or whether they intended everything they wrote to be taken literally, or whether they thought of truth primarily in factual, empirical terms (as we tend to do) or primarily in theological terms (so that the truth of the Gospels would lie less in the accuracy of their factual reporting than in their conveying the significance of Jesus). Also, we cannot be sure that ancient authors such as the Evangelists would draw the lines between myth and history or between truth and embellishment precisely where we would draw them.

This issue arises most sharply in relation to the miracle stories. The more spectacular ones, such as walking on the sea, stilling the storm, or turning water into wine, look theologically motivated and historically dubious. Such accounts raise a particularly acute test case for the historical worth of the Gospels (that is, their worth as sources of historically reliable information about the flesh-and-blood figure Jesus of Nazareth). If all the miracle stories are pious inventions, then we should have to conclude that the Gospels are virtually valueless as historical sources. They might incidentally contain a few snippets of Jesus' teaching, and they might still be correct in asserting that he died by crucifixion, but that would be all. All four Evangelists represent miracle-working as integral to Jesus' ministry, and if that was not the case, then their portraits of Jesus are fundamentally misleading. If the Gospels have so falsified the picture of Jesus as to make him out to have gained a widespread reputation as a miracle-worker when he was no such thing, then the historical Jesus is forever lost to us; even if the real Jesus were somehow encoded in such greatly distorted accounts, there would be no way we could know it.

Yet it is not a case of all-or-nothing, of either unquestioning acceptance or extreme doubt. It is perfectly possible to believe that the portrayal of Jesus as a miracle-worker has a sound basis in the real Jesus of Nazareth while also thinking that the portrayal has grown in the telling. A great deal of historical-Jesus scholarship does just this. But this means we have to exercise critical discernment towards the miracle stories, judging some to be more historically reliable than others, and this raises further problems. On the face of it miracle stories, by their very nature, are accounts of highly unusual or even seemingly impossible events. How is one to assess the historical plausibility of such events, given that a normal procedure in critical historical research is to be sceptical of reports that purport to tell of highly implausible events? Is there any method that can be applied that does not end up being a thinly disguised form of arguing in a circle, whether a credulous circle or a sceptical one?

The best place to start is to clarify what we mean by 'miracle'. In common speech it is sometimes used very loosely to express the speaker's surprise, as in, 'It's a miracle! John actually bought a round of drinks today!' Conversely, it is often used in a precise sense to refer to an alleged breach of the laws of nature, so that something is not regarded as a 'real miracle' unless any natural explanation is ruled out and the event appears physically impossible (like walking on water). Often it is used with religious overtones: Jesus walking on the water is a miracle; Waldo Mysterio walking on the water is a magician possessed of unusual psychic powers; a visiting alien from the Andromeda Galaxy walking on the water is employing highly advanced technology; only the first is counted as a miracle since, of these three, only the first is perceived to have any religious significance. 'Miracle' is also employed as a quasi-literary classification;

when we talk about the Gospel miracle stories we are often referring to a set of incidents involving exorcism (casting out demons), other forms of healing, or more extraordinary deeds that have been conventionally labelled 'miracles' regardless of any detailed investigation of their scientific plausibility.

The element of surprise is common to all these notions of miracle (if something did not look in the least surprising it would be pointless to call it a miracle), but otherwise there is the danger of confusing two quite different concepts. One of these is the notion of a breach of the laws of nature. This is problematic in itself since it is unclear in such a definition whether 'laws of nature' means how nature actually behaves, or how it ought to behave according to the best scientific theories currently available. The latter of these is probably the more useful way of taking it, since we may not in fact know how nature actually behaves under all circumstances, and on the former way of taking it a breach of the laws of nature would have to mean an occasion when nature does not actually behave as it actually behaves, which is simply incoherent. But even in the second sense a breach of the laws of nature is not necessarily a miracle. If the Tower of London were suddenly to turn into a block of green cheese or the Pentagon to launch itself into orbit for no apparent reason, we might well conclude that the laws of nature (in the second sense) had been breached, but if such events lacked any apparent significance they would be just bizarre events, not miracles. This type of event is thus better given some name other than 'miracle'; this book will use the term 'scientific anomaly' or just 'anomaly'.

Some of the biblical miracle stories, such as the sun standing still for Joshua, or Jesus walking across the Sea of Galilee, would also constitute anomalies if they occurred, but this cannot be the defining characteristic of biblical miracle stories. For one thing, the biblical authors had no notion of scientific anomaly, since they did not share our idea of 'laws of nature', which presupposes a concept of nature as a self-sufficient closed system. 'Nature' in this sense is a post-Enlightenment way of avoiding the term 'creation', and it is the latter term that would be closer to biblical thought. Of course the ancients, and the biblical authors among them, were well aware that creation usually behaved in a broadly regular fashion, otherwise they would not have been surprised by apparent exceptions to that regularity, but the biblical authors generally supposed that the regularity of creation was due to the governance of its Creator, not to some necessity inherent in the system. Again, the ancients tended to work with a notion of causality different from ours. We tend to think primarily in terms of mechanism, while they tended to think primarily in terms of agency; while we would ask, 'What could have caused this?' they would ask, 'Who could have done this?' Against this background, a miracle would be something beyond normal human capacity, so that the answer to 'Who could have done this?' would have to be someone superhuman. Superhuman agencies might themselves be divided into the divine and the demonic; an extraordinary deed performed by demonic power would be magic; an extraordinary deed performed by divine power would be a miracle.

This does not mean that the ancients lacked any concept of mechanism, any more than we lack any concept of agency. The issue is rather which type of causality is regarded as more interesting in the face of an unusual event, and the point is that most ancients, including the biblical authors, would tend to be more interested in the question, 'Which agent caused this?' than 'What mechanism caused this?' Answers to these two different types of question are not mutually exclusive. If the telephone rings in my room and someone asks, 'Why is that phone ringing?' I could with equal accuracy reply either 'Because someone wants to speak to me' (the agency explanation) or 'Because an electric current is passing through its bell' (the mechanism explanation). Which explanation is the more appropriate would depend on the purpose of the question.

For the biblical authors a miracle was not primarily a breach in the natural order; it was primarily a significant act of God. It would, of course, have to be a suitably surprising, unusual act of God, or there would be no reason to regard it as a miracle; a miracle is an event that excites wonder through being strikingly unexpected. So perhaps the best definition of a miracle in the biblical sense is 'a strikingly surprising event, beyond normal human capacity, believed to be a significant act of God'. Such an act could be worked either directly on God's initiative, or in response to prayer, or through some suitable intermediary such as a prophet or an angel.

'Miracle' is in any case our word. None of the Evangelists employed a Greek word that is exactly equivalent in semantic range to the modern English 'miracle'. The words the Evangelists used include *dunameis* (powerful deeds), and *sēmeia* (signs; used in a positive sense by John and usually in a negative sense by Matthew, Mark and Luke). They avoid the word *thauma* (wonder), which might come a little closer to the English 'miracle', although they use the verb *thaumazein* (to wonder), to describe people's reactions to both miraculous and non-miraculous events. The 'biblical' definition of 'miracle' just given is thus a modern proposal for describing the defining characteristics of miracle stories in the Bible (and in other ancient Jewish writers) rather than a definition of any term actually used by any of the Evangelists.[2]

It follows that a biblical miracle need not be a scientific anomaly in the modern sense. It is enough that people, or at least some people, thought it miraculous at the time, that is that they regarded it as a religiously significant and strikingly surprising act of God. Many of the Gospel healing stories come into this category; at this remove we simply do not possess the information to decide whether they describe anomalous events or not (the sufferers' symptoms are not described with sufficient accuracy, nor are the healed sufferers now available for medical examination). As we shall see, the same applies to the exorcism stories. People at the time may well have thought that Jesus' unusually effective ability to heal people and cast out demons showed that God was at work through him, in which case these deeds would have been regarded as miraculous, but they cannot now be ruled out as impossibly anomalous, and equally, they cannot be hailed as anomalous 'proofs' of Jesus' divinity.

Some of the reported miracles of Jesus would have constituted anomalies had they actually occurred, such as walking on the sea, stilling the storm, turning water into wine, and feeding large crowds from impossibly meagre resources. These will be addressed in more detail in Chapter 7, but it should be clear from the outset that they raise particular problems. In particular, they invite the question whether, given that the Gospels record such seemingly impossible events, there is any reason for supposing they contain any historical truth at all. Could they not be dismissed as pure myth, or religious fantasies with only the most tenuous link to real history? A position of total (or near-total) scepticism towards the value of the Gospels as historical sources is perfectly coherent, in that it can be held without self-contradiction. Neither can it be conclusively disproved. Whether it is particularly plausible is another matter; to many it might seem just as plausible, if indeed not a good deal more plausible, to suppose that the Gospels represent Jesus as being a certain type of figure because that was the type of figure he was.

Either Jesus was a sufficiently noteworthy figure to make some impression on the traditions about him, or he was not. If he was not, then it is far from clear why anyone should have bothered with him after his death, or, indeed, why the Gospels and the rest of the New Testament should ever

---

[2] T. Alec Burkill, 'The Notion of Miracle with Special Reference to St Mark's Gospel', *ZNW* (1959), 33–48.

have been written. That is not to say that it would be impossible to devise theories that account for the rise of beliefs about Jesus that bore no relation to a historical Jesus of Nazareth, but there seems to be no reason to prefer such theories unless the seemingly more obvious explanation (namely that Jesus of Nazareth was a person of some consequence) has been tested to destruction and found wanting. But if Jesus was a person of sufficient note to make a definite imprint on the traditions about him, then there must be some limits to how far those traditions could distort the kind of person he was, and in particular, what he was noteworthy for. Some stories might grow in the telling, and others might be wholly apocryphal, but there would be some limit to the kind of thing that could be asserted. We can imagine all sorts of fanciful and exaggerated stories being told about such famous characters as Napoleon Bonaparte and Ludwig van Beethoven, but it is most unlikely that any of them would make Beethoven out to be a great general or Napoleon a great composer. Thus, if the four Gospels all make Jesus out to have been a notable miracle-worker, then it is highly plausible that this was a significant part of what the historical Jesus was in fact renowned for (even if we must suppose that his miracles were in fact restricted to healing and exorcism).[3] We shall therefore take this (namely that Jesus was a notable healer-exorcist) as our working hypothesis.

We can go on to test this working hypothesis by seeing if a reasonably plausible account can be given of Jesus as a miracle-worker on the basis of the evidence available. Such an account must not only explain how such a figure might have fitted into his cultural and historical context, but also what kind of significance might have attached to him, and how it might have contributed to other beliefs about Jesus. If such an account decides that certain miracles are too anomalous to be regarded as historical events, then it will need to give some account of how they nevertheless came to be included in the Gospels.

It must be stressed that any such account will be hypothetical. Books on the historical Jesus sometimes create the impression that they are working deductively, sifting the evidence to arrive at more or less certain conclusions about what Jesus said and did and what he meant by what he said and did. Such an approach is illusory; some notion of the historical

---

[3] A comparable argument in relation to the Jesus tradition as a whole is made by Dale C. Allison, *Jesus of Nazareth: Millenarian Prophet* (Minneapolis: Fortress, 1998), 45–51; cf. Morton Smith, *Jesus the Magician* (London: Victor Gollancz, 1978), 8–16 and James D. G. Dunn, 'Eyewitnesses and the Oral Jesus Tradition', *JSHJ* 6.1 (2008), 85–105 (86, 102).

Jesus must already exist to guide the selection of facts and the kind of interpretation given to them. The kind of conclusions we should like to be able to draw about the historical Jesus are underdetermined by the evidence, and no historical enquiry can proceed without some theoretical framework to guide it. If one or more theories about Jesus' miracle-working can be constructed that seem at least reasonably plausible (both in terms of internal consistency and in fitting such data as we have), then we have some reason to trust the viability of our initial working hypothesis (that the historical Jesus made a sufficient impact on the traditions about him that the impact can still be discerned in the Gospel accounts). To the extent that we can come up with a theory that seems more plausible than any of its competitors, we can feel some confidence that things actually happened more or less that way.

The rest of this book will be an exercise in trying to construct such a theory about the miracles of Jesus. The next two chapters will examine what miracle might have meant to Jesus' contemporaries. Chapter 3 will then explore what social-scientific approaches such as cross-cultural anthropology can contribute to our understanding of healing and exorcism. Chapters 1 to 3 will thus fill in much of the cultural background that any account of Jesus' miracles needs to fit.

The next stage will be to look at the evidence specific to Jesus. Chapter 4 will survey the potential sources for Jesus' miracle-working activity. The Gospels are obviously one source, so the main question to be considered is whether there are any others. The answer will be mainly negative, except to the extent that we shall find little if anything that contradicts the view that Jesus was a miracle-worker, and much that is at least consistent with it. Chapter 5 will take a closer look at the Gospel of Mark. There are a number of reasons for focusing on this particular Gospel. On the assumption of Markan priority, Mark is the earliest Gospel and is the main source for the portrayal of Jesus as miracle-worker in at least two of the other Gospels (Matthew and Luke). He also has the highest concentration, and arguably the most interesting use, of miracle stories.

Chapter 6 will sketch in the particularities of Jesus' historical situation and then attempt to use the findings of the previous five chapters to suggest how healings and exorcisms functioned in the ministry of the historical Jesus. To the extent that this account is plausible we shall have succeeded in vindicating our initial working hypothesis. But one major step in the argument will still remain, namely what to make of the so-called 'nature miracles' (such as the feeding stories and sea miracles) that do not fit into the account given in Chapter 6. This will be the subject of Chapter 7. Finally, Chapter 8 will draw the threads of the discussion together and suggest their implications both for historical-Jesus research and for theology.

1

Miracle in Israel

According to the Gospels, Jesus performed most of his miracles in and around Jewish Palestine, especially Galilee. Assuming this reflects the ministry of the historical Jesus, it would be helpful to know what other Jews from around the same time thought about miracles. Although the Jewish scriptures were the most widely influential texts among Second Temple Jews, they are far from the only witnesses to what Jesus' Jewish contemporaries thought, and it is in any case important to enquire how the scriptures were read and interpreted. Moreover, Second Temple Judaism was highly diverse, so we should not assume that all Jews thought the same. (Strictly speaking the Second Temple period stretches from the return from exile and subsequent rebuilding of the temple, around 540 BCE, to the destruction of the temple in 70 CE; in practice the term is often used with the latter half of this period particularly in mind).

We shall start by looking at the range of sources available. From there we shall go on to review what these sources can tell us about how various Jewish groups at the time of Jesus understood miracle, and what other miracle-working figures were around. In the following chapter we shall explore demonology and exorcism and then take a quick look at miracles in the wider Graeco-Roman setting. We shall then be in a position to summarize the significance of miracles in Jesus' milieu.

Sources

The importance of the scriptures for first-century Jews is evident from the large number of surviving works that interpret or build upon them. Notable among these are the various examples of 'rewritten Bible'. These are works that retell the story of all or part of the Old Testament, often with expansions, contractions, shifts of emphasis, and explanatory additions. Such works are important, both for showing how some Jews interpreted their scriptures, and as an indication of what extra-scriptural traditions about biblical narratives were current at the time.

The single most important source of information about first-century Judaism is Josephus, a Jewish historian roughly contemporary with the Evangelists. The most notable example of rewritten Bible is his *Jewish Antiquities*. The first half of this work is a retelling of the narrative books of the Old Testament in the form of Hellenistic history, while the remainder continues the story of the Jewish people down to the outbreak of the Jewish War in 66 CE. Other notable examples of rewritten Bible are found in the works of Philo of Alexandria, a contemporary of Jesus who produced many volumes of allegorical interpretation of Scripture (mainly the Pentateuch), but also wrote more straightforward accounts of the careers of Abraham, Joseph and Moses; Philo's *Life of Moses* is particularly rich in material on the miraculous. Both these authors wrote in Greek with the wider Graeco-Roman world clearly in view. Pseudo-Philo's *Book of Biblical Antiquities* (*L.A.B.*) seems aimed more at fellow Jews. It was almost certainly originally written in Hebrew, perhaps shortly after the destruction of the Second Temple in 70 CE, and retells the biblical narrative down to the death of King Saul (Pseudo-Philo is so called because *L.A.B.* was once erroneously attributed to Philo of Alexandria, and though that has long been recognized as a mistake the identity of *L.A.B.*'s author has remained unknown). An earlier book called *Jubilees* narrates the contents of Genesis and the opening chapters of Exodus. *Jubilees* has little to say on miracle, but is of interest for its demonology. A fragmentary text known as the *Genesis Apocryphon*, discovered at Qumran (a site in the Judaean desert near the Dead Sea), seems also to belong to this genre, and is noteworthy for an account of an exorcism or healing performed by Abraham. The fragments of *Artapanus* (preserved mainly in documents written by the early church historian Eusebius of Caesarea) also retell the life of Moses, in a way that highlights the miraculous and makes Moses into a quasi-magician.

In addition to texts that retell some part of the biblical narrative there are those that reflect upon it. Noteworthy in this respect are the two great wisdom books from the Apocrypha (roughly speaking, the collection of books included in ancient Greek and modern Roman Catholic Bibles but not regarded as canonical by Jews or Protestants): the Wisdom of Solomon and the Wisdom of Ben Sira (also known as Sirach or Ecclesiasticus). The latter recalls a number of miracles associated with prophets in its 'praise of famous men'; the former presents a distinctive interpretation of the exodus miracles through a series of comparisons between the plagues visited on the Egyptians and the blessings afforded the Israelites in the wilderness.

In some texts the link with the biblical text is quite tenuous. For example, the *Book of the Watchers* in *1 Enoch* 1—36 takes off from the story of the 'sons of God' who mate with human females in Genesis 6.1–6 and alludes to the story of the flood, but it largely goes its own way. It has nothing to say about miracle as such, but its account of the origin of evil is important for appreciating at least one strand of Jewish demonology, a strand that is also found in *Jubilees* and some of the Dead Sea Scrolls (the name given to those texts discovered at Qumran between 1947 and 1979).

The texts just surveyed provide the most important sources for what Jesus' Jewish contemporaries thought about miracles and demonology, although other texts from the Apocrypha and Pseudepigrapha (ancient Jewish and Christian writings that were never regarded as canonical) provide some additional evidence. It is worth noting that most of the surviving texts are the products of the relatively well educated urban elite. The various views of Judaism that they give us are thus, in the main, likely to be variants of the 'great tradition', Judaism as seen from the perspective of the well-to-do. The views of peasant farmers, fishermen and craftsmen in rural Galilee (for example) are scarcely represented, yet theirs is likely to be a perspective closer to that of the original Jesus tradition. We must therefore be careful about assuming that the significance of miracles in the ministry of the historical Jesus can be read off purely from surviving Jewish texts. These texts have a built-in upper-class bias that may differ from the point of view both of Jesus and of most of his earliest followers. They are nevertheless the best evidence we have for how Jesus' contemporaries understood miracle.

Concepts of miracle

It was pointed out in the Introduction that 'miracle' is an elastic term, and it is certainly no less so when applied to what first-century Jews thought. No Greek or Hebrew term exactly corresponds to the modern English word 'miracle', although there are a number of terms in both languages that are often used to denote events that we should describe as 'miracles'. The Hebrew scriptures, for example, use *'oth* ('sign'), *mopeth* ('portent') and *pele'* ('wonder'), and this vocabulary is often reflected in that of first-century Jewish writers.[1] Other Jewish writers use a more elaborate

---

[1] See C. F. D. Moule, 'Excursus 1: The Vocabulary of Miracle' in C. F. D. Moule (ed.), *Miracles: Cambridge Studies in their Philosophy and History* (London: Mowbray, 1965), 235–8.

vocabulary. Josephus, for example, in addition to using the biblical *sēmeion* (sign) to denote miracles often uses the term *paradoxon* (something contrary to expectation), but seems shy of using *thauma* (wonder) of the miraculous. Philo, on the other hand, is happy to apply *thauma* to miracles, and even happier to use compounds formed from *thauma* (especially forms of *thaumatourgeō*, to work a wonder).

Philo was a writer thoroughly versed not only in the Jewish scriptures but also Greek philosophy. For Philo, a miracle is a special act of God (perhaps performed through a human intermediary) that accomplishes something otherwise impossible. As such, it is an objective proof of divine action that should be apparent even to a hostile observer. In Philo's narration of the biblical story, miracles tend to be sharply demarcated from other types of event. He is aware that educated readers may be sceptical about miracles, but stoutly defends them on the grounds that everything is possible to the God who created all that is. In this, Philo comes closest of all ancient Jewish writers to the notion of miracle as an anomaly made possible only by God's omnipotence.

The only other Jewish writer who appears at all reflective on the nature of miracle is Josephus. For Josephus, a miracle is a strikingly surprising event that believers perceive as an act of God. Unlike Philo, Josephus allows a certain epistemological ambiguity to miracles; although hostile observers ought to acknowledge God's power in the miraculous, it is at least possible for them not to do so, and instead to attribute the miracle to magical or natural causes. In Josephus, miracles tend to be but the most spectacular examples of God's providence, and there is a corresponding tendency for the truly miraculous to shade into the merely providential. Like Philo, Josephus is aware that miracle stories may stretch the credulity of some of his readers. He deals with this by repeatedly saying that on such matters each reader is entitled to his own opinion, but he nevertheless makes it clear that he believes in the miracles he narrates. His appeal, however, is not so much to God's omnipotence as to his providence and to the reliability of the biblical account. In common with Philo, he occasionally suggests a rationalizing explanation of a miracle where one occurs to him, but this nowhere undermines his conviction that miracles are real acts of God.

The Wisdom of Solomon, which may have originated from a milieu not unlike Philo's, engages with popular philosophy, and even offers a quasi-philosophical explanation of miracle in terms of the interchange of the properties of the elements (Wisdom 19.18; cf. *QG* 4.51). Yet there is no consistently used miracle vocabulary, and very little in the text that explicitly indicates that its author saw miracles as a distinct class of events. Instead, miracles are implicitly indicated by the structure of the comparisons mentioned above, in which Egyptian plagues are contrasted with wilderness blessings.

Pseudo-Philo reproduces the biblical language of signs, portents and wonders (*signa, prodigia* and *mirabilia* in the surviving Latin translation). These words tend to appear in summaries rather than in the detailed description of miraculous events, although it is often apparent that the summaries are referring to miracles. Pseudo-Philo is particularly concerned to stress the divine control of events, and the *prodigia* and *mirabilia* he describes are usually striking divine interventions that punish the guilty or protect the righteous. Pseudo-Philo seems more interested in the effectiveness of these divine acts than in how surprising they are. He sometimes uses *signum* simply as another term for such events, but he also uses it in the more precise sense of a sign that reveals God's will to a faithful enquirer. Such signs may or may not be miraculous: they include water becoming both fire and blood for Gideon (*L.A.B.* 35.7) but also Sisera merely asking for a drink of water (*L.A.B.* 31.5).

The second half of the Moses fragment in *Artapanus* relates a number of miracles in connection with Moses (based mainly on the Exodus account), but it is debatable whether Artapanus' Moses should be described as a miracle-worker or a magician. Elsewhere it becomes increasingly difficult to discern a concept of miracle that is not simply a reflection of the way we choose to identify miracles in the text. It would be fair to say, though, that miracles in Jewish texts are more often significant acts of power than mere wonders, though there must of course be something marvellous about them for them to count as miracles. There is also a strong tendency for miracles to be seen in personalistic terms: God does not so much intervene in the course of nature as exert his authority over creation; his miracle-working power is more like political power than physical power. Thus, for example, in the course of describing God's power to work miracles, Philo remarks, 'God has *subject* to Him, not one portion of the universe, but the whole world and its parts, to minister as slaves to their master for every service that He wills' (*Moses* 1.201), while Wisdom 19.6 speaks of creation complying with God's *commands* in the performance of miracles. In a similar vein the Gentile centurion at Matthew 8.5–13 // Luke 7.1–10 expects Jesus to be able to cure his servant by word of command, since he too is a man both in and under *authority*. In Mark's Gospel, onlookers remark on Jesus' authority to command not only unclean spirits (Mark 1.27), but also the wind and sea (Mark 4.39–40).[2]

Types of miracle

The Synoptic Gospels, that is Matthew, Mark and Luke, give the impression that Jesus' miracles were predominantly healings and exorcisms, with just a handful of nature miracles (for a list of these miracles see p. 145). With the exception of the cursing of the fig tree (Mark 11.12–14, 20–25; Matthew 21.18–22), they are all beneficial in their effect, and in no case is any human being harmed or punished. Some of these miracles resemble those narrated in the Old Testament. The feeding stories (Mark 6.30–44; 8.1–9 and parallels), located in the wilderness, loosely recall the gift of manna in the wilderness, though they far more closely resemble the story of Elisha feeding a hundred men from twenty loaves in 2 Kings 4.42–44. The sea miracles (Mark 4.35–41; 6.45–52 and parallels) may vaguely resemble the crossing of the Red Sea (Exodus 14), but unlike that event, they involve no drowning of pursuing enemies and no spectacular division of the waters (features which tend to be stressed in nearly every Jewish retelling of this story). In fact, the two sea miracles resemble other Old Testament passages rather better: for example the stilling of the storm at Jonah 1.4–16 or the account of the seafarers' deliverance in Psalm 107.23–32.

In Jewish Second Temple literature as a whole, however, healing stories are rare and stories about exorcism are even rarer, while spectacular miracles of national deliverance, punishment of the wicked, provision in need, or accreditation of God and his messengers are far more common. In part this reflects the types of miracle contained in the Old Testament, in which there are no exorcisms, few healing stories, but quite a few miracles of the other types. Since a great deal of the Second Temple literature involving miracle is a retelling of or reflection on parts of the Old Testament, it is not surprising that this pattern should be reproduced. It is noteworthy, however, how some writers play down even the few Old Testament healing miracles there are. For example, Josephus reproduces most of the miracles in the Old Testament (and describes several post-biblical miracles as well), but he omits several healing miracles from the

---

[2] For a fuller discussion of the texts surveyed in this section, see Eric Eve, *The Jewish Context of Jesus' Miracles* (JSNTSup, 231; Sheffield: Sheffield Academic Press, 2002), chs 2–5, 8–9.

Elisha cycle and makes nothing of such healing miracles as might be gleaned from the Pentateuch (such as the remission of Miriam's leprosy at Numbers 12.9–16, the deliverance of the Israelites from the fiery serpents at Numbers 21.6–9 or Aaron's intercession against the plague at Numbers 16.41–50). On the other hand, Josephus does provide one of the few exorcism stories in Second Temple Jewish literature (*Ant.* 8.45–9), and does allude to exorcistic practices elsewhere (*Ant.* 6.166–9; *J.W.* 7.185). Philo is even less interested in miracles of healing and exorcism. Although he frequently mentions healing in both physical and spiritual senses, he never once narrates a healing miracle, and since he dismisses popular demonology as superstition, he shows no awareness of exorcism.[3]

Like Philo, neither Pseudo-Philo nor *Jubilees* narrates any healing miracles. Ben Sira, on the other hand, does allude to some of the healing (and resuscitation) miracles associated with Elijah, Elisha and Isaiah. There is a healing story of sorts in the version of Abraham's and Sarah's dealings with the king of Egypt in the *Genesis Apocryphon* (a fragmentary text found among the Dead Sea Scrolls). Another Sarah is delivered from a demon in the book of Tobit, whose eponymous hero is cured of blindness, but here the procedure looks more medical than miraculous. The comparisons in the Wisdom of Solomon pick up on a couple of the instances of deliverance from disease and death in the wilderness narratives of Numbers (Wisdom 16.5–14; 18.20–25). Finally, 2 Maccabees 3.31–34 narrates the miraculous recovery from injuries of one Heliodorus at the request of the high priest, though what he recovers from is a miraculous assault that punishes him for raiding the temple funds.

Elsewhere in Second Temple literature there are virtually no healing stories (exorcism is a separate issue which will be dealt with in the next chapter). Jesus thus stands out in the Jewish literature of the time as being the only person about whom a whole series of healing miracle stories are told. To find anything comparable in Jewish tradition we have to go back to the stories about Elijah and Elisha in 1 and 2 Kings, but even then Jesus is credited with far more healings than any other figure (especially when

---

[3] For further reading on miracles in Josephus and Philo, see G. MacRae, 'Miracle in the *Antiquities* of Josephus' in C. F. D. Moule (ed.), *Miracles: Cambridge Studies in their Philosophy and History* (London: Mowbray, 1965), 129–47; Otto Betz, 'Miracles in the Writings of Flavius Josephus' in Louis H. Feldman and Gohai Hata (eds), *Josephus, Judaism and Christianity* (Leiden: Brill, 1987), 212–35; Erwin R. Goodenough, *An Introduction to Philo Judaeus* (New Haven: Yale University Press, 1940); Harry Austryn Wolfson, *Philo*, vol. 1 (rev. edn; Cambridge, MA: Harvard University Press, 1968); David Lenz Tiede, *The Charismatic Figure as Miracle Worker* (SBLDS, 1; Missoula, MT: SBL, 1972); and Eve, *Jewish Context*, chs 2–3.

one takes into account such summary passages as Mark 1.32–34; 3.9–12; 6.5, 53–56, which suggest that Jesus performed many more healings than are narrated in detail).

This may in part be due to the social location of the different texts. Ben Sira and Philo both regard professional physicians as the normal channels of God's healing power (Sirach 38.1–15; *Alleg. Interp.* 3.178). No doubt they belonged to a stratum of society that had access to professional medical care. The Gospels, on the other hand, are among the few texts surviving from antiquity that take seriously the concerns of the great majority of ordinary people, who were living more or less at subsistence level. It is unlikely that such people would be able to afford professional physicians, but they would certainly get ill and require treatment, which they would have to find elsewhere (as we discuss further in Chapter 3).

The miracles that attract the most attention in surviving Jewish literature are those associated with the exodus and, to a lesser extent, the conquest. Again this is largely a reflection of the distribution of the miracle stories in the Old Testament. Thus, for example, roughly 40 per cent of the miracles narrated in the first half of Josephus' *Antiquities* (the part that retells the Old Testament narrative) are connected with Moses. Again, the main work in which Philo narrates miracles is his *Life of Moses*, which naturally concentrates on the exodus and wilderness events. Elsewhere Philo concentrates his biblical exegesis mainly on the Pentateuch. He thus focuses mainly on the miracles of the exodus (and subsequent wilderness wanderings), although he also deals with some miracle stories from Genesis. Although the Wisdom of Solomon alludes to one or two miraculous incidents in Genesis (the destruction of Sodom and Gomorrah and Lot's wife turning into a pillar of salt, Wisdom 10.6–7), it is precisely with the miracles of the exodus and wilderness wanderings that it is concerned in Chapters 11—19. And when Wisdom 5.17–23 describes the mighty acts that God *will* do on behalf of his people, this is very much in terms that recall the exodus miracles (cf. Wisdom 19.22). Since the only substantial fragment of *Artapanus* that survives is that on Moses, the miracles he narrates are also mainly connected with the exodus. Likewise the *Exagōgē* of Ezekiel the Tragedian is a rewriting of the exodus story in the form of a drama, so once again it is precisely the miracles associated with the exodus that it describes.

Although the Dead Sea Scrolls from Qumran contain virtually nothing that looks like a nature miracle, such allusions as it does contain are to the exodus. There is a brief reference to the Red Sea crossing in the *War Scroll* (1QM 11.10), in the context of recalling God's past interventions in the hope that he will do something similar in the eschatological (end-time) war to come (for a fuller discussion of the meaning of 'eschatological' see pp. 129–30 below). There is also a general admonition to 'remember his miracles which he did in Egypt' at 4Q185 1.15. *Jubilees* (a work that seems quite close in thought to the Qumran sectarians) shows very little interest in miracles; it narrates the miracles of the exodus in very abbreviated form, but these are the only miracles it narrates at all.

There are exceptions to this focus on the exodus miracles. Pseudo-Philo narrates the biblical story from Adam to the death of Saul, but though he includes the miracles associated with Moses, he spreads his miracle stories evenly throughout the course of his narrative. Although the exodus is paradigmatic for Pseudo-Philo, his interest in good leadership and God's continuing control of events makes him unwilling to confine either to a particular period in Israel's history. Ben Sira's 'praise of famous men' (Sirach 44—50) mentions miracles associated with several figures, but is remarkably restrained in his account of Moses; this may be because he is more interested in Aaron as the founder of the Levitical priesthood. Moreover, there are many Second Temple Jewish texts that make no mention of any miracles of any kind, or, even when they do, make no mention of the exodus.

Nonetheless, it remains true that it is the miracles associated with Moses, the exodus and the wilderness wanderings that receive the greatest attention in Jewish literature. This is hardly surprising, since it was precisely the exodus to which Jews looked back as the paradigmatic saving event in their history. It is also that part of their story that contains some of the more memorable and spectacular biblical miracles, such as the ten plagues visited on Egypt, the deliverance of the Israelites and drowning of Egyptians at the Red Sea, and the miraculous provision of manna, quails and water in the wilderness. There is also evidence to suggest what one might in any case suspect, namely that it was precisely these events that many Jews regarded as the model for future deliverance. We have already seen this in connection with the Wisdom of Solomon at Wisdom 5.17–23 and the reference to the Red Sea crossing in the War Scroll from Qumran. It also seems to have been presupposed in the miracles promised by many of the sign prophets described by Josephus (who will be discussed below). Although the description of the end-time events in apocalyptic works tends to include what we would think of more as cosmic upheavals than as miracles, references to the exodus events also occur. The book of Revelation is partly indebted to the ten plagues of Egypt for its description of the end-time woes. The roughly contemporary

Jewish apocalypse *4 Ezra* (= 2 Esdras 3—14) envisages an eschatological exodus for the ten lost tribes, in the course of which 'the Most High performed signs for them, and stopped the channels of the river until they had passed over' (*4 Ezra* 13.44), a miracle that recalls both the crossing of the Red Sea and Joshua's crossing of the Jordan prior to the conquest of the land. *2 Baruch*, an apocalypse that may be dependent on *4 Ezra*, envisages the dawn of the messianic age as a time of miraculous plenty when 'the treasury of manna will come down again from on high' (*2 Baruch* 29.3–8). Although the uncharacteristically militant outburst at Sirach 36.1–17 makes no explicit mention of the exodus, the language in which the appeal for divine intervention is couched ('Show signs anew, and work further wonders; make thy hand and thy right arm glorious') certainly resembles that in other passages where the exodus events are recalled (e.g. Baruch 2.11; Deuteronomy 4.34; 5.15; 7.19; 9.29; 11.2–3; 26.8; 2 Kings 17.36; Psalm 136.12; Jeremiah 32.21).

The exodus miracles are not the only miracles of divine deliverance and defeat of enemies recalled, just as Second Temple Jewish literature contains stories of miraculous provision besides those of the wilderness period. Both the *Jewish Antiquities* of Josephus and the *Biblical Antiquities* of Pseudo-Philo recall the miracles that helped the Israelites against their foes in the time of Joshua and the Judges (e.g. *Ant.* 5.27, 60, 205; 6.27; *L.A.B.* 30.5; 31.2; 32.10–11). Several texts refer to the deliverance of Jerusalem through the Angel of the Lord slaying 185,000 Assyrian troops in the time of King Hezekiah (1 Maccabees 7.41; 2 Maccabees 8.19; 15.22; Sirach 48.21; *Ant.* 10.21; cf. 2 Kings 19.35–36).

Because Josephus includes the whole scope of biblical history in his works, it is he who supplies the greatest number of stories of miraculous provision outside the exodus account. This includes the provision of food for Elijah and the miraculous productions of oil (*Ant.* 8.319, 322, 349; 9.48–50), but, interestingly, not Elisha's feeding of 100 men from 20 barley loaves (2 Kings 4.42–44). It also includes several stories of provision of water, through a private spring that appears specially for Samson (*Ant.* 5.303) and frequently by means of unexpected rainfall (*Ant.* 8.346; 14.22, 390; 18.285).

Although there are few stories of deliverance from illness (or demons) in Second Temple literature, there are several stories of deliverance from other kinds of danger, many of them again occurring in Josephus' retelling of the Old Testament. These include the stilling of the storm that saves Jonah's fellow passengers when Jonah is cast into the sea and Jonah's subsequent safe arrival on land (*Ant.* 9.212–13), Daniel's three friends

emerging unscathed from the furnace (*Ant.* 10.214) and Daniel surviving
his incarceration in the lions' den (*Ant.* 10.258–62). Josephus also narrates some stories of quasi-miraculous deliverance from after the biblical
period, such as King Herod's providential escape from a building that
collapses in Jericho (*Ant.* 14.455; *J.W.* 1.331), and the Alexandrian Jews'
rescue from being trampled by elephants at Ptolemy Physcon's command
(*Ag. Ap.* 2.53–4; cf. 3 Maccabees 5—6). Pseudo-Philo's retelling of part
of the Old Testament includes a number of deliverance miracles not
found in the biblical account, such as Abraham's rescue from a furnace
(*L.A.B.* 6.15–18) and the rescue of faithful men punished by the idolatrous Jair (*L.A.B.* 38.3–4).

Miracles that deliver individuals, faithful groups, or Israel as a whole
from danger can also have the effect of punishing those who threaten them.
The most obvious examples of this are the ten plagues inflicted on Egypt
to force Pharaoh to let the people go, and the subsequent drowning of the
pursuing Egyptians in the Red Sea (Exodus 7—14). The story of the wilderness wanderings provides several more spectacular examples such as the
punishment of Korah's rebellion (Numbers 16). Josephus goes on to narrate a number of punishment miracles, perhaps the most spectacular of
which is the sequence of events following King Uzziah's attempt to offer
a sacrifice (*Ant.* 9.225): not only is the king smitten with leprosy, as in 2
Chronicles 26.19, but there is a great earthquake that splits the temple
and causes half the western hill to break off and roll round (cf. Zechariah
14.4–5). Philo mentions no miracles later than the Pentateuchal period,
but he does allude to several punishment miracles in Genesis. Thus,
for example, he regards the punishment of Sodom and Gomorrah as a
punishment for wickedness (*QG* 4.51), although also as an act of mercy
towards the rest of humanity, to prevent the earth becoming depopulated
through the spread of their homosexual practices (*Abraham* 136–41). Philo
likewise recalls how God punished the Egyptian king 'with all manner
of scarce curable plagues' for abducting Abraham's wife (*Abraham* 92–8),
although Philo also stresses God's mercy in protecting Abraham and
Sarah. Pseudo-Philo narrates a number of punitive miracles, such as the
punishment of the idolatrous Micah (*L.A.B.* 44.9; 47.12) and of those who
tried to burn Abraham (*L.A.B.* 6.15–18) and the faithful non-idolaters
persecuted by Jair (*L.A.B.* 38.3–4). Wisdom 11—19 is built round a series
of contrasts between the wilderness blessings granted to the Israelites
and the punishments that befell the Egyptians. Divine punishments are
also described in a few other texts. At *Jan. Jam.* 26a the sorcerer Jannes
opposes Moses' signs and wonders by replicating them and is duly struck

with an ulcer. At 3 Maccabees 2.21–24 God punishes Ptolemy for trying to enter the Holy of Holies. Alcimus is paralysed and then dies in agony for ordering the sanctuary wall torn down (1 Maccabees 9.54–57), while Antiochus is seized with an unremitting pain in his bowels for planning to vent his anger on the Jews of Jerusalem (2 Maccabees 9.5).

Sometimes, then, it is general wickedness that is punished; more often it is opposition to God's people, God's messengers, or God himself (through idolatry, disobedience or disrespect). It hardly needs saying that this type of miracle is entirely absent from the Gospel account of Jesus (the withered fig tree is hardly an exception, for there no human being is punished), although it can occasionally be found in Acts (Acts 5.1–11; 13.4–12).

Quite a few miracles in Second Temple literature do not correspond neatly to any of the types so far discussed, but the only other category that need concern us is that of evidential miracles (i.e. miracles designed to supply evidence of divine intent). These scarcely appear at all outside the pages of Philo, Josephus, and Pseudo-Philo, and they function differently for each of these three authors. In the first half of Josephus' *Antiquities* the word *sēmeion* tends to be restricted to a (usually miraculous) sign that authenticates a prophet or other spokesman of God. In Pseudo-Philo, a *signum* is often a (not necessarily miraculous) sign by which a faithful enquirer may discern God's will. Although miracles in Philo occasionally accredit God's messenger (usually Moses), they are more often divine acts that offer direct proof of God's will and being. Sirach 48.23 alludes to the sign of the reversing sun given to Hezekiah, but elsewhere in Second Temple literature signs and wonders are just as likely to be used by the wicked in order to mislead (*Jan. Jam.* 26a; Beliar at *Sib. Or.* 2.167; 3.63–70; Aod the magician at *L.A.B.* 34).[4]

Miracle-working figures

Jesus was not the only Jewish exorcist around at the time (we shall look at exorcism more closely in Chapter 3), and there were very likely other Jewish healers, though we hear little about them, but the evidence for other miracle-working figures in the Israel of Jesus' day is quite sparse.

---

[4] For a fuller discussion of miracle in the texts discussed here see Eve, *Jewish Context*, chs 2–9, and John P. Meier, *A Marginal Jew: Rethinking the Historical Jesus*, vol. 2: *Mentor, Message, and Miracles* (New York: Doubleday, 1994), 535–601.

Apart from exorcists the only known candidates for contemporary miracle-workers are the charismatic holy men depicted in rabbinic literature and the sign prophets reported by Josephus.

Charismatic holy men

The view has become popular (due mainly to the work of Geza Vermes) that around the time of Jesus there was a class of charismatic miracle-working holy men, with whom Jesus may usefully be compared. These charismatic holy men are taken to be exemplified especially by Honi the Circle Drawer and Hanina ben Dosa. Honi the Circle Drawer was famous for making rain in the first century BCE. Hanina is said to have lived in the first century CE, and to have worked a number of miracles, including some healings which resemble those attributed to Jesus (see below).[5]

When one examines the evidence more closely, however, the picture begins to dissolve. The earliest rabbinic evidence for Honi is contained in the Mishnah (at *m. Ta'an.* 3.8), which was probably committed to writing around 200 CE.[6] The Mishnah is a collection of rabbinic rulings on *halakah*, i.e. laws and their interpretation, and is not at all concerned with historiography. Its story of Honi is often read as though it presented him as a powerful miracle-worker, able to persuade God to produce just the right kind of rain to order, but in fact it does just the opposite. The text portrays Honi as an over-confident boaster who tries to blackmail God by standing in a circle and refusing to budge until God sends rain. God makes fun of Honi by sending rain that is too light, then too heavy, then moderate in quality but too long in duration, so that Honi is unable to stop it (making him a little like the sorcerer's apprentice). A rabbi is given the last word by commenting on Honi's childish behaviour. The function of the story may be to exalt the learned rabbi at the expense of the charismatic, and it thus perhaps represents a response to a perceived challenge to rabbinic authority from charismatic miracle-workers.[7] To be sure, in the much later Babylonian Talmud (a massive expansion of the Mishnah with a great deal of 'commentary' which was set down in writing perhaps around 500 CE) the Honi material is reworked and he has been transformed into a respectable rabbi with a pair of humble rain-making

---

[5] Geza Vermes, *Jesus the Jew* (2nd edn; London: SCM Press, 1983), 69–82.

[6] For an explanation of rabbinic literature, see Günter Stemberger, *Introduction to the Talmud and Midrash* (2nd edn, ed. and tr. Markus Bockmühl; Edinburgh: T. & T. Clark, 1996).

[7] Jacob Neusner, *Judaism: The Evidence of the Mishnah* (Chicago: University of Chicago Press, 1981), 307–28.

grandsons. This, however, reflects a much later situation (perhaps that of the fifth or sixth centuries CE) when miracle-working had become more respectable among rabbis. It gives us no reliable historical information about a Second Temple figure.

Josephus also describes an Onias (*Ant.* 14.22–4) who is a righteous man who successfully prayed to God to end a drought. Josephus mentions this to explain why one faction in the civil war between Aristobulus and Hyrcanus asks Onias to pray against the other; Onias refuses and is stoned to death by an angry Jewish mob. If Josephus' Onias is the same as the Mishnah's Honi (as seems likely), then he seems to have been notable as a devout man of prayer, who on one occasion successfully prayed for rain. This hardly makes him a charismatic miracle-worker comparable to Jesus.

Neither Josephus nor any other contemporary source mentions Hanina ben Dosa. The earliest records of Hanina appear in the Mishnah and Tosefta (a second collection of *halakah*, dating from around the mid-third century CE), but these Tannaitic (first- to early third-century CE) traditions tell us very little about him. According to *m. Sotah* 9.15, 'When R. Hanina b. Dosa died the men of deed ceased,' which suggests that Hanina was notable for his deeds, but does not indicate what those deeds were. From *m. Ber.* 5.5 we learn that Hanina could tell from the feel of his prayer whether the sick person he prayed for would recover or not, but this does not tell us whether Hanina's prayers for the sick were especially efficacious. A passage about reciting prayer at *t. Ber.* 2.30 states that on one occasion Hanina did not interrupt his recitation of the prayer even when a poisonous lizard bit him; Hanina remained unharmed but the lizard was later found dead (by Hanina's students). How Hanina's students identified the lizard as the same one that bit their master is left unexplained, a problem that indicates the legendary nature of the tale (as does the theme of the righteous person surviving a poisonous bite, cf. Acts 28.3–6). In any case, the story does not make Hanina out to be a miracle-worker, but instead emphasizes God's care for the devout.

There are several miracle stories associated with Hanina, but these come from much later sources, the two Talmuds (especially the Babylonian Talmud). To be sure, many of the traditions that appear in the Talmuds could be a great deal earlier than their final redaction, but the nature of the Hanina material leaves plenty of room for doubt that it comprises reliable information about a historical figure of the first century CE. This can be seen in the development of the story about Hanina and the poisonous lizard; according to *b. Ber.* 33a Hanina rids a village of a poisonous reptile by deliberately placing his heel over its hole; when the reptile emerges it bites Hanina and dies. As in the case of the earlier story in the Tosefta, the witnesses declare, 'Woe to the man whom a lizard meets, but woe to the lizard which R Hanina b. Dosa meets!' The story has clearly grown in the telling.[8]

Most of the other stories about Hanina look equally dubious. Hanina is journeying home when it begins to rain. He exclaims to God that he is in distress while the rest of the world is at ease. The rain stops. On his return home he exclaims that he is at ease while the rest of the world is in distress. It starts to rain again. On another occasion Hanina's wife throws smoke-making material onto her oven to hide the fact that she has nothing to cook for the Sabbath. When a prying neighbour calls to investigate, the oven is miraculously filled with loaves. Hanina's wife complains about their poverty. Hanina prays and a hand appears offering him a golden table leg. But he then dreams that in the world to come he would be eating at a two-legged table while the pious would be eating at three-legged tables; he therefore prays for the golden leg to be taken away again, and it is. Hanina's daughter is upset because she poured vinegar instead of oil into the Sabbath lamp. Hanina tells her that he who commanded the oil to burn will also command the vinegar to burn, and the vinegar burns all day. Hanina's goats are accused of causing damage. He says that if they are guilty, bears will devour them, but if they are innocent they will each bring a bear home on their horns, which they duly do. Ikku, a neighbour of Hanina, was building a house but found that the beams were not long enough to reach the walls. At Hanina's orders the beams lengthened to protrude one cubit on either side (*b. Ta'an.* 24b–25a).

Given that these stories appear in writing some four or five centuries after the events they purport to describe, and that the Babylonian Talmud is not primarily interested in recording history, and that the events described look more than a little improbable, to treat this material as providing reliable information about a first-century miracle-worker is about as plausible as using mediaeval Arthurian legends to uncover the historical Merlin. The stories in the Talmud were recorded for didactic rather than historiographical purposes, and as such tell us a great deal more

---

[8] Baruch M. Bokser, 'Wonder-Working and the Rabbinic Tradition: The Case of Hanina ben Dosa', *JSJ* 16 (1985), 42–92.

about the concerns of Babylonian rabbis in the Amoraic period (from the early third century to about 500 CE) than about first-century history. As in the case of Honi, these stories about Hanina appear to reflect a period where miracle-working has become not only respectable but even desirable among rabbis, provided it is done on rabbinic terms. The figure of Hanina is accordingly developed into a miracle-working rabbi to exemplify the new ideal (much as mediaeval ideals of chivalry were read back into the stories about a fifth-century warlord called Arthur).

This is apparent not least in the two healing stories attributed to Hanina which most resemble the healing stories of the Gospels. These stories occur together at *b. Ber.* 34b. The first bears several points of resemblance to the story of Jesus healing the Capernaum official's son (John 4.46–54). In the Hanina story the son of R. Gamaliel falls ill and the rabbi sends two scholars to Hanina to ask him to pray for him. Hanina does so, and then announces that the fever has left him, going on to explain, 'If my prayer is fluent in my mouth, I know that he is accepted: but if not, I know that he is rejected' (precisely the words attributed to Hanina in the Mishnah, at *m. Ber.* 5.5, outside the context of a healing story). When the scholars return to Gamaliel they find that the fever had left his son at precisely the moment Hanina said. In the second story Hanina is studying the law with the great rabbi Johanan ben Zakkai when the rabbi's son falls ill. Hanina prays at the rabbi's request and the son recovers. The rabbi's wife then wonders whether Hanina is greater than the rabbi; ben Zakkai counters that, on the contrary, he, the rabbi, is like a nobleman before the king (who can only appear in accordance with court protocol), while Hanina is like a favoured servant (who is more free to beg favours from the king). These stories associate Hanina with two great first-century rabbis, thus bringing him firmly within the rabbinic fold. But the second story also firmly subordinates the miracle-worker to the rabbi. Hanina is expressly ben Zakkai's *pupil*, and the rabbi roundly asserts his superiority at the end of the story. The Gamaliel story may have developed out of the earlier saying at *m. Ber.* 5.5 (see p. 14 above), perhaps under the indirect influence of the similar story in John's Gospel (John 4.46–54; cf. Matthew 8.5–14 and Luke 7.1–10), which had been around for several centuries by the time the Babylonian Talmud was committed to writing.

Hanina ben Dosa probably existed, but the earliest traditions about him suggest a devout man of prayer who coined a few pithy sayings, rather than a charismatic miracle-worker, and it is almost impossible to form any clear picture of the historical Hanina. The traditions about Hanina and

Honi thus cannot form a reliable basis for postulating a class of charismatic holy men contemporary with Jesus.[9]

The sign prophets

Josephus describes a number of figures operating in Jewish Palestine from the time of Pontius Pilate to the destruction of Jerusalem in 70 CE, all of whom promised some kind of sign and appeared to claim some kind of prophetic function. There are few grounds for doubting the existence of these 'sign prophets', though we must be wary of the way Josephus assesses them. We should also keep in mind that 'sign prophet' is a modern scholarly label employed as a convenient designation for a number of figures that appear in the pages of the *War* and the *Antiquities*, not a category employed by Josephus. It may also be that Josephus makes some of these figures appear more alike than they actually were by shaping his accounts of them according to a standard form, since he wishes to paint them all as false prophets.

The earliest of these 'sign prophets' was the Samaritan who appeared when Pilate was governor (*Ant.* 18.85–7). This man led a mob to Mount Gerizim promising to reveal the sacred vessels that Moses had allegedly deposited there. Further followers made their way to join this armed gang, but Pilate intercepted them with a force of infantry and cavalry, killing many of them in battle and taking many prisoners.

Perhaps the two most notable 'sign prophets' are those also alluded to (in a somewhat confused way) in Acts. Theudas (*Ant.* 20.97–9; cf. Acts 5.36) persuaded a large group of people to follow him to the Jordan river, which he promised to part to allow them to pass over. This plan was forestalled by the Roman procurator Fadus sending a squadron of cavalry, which duly killed Theudas and some of his followers, and captured many others. The Egyptian false prophet (*J.W.* 2.261–3 // *Ant.* 20.169–72; cf. Acts 21.38) led a large body of people from the desert to the Mount of Olives. According to the *War* he proposed to enter Jerusalem and overwhelm the garrison by force, but according to the *Antiquities* the Egyptian first planned to make the walls of Jerusalem collapse at his command. Felix, the Roman governor on this occasion, once again employed the standard Roman method of controlling the followers of these would-be prophets, despatching a large force of infantry

---

[9] For further critiques of Vermes's use of Honi and Hanina, see Eve, *Jewish Context*, 272–95; Meier, *Marginal Jew*, 2.581–8; W. Scott Green, 'Palestinian Holy Men: Charismatic Leadership and Rabbinic Tradition' in *ANRW* II.19.2, 619–47.

and cavalry which duly slew some of the mob and captured many others, though on this occasion the Egyptian himself escaped.

Most of the other 'sign prophets' are described in less detail. While Felix was governor a group of 'impostors and deceivers' led a mob into the wilderness with promises of 'signs of liberation' (*J.W.* 2.258–60) or 'unmistakable marvels and signs' (*Ant.* 20.167–8). Felix once again sent troops to suppress them. Festus took similar action when the 'dupes of a certain impostor' followed him into the wilderness on the basis of promises of 'salvation and rest from troubles' (*Ant.* 20.188). Two other figures often counted among the sign prophets seem to be a bit different. As Titus' troops were successfully storming Jerusalem, a would-be prophet led a large crowd to the temple court where, he said, they would receive the signs of their salvation; they were in fact put to death by the Roman soldiers, some perishing as a result of a fire, others killed by the soldiers while trying to escape the flames (*J.W.* 6.283–7). Finally, a story about one Jonathan the weaver set in Libya after the suppression of the revolt in Palestine looks suspiciously like an attempt by Josephus to assimilate a political rebel to the earlier sign prophets (*J.W.* 7.437–50), especially since the parallel account at *Life* 424–5 refers to Jonathan purely as an insurrectionist.

If one excludes the last two figures, the remainder do seem to have a number of features in common. They lead people to a specific place; they generally offer (but apparently fail to produce) a sign; they promise this-worldly salvation; they are without exception suppressed by Roman arms; they operate within Jewish Palestine; and they are generally associated with the wilderness. Some caution must be employed in interpreting this data, especially since Josephus is as much spin doctor as historian, and he is particularly looking for lunatic fringe groups on which to pin the blame for the rebellion against Rome. Again, as Rebecca Gray has pointed out, there may be several reasons for retiring to the wilderness and one should not assume that they were the same in each case.[10]

That said, it does appear that most of these figures were aiming to re-enact some episode of the exodus–conquest tradition. The Egyptian's promise to make the walls of Jerusalem collapse at his command recalls the similar story about Joshua and the walls of Jericho (Joshua 6.1–21). Theudas' promise to part the Jordan recalls both the crossing of the Red Sea (Exodus 14) and Joshua's crossing of the Jordan to invade the

---

[10] Rebecca Gray, *Prophetic Figures in Late Second Temple Jewish Palestine: The Evidence from Josephus* (Oxford: Oxford University Press, 1993), 137.

promised land (Joshua 3). The Samaritan explicitly hoped to find sacred vessels associated with Moses, and his followers were armed, as if in preparation for a holy war. The other figures are described more vaguely, but the association of signs and wonders with the wilderness seems most naturally to recall the exodus period. Moreover, the Romans evidently regarded all these movements as sufficiently threatening to require a substantial body of troops to suppress them. It is thus most probable that these would-be prophets saw themselves as performing a Moses- or Joshua-like role, re-enacting some aspect of the exodus–conquest tradition for the liberation of Israel from Rome. This lends further support to our earlier conclusion that it was miracles of the exodus tradition that excited the most interest among Jesus' Israelite contemporaries. It further shows that this interest had popular currency, and was not simply a feature of texts produced by the literate elite. It also shows the readiness of large numbers of people to follow a plausible prophet who could promise spectacular signs.[11]

Types of miracle-worker

Although we have found little evidence of other actual Jewish miracle-workers from around the time of Jesus (given that the sign prophets seem not to have delivered on their promise of miracles), we should investigate to what kind of figures miracles tend to be attributed in Second Temple literature. In nearly every case, it is God who is the real miracle-worker, though he may sometimes choose to act through a human intermediary or in response to the prayer of a human intercessor.[12] In the literature of his time, Jesus is almost unique in being portrayed as a human miracle-worker (in the full sense of being the apparent source of the miraculous power he employs) about whom a number of miracle stories are told.

God is often portrayed not only as the ultimate source of miraculous power but as the sole agent of the miraculous. Most of the miracles in Philo are performed without the aid of any human intermediary, apart

---

[11] On the sign prophets see further Gray, *Prophetic Figures*; P. W. Barnett, 'The Jewish Sign Prophets AD 40–70: Their Intentions and Origin', *NTS* 27 (1981), 679–97; Richard A. Horsley and John S. Hanson, *Bandits, Prophets, and Messiahs: Popular Movements in the Time of Jesus* (New Voices in Biblical Studies; Minneapolis: Winston Press, 1985); Gerd Theissen, *Miracle Stories of the Early Christian Tradition* (ed. John Riches, tr. Francis McDonagh; Studies of the New Testament and Its World; Edinburgh: T. & T. Clark, 1983), 243–5; Eve, *Jewish Context*, 296–325.

[12] These distinctions are borrowed from Werner Kahl, *New Testament Miracle Stories in their Religious-Historical Setting: A Religionsgeschichtliche Comparison from a Structural Perspective* (FRLANT, 163; Göttingen: Vandenhoeck & Ruprecht, 1994), 76.

from Moses and Aaron. Pseudo-Philo again attributes most of the miracles he narrates directly to God without any human intermediary, the chief exception once again being Moses. Many other miracles are attributed to God throughout Second Temple literature, while several others are attributed to angels acting as his agents.

Some human agents are associated with the miraculous in Second Temple texts. In Josephus' *Antiquities* roughly 60 per cent of the miracles are associated with the prophets (including Moses, with whom roughly 40 per cent of the miracles are associated). Ben Sira also tends to associate miracles and prophets. In Philo, Moses and Aaron are the *only* human figures who play a role in the miraculous. Artapanus, Ezekiel the Tragedian and Demetrius the Chronographer also focus on the miracles associated with Moses, though this is, of course, a direct result of the subject-matter of their surviving works. Overall, the impression created is that many Second Temple Jews would most naturally associate miracle-working first with the figure of Moses, and second with miracle-working prophets like Elijah and Elisha, but would tend to see these figures as people through whom God works or who successfully pray to God to intervene, rather than as workers of miracles in their own right.

This would explain why some people apparently thought Jesus was a prophet (e.g. Mark 6.15; 8.28; Luke 7.16; 13.33; 24.19; John 9.17), but it does not explain why he should be thought of as the Messiah (the 'anointed one') or Son of David, which are ostensibly royal titles. Miracles are occasionally associated with kings. Sirach 48.17–22 portrays Hezekiah as successfully interceding for deliverance from Sennacherib's army. More relevantly, some texts (notably Josephus, Pseudo-Philo and 11Q5/11Q11) credit David and Solomon with expertise in countering demons. The tradition of Solomon's magical wisdom is later developed much further in Jewish magical texts and works like the *Testament of Solomon*.

A firmer basis for associating a Davidic king/messiah with the kind of miracle-working portrayed in the Gospels is provided by the eschatological Davidic Shepherd tradition, especially as expressed in Ezekiel 34. This passage first condemns the existing shepherds of Israel for failing to feed the sheep, heal the sick, bind up the crippled and seek out the lost (Ezekiel 34.1–6). It goes on to promise that God himself will seek out his sheep, rescue them and feed them, bind up the crippled, strengthen the weak, and seek the lost (Ezekiel 34.11–16), and that he will set his servant David over them to feed them and be their prince (Ezekiel 34.20–24). Young S. Chae has argued in some detail that this (often Davidic) shepherd tradition is also found both in other parts of the Old Testament (e.g.

Micah 2.12–13; 5.2–4; Zechariah 11.4–17) and in subsequent Second Temple literature (e.g. *1 Enoch* 85–95; *Psalms of Solomon* 17.40; and various Dead Sea Scrolls), so that it would still have been current in Jesus' day. He further demonstrates how this shepherd tradition fits far better with the healing son of David in Matthew than does an exorcizing Solomonic figure.[13] The similarities between the good shepherd of Ezekiel 34 and the Matthean Jesus are particularly apparent, but these similarities are hardly restricted to the Gospel of Matthew; all four Gospels portray a Jesus who heals and feeds people, and it is in relation to the eschatological Davidic shepherd that such activities can most easily be seen as matching some form of messianic expectation.

Moses is another figure who partly matches this shepherd pattern, and given the association of miracles with Moses and Moses' role as the archetypal deliverer of Israel, one may wonder whether at least some Jews expected the Messiah to be Moses-like. There are certainly later rabbinic sayings along these lines (e.g. the *Midrash on Ecclesiastes* 1.21).[14] Moreover, although Jewish tradition more often sees Moses as a prophet than as a king, Philo's *Life of Moses* narrates Moses' career under the heading of king before going on to consider him as prophet, priest and law-giver. Thus, although direct evidence from the first century is lacking, it would seem likely that the notions of Davidic Messiah and Mosaic Prophet could become mingled in at least some sectors of the popular imagination concerning what an eschatological deliverer should be like.[15]

A note on magic

Miracle-working did not always have positive associations in Jewish texts. We have already seen that Josephus evaluated many of the 'sign prophets' as *false* prophets. Mark 13 shows a similar reserve towards false prophets who show signs and wonders, and the tradition of suspecting them may well go back to Deuteronomy 13.1–5. Second Temple texts could also attribute miracles to evil figures such as Beliar (*Sib. Or.* 2.167; 3.63–70) or Antichrist (*Apoc. El.* 3.5–12), just as Pseudo-Philo could record that the

---

[13] Young S. Chae, *Jesus as the Eschatological Davidic Shepherd* (WUNT, 2nd series, 216; Tübingen: Mohr Siebeck, 2006); cf. Barry L. Blackburn, *Theios Anēr and the Markan Miracle Traditions: A Critique of the Theios Anēr Concept as an Interpretative Background of the Miracle Traditions Used by Mark* (WUNT, 2; Tübingen: Mohr Siebeck, 1991), 245–8.

[14] For further details see Wayne A. Meeks, *The Prophet-King: Moses Traditions and the Johannine Christology* (NovTSup, 14; Leiden: Brill, 1967), 211–14.

[15] So also Blackburn, *Theios Anēr*, 249–51.

sorcerer Aod led the Israelites astray by showing them the sun at night (*L.A.B.* 34.1–5). Miracles only counted as legitimating if the witnesses to them were willing for whoever worked them to be legitimated; otherwise they could just as easily invite charges of sorcery and false prophecy.

The distinction between magic and miracle may not always be entirely clear-cut. What may appear miraculous to an approving onlooker may be labelled magical by someone less sympathetic. Thus, for example, in the Beelzebul Controversy (Mark 3.22–30 // Matthew 12.24–32 // Luke 11.15–22) Jesus is accused by his opponents of casting out demons by the power of Beelzebul, the prince of demons. This has all the appearance of a classic sorcery accusation, in which a potential rival is undermined through hostile labelling. Such accusations of sorcery against Jesus continue in ancient Jewish polemic against him, and indeed in pagan polemic such as that of Celsus.[16]

It is not only ancient writers who have accused Jesus of being a magician. This is the major thrust of a book by Morton Smith, and is implied to a lesser extent by John Hull's book tracing magical motifs in the Synoptic miracle stories.[17] Both books are problematic. Smith relies too heavily on privileging the perspective of Jesus' opponents and on proposing forced parallels between Jesus' actions and those of magicians that take no account of context. Hull sets up the discussion in such a way as to make it almost impossible for anything to count as miracle rather than magic, not least by being too ready to juggle different definitions of 'magic'.[18]

Gerd Theissen has tried to distinguish magic and miracle in terms of their social function. According to Theissen, magic is performed by techniques that can in principle be learned by anyone, and is a private activity conducted for private reasons (in antiquity, typically harming an enemy or winning the love of a woman). Miracle, on the other hand,

[16] For a convenient, if sometimes overstated, summary of the evidence, see Morton Smith, *Jesus the Magician* (London: Victor Gollancz, 1978), 45–67.

[17] Smith, *Magician*; John M. Hull, *Hellenistic Magic and the Synoptic Tradition* (SBT, 2nd series, 28; London: SCM Press, 1974).

[18] For further criticisms see Susan R. Garrett, 'Light on a Dark Subject and Vice Versa: Magic and Magicians in the New Testament' in Jacob Neusner, Ernest S. Frerichs and Paul Virgil McCracken Flesher (eds), *Religion, Science and Magic: In Conflict and in Concert* (New York: Oxford University Press, 1989), 142–65 (146, 149–50); Howard Clark Kee, *Miracle in the Early Christian World: A Study in Sociohistorical Method* (New Haven: Yale University Press, 1983), x, 211–12 n. 69; Edwin Yamauchi, 'Magic or Miracle? Diseases, Demons and Exorcisms' in David Wenham and Craig Blomberg (eds), *Gospel Perspectives*, vol. 6: *The Miracles of Jesus* (Sheffield: JSOT Press, 1986), 89–183 (93–7).

is a deliberately public activity that only gifted charismatics can perform, and is carried out for social purposes rather than private gain.[19] This is helpful so far as it goes, in that what Theissen classifies as magic would undoubtedly have been classified (and condemned) as magic by most people in antiquity, Jews and Gentiles alike. But it is not so clear that surprising or superhuman deeds performed in public were automatically taken by everyone to be miracles, as the accusations of sorcery against both Jesus and the first-century pagan miracle-worker Apollonius of Tyana make clear. It is also helpful to note the gulf that lies between the portrayal of Jesus' miracle-working as portrayed in the Gospels and the thaumaturgical procedures envisaged in the Greek magical papyri.[20] But the same problem remains: while many of the Greek papyri doubtless describe procedures that everyone in antiquity would have regarded as magical, it is harder to find clear examples of what everyone in antiquity would have regarded as miraculous, particularly in relation to such a controversial figure as Jesus of Nazareth.

Particularly instructive in this regard is the passage in the *Jewish Antiquities* where Josephus describes Moses showing his miraculous signs to Pharaoh (*Ant.* 2.284–7; cf. Exodus 7.8–13). Since Pharaoh is able to get Egyptian magicians to perform the same feats, all he sees is a competition between rival sorcerers. So far as Pharaoh is concerned, Moses was simply 'trying to impose on him by juggleries and magic'. In the face of the Egyptian king's refusal to see a miracle wrought by God, Moses replies:

> Indeed, O king, I too disdain not the cunning of the Egyptians, but I assert that the deeds wrought by me so far surpass their magic and their art as things divine are remote from what is human. And I will show that it is from no witchcraft or deception of true judgement, but from God's providence and power that my miracles proceed. (*Ant.* 2.286)[21]

The point is clear enough: the distinction that matters to Josephus is not whether Moses and the Egyptians are employing visibly different techniques when they turn their rods into snakes before Pharaoh, or even whether they are pursuing radically different aims; the distinction that counts is that Moses' miracles proceed from God's power and providence, while the Egyptians use mere art and cunning. More broadly, in an Israelite context, a miracle comes from God, any other superhuman feat is magic. This

---

19 Theissen, *Miracle Stories*, 231–43.
20 As Meier, *Marginal Jew*, 2.537–52 does to good effect.
21 See MacRae, 'Miracle', 135–6 and Tiede, *Charismatic Figure*, 223–6 for similar discussions of this passage.

is precisely the distinction presupposed in the Beelzebul Controversy. A similar distinction appears to be presupposed in texts as far apart as the description of illegal divination and divinely inspired prophecy in Deuteronomy 18 and Origen's discussion of magic and miracle in *Contra Celsum* 2.51.[22]

The reason for this seems obvious enough. To say that a miracle is performed by the power of God (whether the God of Israel in a Jewish context, or a god revered in a pagan one) is thereby to declare it legitimate, and hence to legitimize whoever worked it. If one were unwilling to accord legitimacy to a particular miracle-worker, because, for example, he was seen as challenging one's own honour and authority, then the only recourse would be to label him a magician. Since accusations of sorcery are generally an effective means of attack in societies that believe in sorcery, it was an accusation from which no controversial figure could be immune.

In practice, both Jews and Gentiles distinguished between black magic, which was harmful, and white magic (such as healing) that was beneficial, generally condemning the former while tolerating the latter. Only one recorded deed of Jesus appears to fall into the former category, namely the withering of the fig tree (Mark 11.12–14, 20–25). According to Mark, Jesus cursed the fig tree, although the withering of the tree looks precisely like the kind of thing that Mediterranean cultures would attribute to the evil eye: 'A tree or vine that suddenly withers is certainly the victim of the eye . . . There are many tales of trees and vines that were green and strong in the morning but that had withered and died from a passing envious eye by nightfall.'[23] This fig-tree incident therefore looks like it may originally have been told as a story against Jesus, which Mark has then worked hard to domesticate (as we shall see in Chapter 5). That said, there is little else to suggest that even Jesus' opponents were able to accuse him of performing harmful black magic. The accusation would rather be that he was performing counterfeit miracles to lead people astray, just like a false prophet.

In an age when causality tended to be seen in terms of agency, the performance of superhuman deeds naturally required the aid of superhuman agents; if not gods, then demons. Someone who cast out demons might

---

[22] See further Eve, *Jewish Context*, 27–8, 361–8.

[23] Regina Dionisopoulos-Mass, 'The Evil Eye and Bewitchment in a Peasant Village', in Clarence Maloney (ed.), *The Evil Eye* (New York: Columbia University Press, 1976), 42–62 (49–50).

be particularly vulnerable to suspicions of consorting with them. The next chapter will explore how demons and exorcisms were seen by Jesus' Israelite contemporaries, before taking a brief look at miracles in the wider Graeco-Roman world.

2

Demons, pagans and the significance of miracle

The previous chapter surveyed Second Temple Jewish notions of healing and miracle-working, but left a number of areas uncharted. One of these is the issue of demonic possession and exorcism (the casting out of evil spirits), a complex topic that will occupy much of the present chapter. Although Jesus worked in an Israelite context, the Graeco-Roman context also needs to be taken into account, so we shall also take a brief look at miracles in the wider Graeco-Roman world. These tasks complete, we shall draw the threads together by summarizing the significance of miracle for Jesus' contemporaries.

Demonology and exorcism

The impression is sometimes given that there was some set of beliefs about demons and exorcism that all Jesus' Jewish contemporaries shared. The reality was probably far more complex. The surviving texts suggest that there was a range of views on these matters, and there are also hints that the most widespread popular views are only to be glimpsed in these texts. Belief in evil spirits of various kinds was clearly widespread, but many Second Temple texts make no references to demons or exorcism at all. Philo only mentions belief in demons to dismiss it as superstition (*Giants* 16). As we shall see, Josephus does mention exorcism on a few occasions, but demons play very little role in his narrative. The texts that seem most occupied with the demonic, on the other hand, such as *1 Enoch*, *Jubilees* and some of the Dead Sea Scrolls, show little or no interest in the types of miracle that interest Philo and Josephus, and represent a quite distinct strand of Judaism.

There is also a temptation to seize on any procedure for countering demonic attacks as a potential parallel to Jesus' exorcisms, but this is also a mistake. Exorcism, as portrayed in the Gospels, Josephus, and one or two other places, is a procedure for casting a demon out of a human being. In these cases the affliction apparently consists of the demon's taking control of the victim's mind. The phenomenon of spirit possession, in the form of a person's normal personality being displaced by that of a possessing spirit, is widely attested in anthropological literature (as we shall see in the next chapter) and there is no reason to doubt that it occurred in biblical times. Demons were often held responsible for causing illness, so one might reasonably extend the term 'exorcism' to the casting out of demons of this type. But as we shall see, many so-called 'exorcistic' texts are concerned less with *expelling* demons than with preventing their attack in the first place.

It is not always clear what form this attack is taking. In the Gospels (and Acts) demons possess individuals. This is true of a few other texts as well. But elsewhere evil spirits are held responsible for all sorts of mayhem. For the purposes of classification it may be useful to identify two distinct views of the demonic: the individual and the cosmic. The demons in the Gospel exorcism stories, Josephus, and several other texts belong mainly in the first category; they attack individuals by possessing them or afflicting them with disease. Those in *1 Enoch* and related texts tend to belong to the latter category; they cause evil on a massive scale by instigating sin and leading people astray. These two categories should be regarded as 'ideal types', measuring rods for the purposes of classification and description, not as two distinct camps into which all Jewish views on the demonic neatly fell. Indeed, on closer examination the Gospels' views of demonology and exorcism straddle this divide, since while on the one hand Jesus' exorcisms are acts against demons of the individual type, on the other they are given cosmic eschatological significance (Matthew 12.28 // Luke 11.20; Luke 10.17–18). This is a point to which we shall return. In other Jewish literature, however, these two views of the demonic are hardly ever commingled.

Enochic demonology

Gabriele Boccaccini has identified a distinctive current in Second Temple Judaism characterized by a particular view of the origins of evil. This view first emerges in *1 Enoch*, and so may be labelled 'Enochic', although it finds its way into later texts as well. On Boccaccini's view this 'Enochic' view was held by the people the classical sources (Josephus, Philo and Pliny) called 'Essenes'.[1]

---

[1] Gabriele Boccaccini, *Beyond the Essene Hypothesis: The Parting of the Ways between Qumran and Enochic Judaism* (Grand Rapids: Eerdmans, 1998).

1 Enoch is a composite text comprising five books of which the first is *The Book of the Watchers* (*1 Enoch* 1—36), which is thought to date from the third century BCE. This section (which is itself composite) contains what turned out to be a highly influential myth of the origin of evil, based on the cryptic account of the 'sons of God' and the Nephilim and 'mighty men' in Genesis 6.1–4.

The story is admittedly not entirely clear, since even within the relevant section, *1 Enoch* 6—11, there appears to be a fusion of two different traditions. The story in Chapters 6 and 7 concerns 200 rebel angels (the Watchers), led by Semhaza, who bind themselves by an oath to take wives from among the daughters of human beings. The offspring of this illicit union are the giants, who set about devouring first all the vegetable produce of the earth, and then all the animal life (human beings included). Chapter 8 introduces a second angelic leader, Azazel, together with a second band of angels whose sin is to reveal to human beings such forbidden knowledge as weaponry, cosmetics, astrology and divination. In Chapter 9 a trio of faithful angels report all these misdeeds to God, and Chapter 10 proceeds to describe the punishment of the rebel angels. Raphael is sent to bind Azazel and bury him in a hole in the desert. Gabriel, meanwhile, is sent to foment mutual destruction among the giants so that they will perish at one another's hands, while Michael is instructed to tell the Watchers what their children's fate will be and then to bind them (the Watchers) under the earth until the day of judgement. At the beginning of Chapter 10 God sends the angel Asuryal to warn Noah of the coming flood.

But neither the flood nor the giants' mutual slaughter succeeds in ridding the world of their baneful influence. Although the giants' bodies are destroyed, they live on in the form of evil spirits that emerge from their bodies (*1 Enoch* 15.8–9). The Watchers are thus shown to be the originators of both human and inhuman evil. Through their teaching they introduce humankind to warfare, sexual temptation and magic, while through their giant progeny they give rise to the evil spirits responsible for disease and other types of human ill beyond human control. The only solution envisaged by *The Book of the Watchers* to these evils are the final judgement and cleansing of the earth.

Evil spirits play only a minor role in *The Book of the Watchers* (and elsewhere in *1 Enoch*), but their role is substantially expanded in *Jubilees* (a work probably dating to between 170 and 140 BCE). Although the story of the Watchers in *Jubilees* is broadly similar to that in *1 Enoch*, the evil spirits that emerge from the bodies of the giants are given a specific role after the flood: they mislead Noah's offspring and set about blinding and killing them (*Jubilees* 10.1–2). These hostile spiritual forces continue to plague humanity in the remainder of the book. At the time of Abraham, Mastema (the chief of the evil spirits) sends birds to rob people of the labours of sowing seeds (*Jubilees* 11.11). After engaging in star-gazing Abraham subsequently prays to be protected from the influence of evil spirits (*Jubilees* 12.20), but he nevertheless falls victim to Mastema's attempt to test him through the sacrifice of Isaac (*Jubilees* 17.16). Cruel spirits led by Mastema elsewhere encourage people to idolatry and warmongering (*Jubilees* 11.4–6). Indeed, throughout the book demons incite Gentiles and wayward Israelites to worship idols, which in turn is regarded as a form of demon worship (*Jubilees* 1.11, 20; 15.31; 19.28; 22.17).

Mastema becomes particularly active at the time of the exodus. He tries to kill Moses to prevent him executing God's judgement on Egypt, and aids the Egyptian magicians against him (*Jubilees* 48.2–3, 9). Curiously, Mastema also takes on some of the roles that the original Exodus story attributed to God: it is Mastema who hardens Pharaoh's heart and encourages the Egyptians to pursue the Israelites (*Jubilees* 48.16–17), and it is all the powers of Mastema that are sent to slay the first-born of the Egyptians.

Although evil spirits play a greater role in *Jubilees* than in *1 Enoch*, their activities never explicitly include possession. They are responsible for disease, idolatry, leading people astray and inciting them to oppose God's will. As such they are as much responsible for human *sin* as human *suffering*. Conversely, their activities are never countered by exorcism. The closest *Jubilees* comes to an exorcism is Noah's prayer for deliverance from the evil spirits that are troubling his children and grandchildren (*Jubilees* 10.1–14). But this results, not in the casting out of demons from individual victims, but in the consignment of nine-tenths of the demons to the place of judgement while the remaining one-tenth are left free to continue their demonic depredations; despite the fact that 'the evil spirits were restrained from following the sons of Noah' (*Jubilees* 10.13), Noah still needs to be instructed in counter-measures that would scarcely be necessary if this restraint were fully effective (*Jubilees* 10.12). The fate of the other nine-tenths of the demons approximates to that of the Watchers: they are bound pending final judgement. This is perhaps the closest that surviving Second Temple literature comes to finding an eschatological significance in an individual act of defence against demonic attacks.

The *Book of Similitudes* (*1 Enoch* 37—71) and the *Testaments of the Twelve Patriarchs* provide two examples of later literature in the same stream of tradition. *1 Enoch* 54 can be read as suggesting that the *Book of Similitudes* has completely identified the evil spirits with the fallen angels, since in this text the binding of Azazel's army still lies in the future.[2] Among other things, the priestly figure (perhaps messianic though not explicitly called so) in *T. Levi* 18 is to bind Beliar, an expectation that again seems to blur the distinction between the evil spirits and the fallen angels. A different type of blurring occurs in the *Testaments of the Twelve Patriarchs* in the role assigned to evil spirits: they act on individuals, like the evil spirits responsible for illness and other types of affliction, but they are responsible primarily for luring people into sin, like the demons who act on a more cosmic scale. Satan/Beliar's main role thus becomes that of chief tempter and deceiver, rather than as head of an army of evil spirits who possess people to take over their personalities or make them ill. The evil spirits of the *Testaments* are thus similar to the Angel of Darkness of the Qumran two-spirits doctrine (for more on which see below), though without the determinism of Qumran.

Demons in the Dead Sea Scrolls

The Qumran spiritual dualism is described explicitly in the *Community Rule* (1QS 3.13—4.1). According to this doctrine, the fate of human beings is determined by the influence that two spirits, the Prince of Light and the Angel of Darkness, have upon them. These spirits prompt people to good or bad behaviour, and the balance of these two spirits within individuals determines whether they *are* good or bad, sons of light or sons of darkness. Yet there are indications that this was by no means the only view of evil spirits held at Qumran. For example, at one point the *Damascus Document* (CD) states, 'Every man who preaches apostasy under the dominion of the spirits of Satan shall be judged according to the law relating to those possessed by a ghost or familiar spirit' (CD 12.2–3).[3] The allusion to the law here is via the Hebrew terms for the two types of spirit condemned at Leviticus 20.27, which seem to be terms relating to illicit forms of spirit possession elsewhere in the Hebrew scriptures. Admittedly this example is not completely clear-cut, since preaching

[2] So Paolo Sacchi, *Jewish Apocalyptic and its History* (tr. William J. Shortt; JSPSup, 20; Sheffield: Sheffield Academic Press, 1996), 228.
[3] The translation is that of Geza Vermes, *The Complete Dead Sea Scrolls in English* (Harmondsworth: Penguin Books, 1998), 141.

apostasy under Satanic influence could refer to someone led astray by the Angel of Darkness rather than someone actually possessed.

A similar uncertainty rests over many of the apotropaic texts (i.e. texts concerned with warding off evil) found among the Dead Sea Scrolls. Thus, for example, the *Songs of the Maskil* (4Q510 and 4Q511) contain an appeal to the majesty of God for the purpose of frightening off evil spirits, referred to in 4Q510 as, among other things, 'the spirits of the destroying angels and the spirits of the bastards'. The phrase 'spirits of the bastards' is probably an allusion to the Enochic account of demonic origins: the 'bastards' are the giants who were born from the illicit union of the angelic Watchers and human females; their spirits are the evil spirits that came out of their bodies. In 4Q510 these spirits are further called, 'the demons, Lilith, the howlers', which suggests a more popular or 'individual-afflicting' view of them. But they are then described as 'they who strike suddenly to lead astray the spirit of understanding and appal their heart'. This could well be understood in terms of the Qumran two-spirits doctrine; the evil spirits should then be seen as agents of the Angel of Darkness trying to draw the sons of light off the path of righteousness.[4] If so, these evil spirits are being blamed for temptation rather than possession. In any case the Maskil's prayer is not strictly an *exorcism*, since the aim is prevention not cure. The Maskil is not attempting to drive a demon out of anyone, or to cure any demonically induced illness, 'Rather the Maskil is, through prayer, erecting or maintaining a spiritual cordon round the Community, *pre-emptively* to keep at bay the forces of darkness.'[5]

Another reference to apotropaic counter-measures occurs in 11Q5 (= 11QPs[a]) and 11Q11 (= 11QapPs[a]). 11Q5 contains a number of canonical and non-canonical psalms. Among the latter the following notice appears:

> David Son of Jesse was wise and brilliant like the light of the sun; . . . YHWH gave him an intelligent and brilliant spirit, and he wrote 3,600 psalms and . . . 4 songs to make music on behalf of those stricken (by evil spirits) . . .   (11Q5 27.2–4, 10)[6]

---

[4] This is also recognized by Philip S. Alexander, ' "Wrestling against Wickedness in High Places" Magic in the Worldview of the Qumran Community' in Craig A. Evans and Stanley E. Porter (eds), *The Scrolls and the Scriptures: Qumran Fifty Years After* (JSPSup; Sheffield: Sheffield Academic Press, 1997), 318–37 (324).

[5] Alexander, 'Wrestling', 321 (emphasis original); cf. Bilha Nitzan, *Qumran Prayer and Religious Poetry* (tr. Jonathan Chipman; STDJ, 12; Leiden: Brill, 1994), 253–9.

[6] Vermes, *Complete Dead Sea Scrolls*, 307.

The notice that David wrote four songs to help those stricken by evil spirits is probably a reference to the story in 1 Samuel 16.14–23, where David plays his lyre to relieve King Saul from the attacks of an evil spirit. 11Q11 contains part of the text of four psalms, which could well be intended to be the four Davidic songs referred to. These include a version of Psalm 91, which later Jewish tradition recommends for use against demonic attack.[7] Unfortunately, the text contains a large number of lacunae which frustrate attempts at a definitive reconstruction. The psalms appear to contain the words an individual is to use to counter a demonic attack, but it is not clear what form the attack is taking. There is nothing in the surviving text that prevents the attack from being a purely moral one; the afflicted individual would then be praying for the power to resist temptation. On the other hand, the fragment could equally well be referring to a demonic attack that is causing illness; the reference to the Davidic songs in 11Q5 together with the later use of Psalm 91 perhaps tips the balance in favour of this interpretation. In that case, 11Q5 and 11Q11 provide evidence for belief in individual-afflicting demons at Qumran, as well as something that comes quite close to an exorcistic procedure.

Evidence for a more popular demonology at Qumran is provided by another small but highly significant fragment, 4Q560. Its significance lies in its similarity to Jewish magical texts that are otherwise attested only from a much later date. It appears to contain the text of a formula for use in an amulet to protect against demonic attack. Here the demons are almost certainly those that cause physical and mental afflictions, rather than mere temptations, since the text refers to 'the male poisoning-demon and the female poisoning-demon' that are forbidden to 'enter the body' and to 'fever and heartburn'. But the text is again apotropaic rather than exorcistic; its purpose is to ward off demons, not to expel demons that have already invaded.

It is not clear that the Dead Sea Scrolls contain any example of an exorcism in the strict sense. The *Prayer of Nabonidus* (4QprNab = 4Q242) is sometimes cited as doing so, on the grounds that the Jewish *gazer* who appears in this fragmentary text alongside the afflicted king is an exorcist who effects his cure. This, however, is far from clear. Despite arguments to the contrary, the obscure word *gazer* is probably better translated 'seer' than 'exorcist', and on the most plausible reconstruction his function is

---

[7] Alexander, 'Wrestling', 325; Nitzan, *Qumran Prayer*, 228, 233.

not to heal the king but to announce God's mercy and demand the king's repentance.[8]

The *Genesis Apocryphon* (1QapGen) comes closer to describing an exorcism. This text again survives only in fragmentary form. It begins with an account of Lamech's suspicion that his wife has become pregnant by one of the Watchers. Lamech asks his father (Methuselah) to ascertain the truth of the matter from his (Lamech's) grandfather Enoch, at which point the text breaks off. It remains fragmentary until the story of Abraham, which includes a considerably expanded account of Abraham's sojourn in Egypt (Genesis 12.10–20). In the biblical account Abraham attempts to pass Sarah off as his sister for fear that the Egyptians will kill him if they know that she is his wife. Pharaoh takes Sarah into his house, and God duly afflicts him with great plagues. Realizing the cause of this, Pharaoh reproaches Abraham for his deceit and sends both Abraham and Sarah on their way.

The expanded version of this story in the *Genesis Apocryphon* makes Abraham appear more innocent and Pharaoh more guilty. It also describes how, when Pharaoh has Sarah forcibly abducted, Abraham implores God not to let Sarah be defiled. God duly sends a pestilential spirit to afflict Pharaoh and his household, and thereby prevent the consummation of his forced 'marriage' to Sarah. Pharaoh sends one Hirqanos to request that Abraham lay his hands on him and heal him, but Lot explains that his uncle cannot do this while Pharaoh is holding his wife. Hirqanos duly reports to Pharaoh that Abraham's wife must be restored to him before he can be expected to pray for Pharaoh's recovery. Pharaoh summons Abraham, rebukes him for his deception, banishes him and Sarah from Egypt, and then requests that Abraham effect a cure. Abraham duly prays and lays his hands on the king, and the king thus recovers, while the evil spirit is rebuked.

This account is noteworthy for several reasons. First, it is almost the only reference in Jewish literature outside the Gospels to healing by the laying on of hands.[9] Second, it clearly is a story that relates the deliverance of an afflicted individual from demonic attack. It is thus important as evidence for the sort of thing that at least some Jews thought evil spirits might do, and the ways in which their attacks might be countered.

---

[8] Eric Eve, *The Jewish Context of Jesus' Miracles* (JSNTSup, 231; Sheffield: Sheffield Academic Press, 2002), 182–9.

[9] See David Flusser, 'Healing through the Laying-on of Hands in a Dead Sea Scroll', *IEJ* 7 (1957), 107–8.

That said, it is also important to notice the way this story *differs* from the Gospel accounts of Jesus' exorcisms. The most significant is that, from Abraham's point of view, the spirit that afflicts Pharaoh is not really hostile; on the contrary, *this* evil spirit was sent by God at Abraham's request for the express purpose of preserving Sarah's sexual purity. Second, the spirit both comes and goes through prayer, but Jesus never exorcizes through prayer (despite what Mark 9.29 may appear to suggest; see Mark 9.25). Third, although Pharaoh is clearly *afflicted* by this evil spirit, he is not, strictly, *possessed* by it; he remains in control of his own mind and speech (unlike the demoniacs described in the Gospels). Finally, there is nothing to suggest that Abraham ever performed any other exorcisms, or that this cure was due to any special ability on Abraham's part; the point is that Abraham's devout prayer was heard and answered by God, not that Abraham possessed special powers.[10]

Tobit

The evil spirit that afflicts Pharaoh in the *Genesis Apocryphon* is a little like the demon Asmodeus who plagues another Sarah in the book of Tobit, in that Asmodeus behaves like a jealous lover who murders Sarah's husbands on their wedding-nights (Tobit 3.7–8). The jealous Asmodeus is finally expelled by the joint efforts of Tobias and Raphael (an angel posing as a distant relative). When Tobias catches a fish, the angel instructs him in the use of its innards for fumigating the demon. When the courageous Tobias subsequently becomes Sarah's eighth husband, fully knowing the fate of the previous seven, he duly burns the fish organs to drive Asmodeus off with the stench. Raphael then pursues the demon to the furthest part of Egypt, where he binds him to prevent his return, while Tobias prays for divine protection (Tobit 8.1–8). This is hardly a close parallel to Jesus' exorcisms. For one thing, the story hardly represents Sarah as possessed; indeed Asmodeus never attacks her directly, only her husbands. Second, the demon is not driven out by word of command, as in the Gospel exorcisms, rather he is driven away by the fumigated fish and bound by the angel Raphael. But the story does contain a number of possible echoes of the Enochic traditions: in particular Raphael was also the name of the angel who bound the Watcher Azazel (*1 Enoch* 10.4–5). Again, the book of Tobit is narrated in such a way as to make the rescue of Tobit and Sarah from their respective afflictions paradigmatic for the deliverance of Israel as a whole from the afflictions of exile (note, for

---

[10] Eve, *Jewish Context*, 177–82.

example, how the conclusion of the book records that Tobias lived to rejoice at the destruction of Nineveh, Tobit 14.15), so in that way the driving away of the demon is given more than purely individual significance.[11]

Josephus

Perhaps the best example of a Second Temple Jewish exorcism story is that provided by Josephus in book 8 of the *Jewish Antiquities*, where, in the course of describing the reign of King Solomon, Josephus boasts that the incantations Solomon composed are still effective down to this day:

> And God granted him [sc. Solomon] knowledge of the art used against demons for the benefit and healing of men. He also composed incantations by which illnesses are relieved, and left behind forms of exorcisms with which those possessed by demons drive them out, never to return. And this kind of cure is of very great power among us to this day, for I have seen a certain Eleazar, a countryman of mine, in the presence of Vespasian, his sons, tribunes and a number of other soldiers, free men possessed by demons, and this was the manner of the cure: he put to the nose of the possessed man a ring which had under its seal one of the roots prescribed by Solomon, and then, as the man smelled it, drew out the demon through his nostrils, and, when the man at once fell down, adjured the demon never to come back into him, speaking Solomon's name and reciting the incantations which he had composed. Then, wishing to convince the bystanders and prove to them that he had this power, Eleazar placed a cup or foot-basin full of water a little way off and commanded the demon, as it went out of the man, to overturn it and make known to the spectators that he had left the man. And when this was done, the understanding and wisdom of Solomon were clearly revealed. (*Ant.* 8.45–9)

It is not clear what form the possession mentioned in this account took, but it could well have been similar to that envisaged in the Gospels, as the language of 'freeing' the possessed men suggests. Moreover, the demon is clearly perceived as an invisible invader; it is drawn out through the nostrils and commanded to overturn a basin of water to demonstrate its expulsion. Interestingly, Josephus seems happy to describe the procedure as almost magical. Although it was God who granted Solomon the knowledge in the first place, Eleazar employs it simply as a technique (*technē*, the word used by Josephus at *Ant.* 2.286 for the Egyptian magicians' merely human art in contradistinction to the divine miracles worked through Moses). Eleazar makes no explicit reference or appeal to

---

[11] Eve, *Jewish Context*, 218–32.

God's power at any point in the procedure, and Josephus sees Eleazar's exorcistic abilities as demonstrating the 'understanding and wisdom of Solomon' rather than the power, glory or mercy of God.

Josephus makes few references to demons or exorcisms elsewhere. There is a brief reference at *J.W.* 7.185 where he describes the properties of an extraordinary root (perhaps the one prescribed by Solomon) which could be found in the neighbourhood of Baaras:

> It possesses one virtue for which it is prized; for the so-called demons – in other words, the spirits of wicked men which enter the living and kill them unless aid is forthcoming – are promptly expelled by this root, if merely applied to the patients.

It is interesting that for Josephus the afflicting spirits are only 'so-called' demons, but are in reality the spirits of wicked men. This is at a considerable remove from the elaborate demonology of the Enochic traditions that sees evil spirits as the offspring of fallen angels, responsible for a wide variety of human ills, and ultimately condemned to final judgement; such a view of the demonic plays no role in Josephus' historiography, in which human beings are held fully accountable for their own misdeeds, without any reference to demonic interference. Although it might have been a useful polemical technique, Josephus never attempts to discredit the many people of whom he disapproves by suggesting they were possessed or otherwise under demonic influence. However perilous arguments from silence may be, this does suggest that Josephus attached very little significance to the role of evil spirits in human affairs.

The only other place where Josephus comes close to narrating an exorcism is in his version of 1 Samuel 16.14–23, where David plays the lyre to relieve King Saul from the attacks of evil spirits (*Ant.* 6.166–9). In 1 Samuel the evil spirit was explicitly said to have been sent from the Lord; by omitting this detail Josephus moves the story closer to the demonology of his own time. According to Josephus the main symptoms of the demonic attacks on Saul were 'suffocation and strangling'; the evil spirits are thus clearly envisaged as belonging to the individual-afflicting type, but not as possessing their victim in the sense of psychic invasion. Pseudo-Philo similarly retells this story to make it more closely resemble an exorcism (*L.A.B.* 60), but there the focus is mainly on the psalm David composed to rebuke the evil spirit. Taken together with Josephus' account of Eleazar and the Qumran texts 11Q5 and 11Q11 this suggests that incantations or psalms attributed to David and Solomon may have been a common means of countering demonic attacks.

Later sources

There are one or two other sources of evidence about Jewish exorcists. Demonology and exorcism are certainly referred to in rabbinic texts (e.g. *b. Me'il.* 17b and *Num. Rab.* 19.8), but these texts date from rather later than the Second Temple period. The first of these texts contains an account of a rabbi casting out a demon by word of command (from the Emperor's daughter), but here the rabbi and demon are working together to secure concessions from the Emperor, so that the possession is a put-up job all along. This story of a demon offering to help a rabbi (and the rabbi's chagrin at having to accept help from such a quarter) is surely told tongue-in-cheek, but it nevertheless presupposes that demons could possess people and that some rabbis had the ability to order them out. The second of these texts concerns an exchange between a pagan and the first-century rabbi Johanan ben Zakkai, in which the pagan tells Johanan that in case of invasion by 'the demon of madness' one brings roots, makes them smoke under the demon, and then sprinkles it with water, whereupon it flees, a method which bears some relation to those attributed to Eleazar (the root) and Tobias (the fumigation). Nonetheless, this is another tongue-in-cheek story, since Johanan is making a spurious rejoinder to the pagan's accusation that the Jewish red heifer ritual looks like sorcery. Again *Numbers Rabbah* dates from much later than the first century, so it is possible that the technique described by the pagan in this story reflects later practices. Nevertheless, there does tend to be considerable continuity in magical practices, so even despite its relatively late date, this rabbinic evidence is of some value.

There are a few references to Jewish exorcisms in non-Jewish texts from the second and third centuries, for example Justin, *Dial.* 85, Irenaeus, *Against Heresies* 2.6.2, and probably Origen, *Contra Celsum* 5.45. One should also mention Lucian of Samosata's 'Syrian from Palestine' (*Philopseudes* 16), conceivably a Jew, who performs exorcisms which bear some resemblance to those narrated in the Gospels (e.g. the epileptic boy and the Gerasene demoniac). Lucian clearly intends this account to be taken with a large pinch of salt, so even if one could be sure that his 'Syrian' was a Jew, his evidence would need to be treated with caution. His satire nevertheless presupposes that such exorcisms are common enough to be talked about but rare enough to be regarded as spectacular.[12]

---

[12] Wendy Cotter, *Miracles in Greco-Roman Antiquity: A Sourcebook for the Study of New Testament Miracle Stories* (Abingdon: Routledge, 1999), 81–2.

Perhaps the strongest evidence for Jewish exorcists from around the time of Jesus comes from the New Testament. In Matthew's version of the Beelzebul Controversy (Matthew 12.22–32) Jesus asks, 'And if I cast out demons by Beelzebul, by whom do your sons cast them out?' (Matthew 12.27). This presupposes the existence of exorcists recognized as legitimate by the Pharisees. The most notable Jewish exorcists in the New Testament are, however, the sons of Sceva lampooned at Acts 19.13–20. This passage contains a number of difficulties that need not be discussed here.[13] The main point is that the existence of Jewish itinerant exorcists is simply taken for granted in this text, whatever one makes of their failure to cast out a particular demon using (or, in Acts' view, misusing) the name of Jesus. A further point worth noting is the terminology Luke employs here. Only here in the New Testament is anyone specifically called an exorcist (*exorkistēs*) or said to attempt to expel a demon by adjuring (*horkizein*) it. The only time *horkizein* occurs in connection with one of Jesus' exorcisms is at Mark 5.7, where, however, the demon attempts to adjure Jesus rather than the other way about, presumably in a failed attempt at magical self-protection.

Summary

If this survey of Jewish views on demonology and exorcism shows anything, it shows that the issue is far from simple. Different Jews had different views on the subject, and we have identified at least four strands: those who, like Philo, regarded demonology as mere superstition or made no reference to it at all; those who, like Josephus, record one or two exorcisms without attaching any great significance to them; the Enochic tradition that attributes considerable importance to the myth of the Watchers, their bastard offspring, and their ultimate (eschatological) defeat, but tends to narrate few miracle stories or exorcisms; and finally the popular demonology dismissed by Philo, possibly transmuted by Josephus, but perhaps most evident in some of the Qumran texts, notably 4Q560, and also, perhaps in the Gospels, Acts, Lucian's *Philopseudes* and some of the rabbinic texts.

Against this background the Gospel accounts of Jesus' exorcisms make him stand out as quite distinct. He is one of the very few named figures of whom an exorcism story is told, and he is the *only* Jewish figure of whom a whole *series* of exorcism stories are told. Again, both the significance and the method of Jesus' exorcisms stand out. The claim made by

---

[13] For a fuller discussion, see Eve, *Jewish Context*, 334–9.

Jesus at Matthew 12.28 // Luke 11.20 ('If it is by the spirit/finger of God that I cast out demons, then the kingdom of God has come upon you') exceeds anything else found in contemporary Jewish literature. There are few if any instances of contemporary Jewish exorcists claiming to be casting out demons by the power of God (as opposed to material means, or incantations written by David or Solomon), though some of the Qumran texts appeal to divine protection against demons, as does Tobias in the book of Tobit. There are no instances of contemporary Jewish exorcists claiming that their exorcisms herald the imminence of the kingdom of God; even the binding of nine-tenths of the demons in response to Noah's prayer in *Jubilees* is some way removed from that. Again, there are few parallels to the expulsion of demons by a simple word of command, as opposed to prayer, incantation, fumigation, and the use of special roots.

The demonology presupposed in Jesus' exorcisms is also correspondingly distinctive. The Gospels are not alone in seeing possession in the form of psychic invasion as the principal form of demonic attack – this also seems to be assumed by Josephus and perhaps the rabbinic texts cited. Neither are they alone in speaking of the binding of demons and the ultimate defeat of the demonic powers; the whole Enochic tradition shares these notions. But nowhere else are these two ideas combined such that the casting out of individual demons is seen as contributing to the ultimate defeat of demonic powers (or else as a sign of their defeat). The possibility for making such a connection certainly existed within the range of Jewish views on demonology, and in different ways both *Jubilees* and Tobit take small steps towards it, but the Gospel exorcism stories seem to represent a distinctive confluence of the Enochic myth, popular demonology, and the type of exorcism story told by Josephus.

Miracle in the Graeco-Roman world

Jesus' immediate milieu was Israelite, so up until now we have concentrated on the understanding of miracle in a Jewish context. But first-century Palestine was by no means unaffected by the wider Graeco-Roman world; still less so were the Evangelists, who wrote in Greek, sometimes for Gentile audiences, and certainly with some knowledge of Graeco-Roman culture. We should therefore take a brief look at how miracle was perceived in this wider environment.

It is often said that belief in miracle was widespread in antiquity, and that miracle-workers (or at least, stories of miracle-workers) were relatively common. Classical form critics such as Rudolph Bultmann and Martin

Dibelius moreover suggested that most of the miracle stories in the Gospels were formed on Hellenistic models for the purposes of missionary propaganda. They and several other scholars have supposed that the Gospel miracle stories are designed to portray Jesus as a *theios anēr* (divine man) for the benefit of a Graeco-Roman audience who would recognize the type and be suitably impressed by it.

All of these assumptions have been challenged, and all of them need qualifying. First, it is a mistake to bracket the whole of Graeco-Roman antiquity together as if attitudes to miracle were uniform across classes, cultures and centuries. There is evidence to suggest that, at least among the educated upper classes, scepticism towards the miraculous reached a peak in the first century BCE, with a gradual increase in credulity setting in over the next five centuries.[14] It is therefore a mistake to take miracle stories from the pagan religious propaganda of the second and third centuries CE as automatically indicative of their use in the first.[15] Second, it is unclear that *theios anēr* was ever a recognized category in antiquity, or that there was ever a significant class of ancient miracle-workers who possessed all the characteristics a divine man was meant to have. It has instead been argued that the Hellenistic *theios anēr* is largely a modern scholarly construct created by compounding the features of a number of different figures from antiquity that do not really appear together until Philostratus' third-century CE portrayal of Apollonius of Tyana.[16] It has also been argued that the category of *theios anēr* is not necessary to account for the miracle stories in Mark, which can be perfectly well accounted for from a Jewish background.[17] Finally, not all miracles – not even all healing miracles –

---

[14] Robert M. Grant, *Miracle and Natural Law in Graeco-Roman and Early Christian Thought* (Amsterdam: Noord-hollandsche Uitgevers-Maatschappij, 1952).

[15] Howard C. Kee, *Miracle in the Early Christian World: A Study in Sociohistorical Method* (New Haven: Yale University Press, 1983).

[16] Carl R. Holladay, *Theios Aner in Hellenistic Judaism: A Critique of the Use of This Category in New Testament Christology* (Missoula, MT: Scholars Press, 1977); Otto Betz, 'The Concept of the So-Called "Divine Man" in Mark's Christology' in D. E. Aune (ed.), *Studies in New Testament and Early Christian Literature* (NovTSup; Leiden: Brill, 1972), 229–40; Howard Clark Kee, 'Aretalogy and Gospel', *JBL* 92 (1973), 402–22. Barry L. Blackburn, ' "Miracle Working Theioi Andres" in Hellenism (and Hellenistic Judaism)' in David Wenham and Craig Blomberg (eds), *Gospel Perspectives*, vol. 6: *The Miracles of Jesus* (Sheffield: JSOT Press, 1986), 185–218. David Lenz Tiede, *The Charismatic Figure as Miracle Worker* (SBLDS, 1; Missoula, MT: SBL, 1972); John P. Meier, *A Marginal Jew: Rethinking the Historical Jesus*, vol. 2: *Mentor, Message, and Miracles* (New York: Doubleday, 1994), 595–601.

[17] Barry L. Blackburn, *Theios Anēr and the Markan Miracle Traditions: A Critique of the Theios Anēr Concept as an Interpretative Background of the Miracle Traditions Used by Mark* (WUNT, 2; Tübingen: Mohr Siebeck, 1991).

are of the same type, and it simply creates confusion to lump them all together regardless of their social context.[18]

Many of the stories of healing miracles in Graeco-Roman antiquity come, not from accounts of charismatic miracle-working figures like Jesus of Nazareth, but from inscriptions at healing shrines such as Epidauros (a kind of ancient equivalent of Lourdes). Although a number of gods, including Isis and Sarapis, came to be associated with healing, probably the chief healing god of Graeco-Roman antiquity was Asclepius. The earliest accounts of Asclepius (e.g. in Homer) make him out to be an earthly, human physician, but long before the time of Jesus Asclepius had become a god, having a miraculous healing cult associated with him. The usual way of obtaining a cure from Asclepius was by 'incubation', that is by sleeping in the shrine of the god overnight and hoping to be visited by him in a dream (often in the form of a snake), following which a cure (or at least the prescription for a cure) might result. This may be illustrated with a couple of brief inscriptions:

> Alcetas of Halieis. The blind man saw a dream. It seemed to him that the god came up to him and with his fingers opened his eyes, and that he first saw the trees in the sanctuary. At daybreak he walked out sound.

> To Valerius Aper, a blind soldier, the god revealed that he should go and take the blood of a white cock along with honey and compound an eye salve and for three days should apply it to his eyes. And he could see again and went and publicly offered thanks to the god.[19]

The second of these examples, from the second century CE, illustrates a change in the nature of these healings that seems to have come about between the Hellenistic and Roman periods: the later healings tend to feature prescriptions for self-cure taking a matter of days rather than instantaneous cures brought about in a dream.[20]

The main thing to note about this kind of healing miracle, however, is that the healing shrines were a recognized institution of antiquity, a place where society could conveniently leave its sick to be taken care of. This is not to downplay the miraculous element in many of these healings, but it is to emphasize that the god performing the miracle was not a visible presence like Jesus or one of the Israelite prophets. It is also to emphasize

---

[18] Gerd Theissen, *Miracle Stories of the Early Christian Tradition* (ed. John Riches, tr. Francis McDonagh; Studies of the New Testament and Its World; Edinburgh: T. & T. Clark, 1983), 231–64.

[19] Cotter, *Miracles*, 18.

[20] Kee, *Miracle in the Early Christian World*, 89.

that a very different social role is played by an institutional healing shrine from that played by a charismatic healer like Jesus.

Charismatic miracle-workers were by no means unknown in Graeco-Roman antiquity. One of the earliest was Pythagoras (sixth century BCE) to whom a number of healing and nature miracles were attributed, including chasing away pestilences and stilling storms at sea.[21] Another in the same tradition was Empedocles (fifth century BCE), also reputed to be a healer and someone who could control the elements.[22] But perhaps the most notable miracle-working figure in the broadly Pythagorean tradition was Apollonius of Tyana, who dates from the first century CE.

Our principal source for the life of Apollonius is Philostratus' account, written early in the third century CE. Apollonius claims to have based much of his account on the diary of one Damis, a travelling companion of Apollonius, though many scholars suspect that Damis is a literary fiction. Nonetheless, it is generally accepted that Apollonius really existed, and that many of the miracle stories told about him in Philostratus' *Life* predate that work, not least because Philostratus exhibits a certain reserve towards them. For example, in narrating a story in which Apollonius raises a girl to life as she is being borne to her funeral pyre (a story which has some resemblance to that of the Widow of Nain's Son at Luke 7.11–17), Philostratus indicates that Apollonius may have detected some sign of life in her that others missed; the story thus becomes one that illustrates Apollonius' wisdom rather than his miraculous power, and this fits in with the tendency to portray Apollonius primarily as a Neo-Pythagorean philosopher.[23]

The similarities between the miracle stories told about Apollonius and those told about Jesus of Nazareth are often exaggerated, not least when the former are seen as relatively infrequent incidents in the context of a fairly long, rambling account of Apollonius' travels round the Roman empire and to exotic destinations such as India.[24] Nonetheless Apollonius is noteworthy as being a charismatic miracle-worker of sorts who apparently flourished at around the time the Gospels were being written. He is also noteworthy as being about the only figure up to his time apart from

[21] Cotter, *Miracles*, 37–8. For a discussion of largely spurious parallels to walking on water see Patrick J. Madden, *Jesus' Walking on the Sea: An Investigation of the Origin of the Narrative Account* (BZNW, 81; Berlin: Walter de Gruyter, 1997), 49–61, and Cotter, *Miracles*, 155–63.
[22] Cotter, *Miracles*, 38–9, 144.
[23] On Apollonius of Tyana see further Morton Smith, *Jesus the Magician* (London: Victor Gollancz, 1978), 84–91.
[24] See Meier, *Marginal Jew*, 2.576–81.

Jesus of whom a number of exorcism stories are told.[25] Given that stories about exorcisms are comparatively rare in texts surviving from antiquity, these accounts are of particular interest as evidence for how possession and exorcism were viewed in the Graeco-Roman world. Two of these stories portray the demon as controlling its victims' behaviour, and in one of them the victim is returned to normality when the demon is expelled, as in the Gospels. In the other case the demon is said to be the ghost of a man fallen in battle, and Apollonius sends it a threatening letter. In the first Apollonius expels the demon with a word of command, and the expulsion is demonstrated by the demon overturning a statue in a manner reminiscent of the story Josephus tells about Eleazar. In neither case is any particular significance attached to the possession or the exorcism beyond the relief given to the people directly affected.

This kind of exorcism is also indirectly attested by Lucian of Samosata at *Philopseudes* 16, as we have seen. Lucian also satirizes other kinds of miracle-working, including would-be charismatic miracle-workers (whom he regards as charlatans). This indicates that such figures may have been more common than the surviving literature suggests, though we should be cautious about too readily assuming that evidence from Lucian's day (second century CE) can be applied to the Graeco-Roman world of Jesus' day.

It cannot be said that such figures were all that common in Graeco-Roman antiquity prior to Jesus' day. Although there were more examples than have been listed here, according to Gerd Theissen:

> The last representative of this type, Menecrates, lived in the 4th century BC. If we except King 'Eunus', who is more like a Hellenistic mercenary captain than the charismatic miracle-workers, for 300 years we hear nothing of charismatic miracle-workers. Our sources may of course be incomplete, but even if we assume that there were more charismatic miracle-workers than we know of, they can hardly have had a very large following. In the first century AD this changes. Particularly in the eastern part of the Roman Empire charismatic miracle-workers appear.[26]

The first-century examples Theissen goes on to give include Apollonius of Tyana, the Indian sage whom Apollonius meets on his travels, a miracle-worker reputed by Plutarch to have lived on the Red Sea, the Samaritan Simon Magus (Acts 8.9–24), and a number of Palestinian figures. The catalogue is not large, especially when historically dubious

---

[25] See Cotter, *Miracles*, 83–9.
[26] Theissen, *Miracle Stories*, 271–2.

figures such as Hanina ben Dosa are excluded. The evidence suggests that the Gospels were written when interest in charismatic miracle-workers may have been on the increase, but hardly at a time when charismatic miracle-workers were an established type to which a new hero would be expected to conform.

It is noteworthy that at the time of Jesus, charismatic miracle-working seems to have been largely an eastern phenomenon. We know of virtually no western, and specifically no Roman miracle-workers. Miracles in Roman historiography tended to take the form of signs and portents revealing divinely shaped destinies, particularly in relation to a ruler or dynasty.

The one partial exception constitutes arguably the most interesting Graeco-Roman parallel to the Gospel healing stories. In addition to a number of portents of the more traditional Roman sort relating to Vespasian's rise to power, a pair of healing miracles were attributed to him.

Vespasian was the general sent by Nero to put down the Jewish Revolt of 66–70 CE. After Nero's death Galba, Otho and Vitellius each tried to seize the imperial throne, but each lasted only a few months before being fatally dislodged by the next. On 1 July 69, the Roman legions stationed in Alexandria acclaimed Vespasian emperor, and his own troops quickly followed suit. In order to consolidate his position Vespasian repaired to Alexandria in November 69 while his confederate Mucianus led an army on Rome. It was while he was in Alexandria in late 69 or early 70 that Vespasian apparently healed two men with the aid of the god Sarapis. According to the account in Suetonius, *Vespasian* 7.2–3:

> Vespasian as yet lacked prestige and a certain divinity, so to speak, since he was an unexpected and still new-made emperor; but these also were given him. A man of the people who was blind and another who was lame, came to him together as he sat on the tribunal, begging for the help for their disorders which Serapis had promised in a dream; for the god declared that Vespasian would restore the eyes, if he would spit upon them, and give strength to the leg, if he would deign to touch it with his heel. Though he had hardly any faith that this could possibly succeed, and therefore shrank even from making the attempt, he was at last prevailed upon by his friends and tried both things in public before a large crowd; and with success.

The story is also reported in Tacitus, *Histories* 4.81 and Cassius Dio, *Roman History* 65.8.2.[27] Tacitus' account is a little longer, and contains a few differences of detail; for example according to Tacitus (and Cassius Dio) the second man had a useless hand rather than a lame foot. Tacitus

---

[27] Cotter, *Miracles*, 40–2.

also states that the reluctant Vespasian consulted physicians about the medical possibility of the cures before attempting them, the effect being to play them down through rationalizing explanations. Tacitus concludes by remarking that 'both facts are told by eye-witnesses even now when falsehood brings no reward', but the impression given is that this kind of story fits a little awkwardly into the account of a Roman emperor. Both Tacitus and Suetonius suggest that these miracles served to legitimate Vespasian's claim to the throne, but they do not really explain why beyond gesturing vaguely towards the favour of the gods.

There is almost certainly more to this story than meets their Roman eyes. The accounts of Vespasian's healings were part of a package of propaganda aimed at an eastern audience at a time when Vespasian's claim to the throne was anything but secure and the aspiring emperor needed to consolidate his support in the east. Other parts of the propaganda painted Vespasian in quasi-messianic terms, even applying to him an ancient prophecy (almost certainly a Jewish messianic prophecy) that one from Judaea would rise to rule the world (Josephus, *J.W.* 6.312; Tacitus, *Histories* 5.13; Suetonius, *Vespasian* 4.5). Moreover, Vespasian's healing miracles need to be understood in the context of the Egyptian ruler cult in general and the cult of Sarapis in particular. Whatever actually happened in Alexandria, what was made to appear to happen was not simply Vespasian enjoying the favour of a local deity, but Vespasian in some sense becoming identified with that deity, just as the Pharaohs of old had been acclaimed sons of Ra.[28] None of this would have played well with a Roman audience, so this kind of propaganda was quickly dropped once Vespasian was safely installed as emperor in Rome, but in Egypt and the rest of the east its meaning would have been clear enough: Vespasian was the quasi-messianic, divinely appointed agent to bring salvation and restore peace to the divided Roman world.

Vespasian's use of spittle to heal a blind man is commonly recognized as a parallel to Jesus' use of spittle to heal the blind man of Bethsaida (Mark 8.22–26), but it is less often remarked that the time when the story about Vespasian would have been current propaganda was very close to the time when Mark wrote his Gospel. Given that the use of spittle or other material means is uncommon in the healing stories about Jesus, it is tempting to suppose that Mark borrowed this motif from the Vespasian story (otherwise it is an odd coincidence that both stories emerged at almost the same time). This seems all the more likely given that Mark is anxious

---

[28] Albert Henrichs, 'Vespasian's Visit to Alexandria', *ZPE* 3 (1968), 51–80.

to portray Jesus as a messianic Son of God in a manner that both contrasts and competes with the kind of claims being made for Vespasian (see Mark 10.42–45). This is not to suggest that Mark borrowed the story in its entirety from that about Vespasian; neither is it to deny that Mark's account of the Blind Man of Bethsaida performs other functions unrelated to Vespasian; but it is to suggest that Mark's telling of this story has probably been influenced by the Vespasian story with the intent of providing a polemical contrast between the styles of salvation and leadership offered by Vespasian and Jesus.[29] Of all the Graeco-Roman miracle stories, the accounts of healings performed by Vespasian may thus be the most relevant for understanding the Jesus miracle tradition.

The significance of miracles

Having surveyed the material, we can finally discuss what significance was attached to miracles at the time of Jesus. In the case of three of the Jewish writers we have mentioned – Josephus, Pseudo-Philo and Philo – this is fairly clear, since their surviving works are sufficiently extensive for a pattern to emerge.

For Josephus, miracles are the most striking examples of the workings of God's providence, which is understood as God's retributive justice working itself out in history. Indeed, at *Ant.* 1.14 Josephus expressly states that the main lesson to be drawn from his history is that those who obey God and ancestral custom prosper beyond belief, while the disobedient are correspondingly punished, and in the main this is borne out by the way Josephus goes on to narrate his history. This theory of divine retribution is carried out even more strictly in Pseudo-Philo's *L.A.B.*, where the function of miracle is often to punish the wicked, rescue the righteous, or protect the covenant people. In Pseudo-Philo miracles also serve to strengthen the insistence on the divine control of events. For Philo of Alexandria, miracle seems to be more important as defining God as the biblical God who acts, rather than the Aristotelian Unmoved Mover, Stoic world-soul, or abstract Platonic Idea that might have resulted from Philo's marriage of Jewish scriptures and Greek philosophy.[30] They may also serve a propagandist function, indirectly glorifying Judaism by showing what great things God did on its behalf.

---

[29] For a full statement of the case, see Eric Eve, 'Spit in Your Eye: The Blind Man of Bethsaida and the Blind Man of Alexandria', *NTS* 54 (2008), 1–17.

[30] Cf. Harry Austryn Wolfson, *Philo*, vol. 1 (rev. edn; Cambridge, MA: Harvard University Press, 1968), 180, 348–9.

As we have already seen, for all three writers miracles sometimes have evidential value: for Josephus, signs may be used to accredit God's agent; for Pseudo-Philo, they may be used by the faithful to discern God's will; for Philo, they demonstrate the reality of God's will and power.

Of these three writers, only Pseudo-Philo shows any interest in any possible eschatological significance for miracles, in a context that suggests a hope for something like the exodus miracles of deliverance in Israel's future (*L.A.B.* 27.7; 28.1). Indeed, the connection between miracles and eschatology is seldom made; where reference is made to signs and wonders at the end-time, this is more often to apocalyptic upheavals than to miracles (e.g. *4 Ezra* 9.3–6). To be sure, there was some expectation of the eschatological defeat of the demonic powers, particularly in the Enochic traditions, but this was not seen as taking place through miraculous exorcisms. Again, *2 Baruch* 29.3–8 does envisage a time of extraordinary plenty in the messianic age, which includes the reappearance of the manna, and a similar hope seems to be expressed at *Sib. Or.* 3.744–51 ('For the all-bearing earth will give the most excellent unlimited fruit to mortals, of grain, wine and oil and a delightful drink of sweet honey from heaven . . .'),[31] but neither text refers to a particular figure who works a specific miracle to provide this abundance.

It is not uncommon to see prophetic texts such as Isaiah 35.5–6 cited as evidence that the Jews expected the Messiah to perform miracles of healing.[32] But there is very little evidence from surviving Second Temple texts that Isaiah 35 was taken up in this way; the most plausible example of a text expressing this kind of expectation would be *Sib. Or.* 8.205–7, but this text could well be of Christian origin. There is a hope for general end-time health, wellbeing and longevity (though not for healing miracles) expressed at *Jubilees* 23.23–31, but this should be understood as the conventional language of national restoration rather than as any kind of expectation for individual healings.

One text that does appear to express an expectation of a Messiah who will perform miracles, in terms that recall Jesus' reply to John the Baptist (Matthew 11.4–5), is the *Messianic Apocalypse* (4Q521). The major surviving fragment of this Qumran text reads:

1. . . . . [the hea]vens and the earth will listen to His Messiah,
2. and none therein will stray from the commandments of the holy ones.

---

31 *OTP* 1.378.
32 See, e.g., A. E. Harvey, *Jesus and the Constraints of History* (London: Duckworth, 1982), 98–119 and the critique in E. P. Sanders, *Jesus and Judaism* (London: SCM Press, 1985), 160–3.

3. Seekers of the Lord, strengthen yourselves in his service!
4. All you hopeful in (your) heart, will you not find the Lord in this?
5. For the Lord will consider the pious (*hasidim*) and call the righteous by name.
6. Over the poor his spirit will hover and will renew the faithful with his power.
7. And he will glorify the pious on the throne of the eternal Kingdom.
8. liberating the captives, restoring sight to the blind, lifting up the b[ent]
9. And f[or] ever I will clea[ve to the h]opeful and in His mercy . . .
10. And the f[ruit . . .] will not be delayed for anyone
11. And the Lord will accomplish glorious things which have never been as [He . . .]
12. For He will heal the wounded, and revive the dead and bring good news to the poor
13. . . . He will lead the uprooted and knowledge . . . smoke(?)[33]

The text is fragmentary, and in many lines there is more than one way of supplying what is missing and translating the result. Nevertheless, at first sight there appear to be some remarkable correspondences to Jesus' ministry. But on closer examination this is less clear. For one thing, the Messiah is mentioned only in the first line. Thereafter it appears to be 'the Lord' rather than 'the Messiah' who is the subject of the actions (liberating captives, restoring sight, healing the wounded, etc.). For another, some of the terms may bear meanings a little different from similar-sounding terms describing the miracles of Jesus' ministry. Thus, for example, 'lifting up the bent' probably refers to helping the down-trodden rather than healing someone's crooked back as in Luke 13.10–13. The word translated 'wounded' more normally means 'slain'; perhaps here the sense 'mortally wounded' is intended. The picture of healing the mortally wounded and reviving the dead might then suggest restoration in the aftermath of a battle rather than healing the sick. Admittedly the interpretation of the text is problematic, so that it may be that the Messiah is intended to be the subject of some of the actions mentioned (such as bringing the good news to the poor, an activity that is never attributed to God elsewhere). The text would be clearer if one could be

---

[33] The translation is basically that of Vermes, *Complete Dead Sea Scrolls*, 244–5, with one or two emendations in the light of Robert H. Eisenman and Michael Wise, *The Dead Sea Scrolls Uncovered* (Shaftesbury: Element, 1992), 21–3; Michael O. Wise and James D. Tabor, 'The Messiah at Qumran', *Biblical Archaeology Review* 18.6 (1992), 60–5; James D. Tabor and Michael O. Wise, '4Q521 "On Resurrection" and the Synoptic Gospel Tradition: A Preliminary Study', *JSP* 10 (1992), 149–62; and especially E. Puech, 'Une apocalypse messianique (4Q521)', *RevQ* 15 (1992), 475–522.

sure how the lacunae were to be completed. But as it stands, it reads more as a description of what God will do in the messianic age than what the Messiah himself will do.

Moreover, it is not even clear that the text looks forward to individual miracles of healing and raising the dead. Such expressions may rather be the traditional language of salvation. What may be in view is not so much a literal reviving of the dead or healing of the mortally wounded as the revival of God's hard-pressed people (cf. Ezekiel 37.1–14; Hosea 6.2). This may well be the language of eschatological salvation, but it is not neces-sarily a prediction of individual healing miracles. Indeed, it may be that several texts that appear to promise physical healing (e.g. Isaiah 29.18–19; 35.5–6 and Psalm 146.7b–8) were in fact understood as poetic descrip-tions of salvation and return from exile.[34] The importance of 4Q521 is thus not that it associates the coming of the Messiah with the literal restoration of sight to the blind, healing, and raising the dead, but that it provides a good example of this kind of language being applied to the end-time in a metaphorical sense. That said, it may be that many of Jesus' contempor-aries (not least those who left no texts behind) took this kind of language more literally. Either way 4Q521 illustrates how an exceptional healing ministry could be related to existing end-time expectations.[35]

Summary and conclusions

As by now should be apparent, we cannot speak of a single, uniform view of miracle at the time of Jesus. What we can say is that for many Israelites, the most significant miracles were those associated with the exodus (and to a lesser extent, the conquest), and that the most notable miracle-working figure was Moses. Hopes for God's miraculous intervention in the future were often expressed in terms that recalled the exodus events. These hopes and interests are, however, largely absent from texts in the Enochic tradition, which have a distinctive view of the origin of evil through the illicit mating of angelic 'Watchers' with human females, and which look forward to the ultimate defeat of the demonic powers.

Outside the New Testament there is little interest in healing miracles in Jewish texts, and Jesus is unique in the surviving Jewish literature of the time in having a whole series of healing and exorcism stories attributed

---

[34] So Hans Kvalbein, 'The Wonders of the End-Time: Metaphoric Language in 4Q521 and the Interpretation of Matthew 11.5 par', *JSP* 18 (1998), 87–110.

[35] For a more detailed discussion of 4Q521, see Eve, *Jewish Context*, 189–96.

to him. The largest number of Graeco-Roman healing stories are associated with shrines like the Asclepium at Epidauros rather than with
charismatic miracle-workers, though the story of Vespasian's healings form
a notable exception of considerable relevance, since they form part of a
pattern of propaganda designed to legitimate Vespasian in quasi-messianic
terms. Vespasian aside, it is far from clear that the Graeco-Roman parallels suggest any type, such as *theios anēr* or divine man, to which stories
of Jesus' miracle-working would tend to be conformed. Whether against
an Israelite or a Graeco-Roman background Jesus stands out as being
exceptional for the number of miracles narrated of him, but it is almost
certainly the Israelite background that is the more relevant for interpreting them. Three features of this background may be particularly pertinent
for interpreting a ministry of healing and exorcism: healing as a hope and
metaphor for national restoration, the tradition of the eschatological
Davidic shepherd who would heal and feed the flock (i.e. Israel), and the
expectation of the final defeat of demonic powers.

So far, we have taken a purely literary approach to filling in the background of Jesus' miracles. In the next chapter we shall see what social-
scientific approaches might have to contribute.

3

Healing and social science

Curing disease and healing illness

As depicted in the Gospels Jesus was a healer, but not a professional physician. He did not cure people by either ancient or modern medical means, but by word of command and the laying on of hands. Neither did he attempt anything resembling a scientific diagnosis of the conditions he cured. The Gospel healing stories describe the various sufferers' conditions in terms of the apparent symptoms, such as deafness, blindness, fever, paralysis, haemorrhaging, or, in an apparently separate category, possession. This applies even where people are said to be suffering from leprosy, since so far as we can tell *lepra* was not what we call leprosy today (Hansen's disease), but functioned as a blanket term for a variety of skin complaints, probably including psoriasis and the like (this is apparent from the descriptions of the symptoms of 'leprosy' described in Leviticus 13—14).[1]

Several writers have pointed out that these conditions could all be psychosomatic and might therefore be responsive to forms of non-medical treatment.[2] While this is true enough, it does leave some unanswered questions. For one thing, the stories of Jesus' healings resemble modern psychotherapy as little as they resemble modern medicine (not least in terms of the speed with which the cures were apparently accomplished). For another, it is not immediately obvious how a first-century healer would possess an unerring instinct for singling out psychosomatic illnesses from organic ones and only attempting to cure the former. It may be, of course, that the Jesus tradition simply dropped reports of unsuccessful cures and exaggerated the speed of the successful ones, but if Jesus' healing ministry

---

[1] See John J. Pilch, *Healing in the New Testament: Insights from Medical and Mediterranean Anthropology* (Minneapolis: Fortress, 2000), 39–54.

[2] e.g. E. R. Micklem, *Miracles and the New Psychology* (London: Oxford University Press, 1922) and L. Weatherhead, *Psychology, Religion and Healing: A Critical Study of All the Non-Physical Means of Healing, with an Examination of the Principles Underlying Them, together with some Conclusions regarding Further Investigation and Action in this Field* (2nd edn; London: Hodder & Stoughton, 1963).

was really such a hit-and-miss affair, it becomes harder to see how it could form the basis of an exceptional reputation.

Jesus is far from being the only person to heal by non-medical means, so it may be that some kind of social-scientific understanding of the healer role will help round out the picture. Instead of trying to tease medical and psychological details out of miracle stories that were never designed to supply them, we may get further by asking what kind of role a healer (or exorcist) might have played in the kind of society in which Jesus operated. One branch of social science that deals particularly with that kind of question is medical anthropology, which may be defined as that branch of cultural anthropology that studies societies from the point of view of health care.[3]

One medical anthropologist whose work has proved particularly influential in this area is Arthur Kleinman. Kleinman conducted a study of competing health-care methods in Taiwan (traditional folk medicine, traditional Chinese medicine, and modern Western-style medicine) and found that the traditional folk-healers were often more effective than the Western-style doctors.[4] But Kleinman's work extends beyond the particularities of Taiwan towards constructing models applicable to any society.

A key distinction Kleinman makes is between *sickness, disease* and *illness* (used in his technical senses rather than everyday ones). For Kleinman, *sickness* is the generic term covering the other two. *Disease* is the organic (or mental/psychological) malfunction afflicting the individual sufferer (such as a broken bone, a cancer, a viral infection, a blocked artery, or a mental illness such as schizophrenia). It is disease in this sense that is diagnosed and treated in modern Western medicine, and corresponding to the disease is the *cure*. In Kleinman's terminology, a disease is cured when a therapist intervenes biomedically to correct the physical or psychological disorder. Both the disease and the cure affect only the patient.

Illness, on the other hand, is a more holistic concept. It is constituted by the sufferer's own understanding of his or her condition (what Kleinman calls the 'explanatory model'). Neither the illness nor the

---

[3] For the application of medical anthropology to Jesus' healings see Pilch, *Healing*; John Dominic Crossan, *The Birth of Christianity: Discovering What Happened in the Years Immediately After the Execution of Jesus* (San Francisco: Harper, 1998), 293–304; and Eric Eve, *The Jewish Context of Jesus's Miracles* (JSNTSup, 231; Sheffield: Sheffield Academic Press, 2002), 350–76.

[4] Arthur Kleinman, *Patients and Healers in the Context of Culture* (Comparative Studies of Health Systems and Medical Care, 3; Berkeley: University of California Press, 1980).

explanatory model should be understood in individualistic terms; the explanatory model will most likely be one shared with the sufferer's social group, and the illness will probably affect not only the individual directly concerned but also the sufferer's friends, family and wider community. Indeed, the sufferer's relationships within these social groupings may well constitute part of the illness. Whereas a disease is *cured* by biomedical intervention, an illness is *healed* when the sufferer (together with those connected with him or her) is satisfied that the problem has been dealt with. The process of healing involves identifying the illness, giving it a socially meaningful explanation, and applying a culturally relevant remedy.[5] Thus, whereas disease and cures are (notionally at least), value-free, objective, scientific concepts, illness and healing generally involve a great deal of subjectivity.

Disease and illness are not mutually exclusive concepts, they are rather two different ways of construing sickness. It is a mistake to suppose that disease is our modern concept while illness is the way the ancients thought about it. On the contrary, Kleinman makes it quite clear that his distinction is a modern one designed for the purpose of cross-cultural comparison. Moreover disease and illness represent ideal types in that elements of both ways of construing sickness may be present in any particular case. There is also no reason to assume that the words 'disease' and 'cure' refer exclusively to the modern Western understanding of medicine; they could equally apply to any understanding that works in terms of correcting naturally occurring bodily malfunctions (including that of traditional Chinese medicine, or the notion of the balance of the four humours in ancient Graeco-Roman medicine).

Although disease and illness are not mutually exclusive, they need not both be present in the same sickness episode. Presumably an illness only exists if the sufferer is aware of it, so that, for example, an early undiagnosed cancer might be a disease but not an illness. Conversely, there may often be an illness without any corresponding disease. In Kleinman's view many illnesses have mental causes even when they manifest physical symptoms. He estimates that up to 50 per cent of patients in both Taiwan and the USA 'suffer from somatic complaints that are due to psychological problems'.[6] He thus regards most illnesses as being anxieties about minimal symptoms, caused not by any serious disease but by psychological and social stress (such as low self-esteem, poverty, unemployment,

---

[5] Kleinman, *Patients and Healers*, 71–82.
[6] Kleinman, *Patients and Healers*, 139–40.

and troublesome relationships). Instead of blaming the actual causes of stress, the sufferer may enter into the socially sanctioned sick role, which often lacks the stigma attached to an admission of mental illness. Given that the underlying problem is social or psychological, '[t]herapeutic response in these cases obviously will follow upon removal of the psycho-social stressor and reduction in anxiety'.[7]

In the Taiwanese culture Kleinman investigated, considerable stigma attaches to any form of mental illness. People with mental or emotional difficulties are thus reluctant to admit to them, even to themselves, so that they tend to experience their problems as some form of bodily disorder instead (a process Kleinman calls 'somatization', from *soma*, the Greek word for 'body', although the corresponding term in modern psychology is probably 'conversion disorder' rather than 'somatization disorder', which is much rarer). Kleinman suggests that somatization of psychological problems is also prevalent among poorly educated people in the West. Although he does not go on to discuss the ancient Mediterranean, it would seem plausible that what holds for both Taiwan and the modern West in this respect would also have held for first-century Palestine.

The apparent bodily symptoms that can result from somatization (in Kleinman's sense) certainly include many of the conditions apparently healed by Jesus, including blindness, deafness, dumbness, fever, paralysis and possession. Given both that Jesus' reported healings seem to be largely confined to conditions of this sort and that the somatization of psychological problems may account for half of all sickness episodes, it becomes more plausible to suppose that Jesus' healings would have been largely confined to cases of this sort. But it would be premature to rush to the conclusion that Jesus was some sort of first-century folk-psychotherapist. There is more ground to travel before we can arrive at any kind of conclusion.

Physicians and folk-healers

The next step is to introduce Kleinman's model of the 'health care system'. By this he means a modern intellectual construct devised for the purpose of cross-cultural comparison, not an entity such as the UK's National Health Service or any of the various health-care providers in

---

[7] Kleinman, *Patients and Healers*, 366.

the USA. Applying the term 'health care system' to the ancient world does not imply that ancient governments took on responsibility for health care;[8] a 'health care system' in Kleinman's terminology is simply a society analysed from the perspective of health care.

Kleinman's model divides all health care systems into three sectors: professional, popular and folk. The professional sector comprises all those who practise medicine with official accreditation (such as doctors and nurses in the modern West). It is not entirely clear how far such a definition is applicable to the first-century Roman empire. Although there were people who made their living as physicians, it is doubtful that there was anything that constituted official accreditation; instead one might perhaps envisage physicians who had undergone training in the tradition of 'scientific' Graeco-Roman medicine.

The popular sector comprises the non-specialist care provided by friends, relatives, neighbours and the sufferers themselves. When a mother puts her sick child to bed and doses him with an aspirin, she is providing health care within the popular sector. If I put myself to bed and dose myself with an aspirin, I am doing the same. Kleinman estimates that between 70 and 90 per cent of all illness episodes in Taiwan and the USA are handled in the popular sector.[9] It is a reasonable guess that the proportion would have been similar in ancient Palestine (or perhaps higher, given the lack of widespread access to professional health care).

The folk sector, which overlaps the other two, consists of anyone who specializes in healing to a greater extent than friends and relatives providing common remedies in the popular sector, but who is not officially recognized as a professional physician. In a society that lacks the political apparatus to accredit professional physicians (or the economic means to employ them), any specialist healer will be a folk-healer, but folk-healers often exist in societies that have a professional sector as well, as Kleinman's discussion of Taiwanese medicine illustrates. In terms of this classification, Jesus plainly belongs in the folk sector. In what follows, any reference to Jesus as a folk-healer must be understood in this sense, namely as someone who possesses specialist healing skills without being a professional physician.

One characteristic of folk-healers that Kleinman emphasizes is that they tend to employ explanatory models that are far closer to their patients'

---

[8] But see Wendy Cotter, *Miracles in Greco-Roman Antiquity: A Sourcebook for the Study of New Testament Miracle Stories* (Abingdon: Routledge, 1999), 206.

[9] Kleinman, *Patients and Healers*, 50.

understanding of their condition than those of professional physicians. It would be an oversimplification to say that folk-healers heal illnesses while professional physicians cure diseases, but there is clearly a strong tendency in that direction, and this tendency forms part of Kleinman's explanation of a question that particularly exercised him: why indigenous folk-healers such as the Taiwanese *tâng-ki* (or shaman) often prove more effective at healing illnesses than Western-style doctors operating in the same culture. As we have seen, in Taiwanese culture (and other cultures besides), illness episodes are often due to the somatization of psychological problems. Traditional healers such as the *tâng-ki* are skilled at dealing with this kind of problem through rituals that are effectively a form of indigenous psychotherapy. In particular, these indigenous healers take their clients seriously by providing explanations for their suffering in terms they can relate to, unlike the Western-style doctors who take what Kleinman castigates as a 'veterinary' approach. Indigenous folk-healers, however, are not *always* more effective than Western-style doctors; where the illness is a manifestation of a serious disease like cancer then professional medical intervention may be essential; but where the disease is minor or non-existent the folk-healer can often be more effective at healing the illness.

This does not mean that healing an illness is simply a matter of providing meaning for the sufferer's condition;[10] it normally involves performing some action believed to be therapeutic, even if the action is largely a ritual or symbolic one. Presumably such actions gain their efficacy from the patients' belief in them, which in turn may be based partly on the patients' trust in the folk-healer and partly on what constitutes a culturally recognized remedy (for example exorcism may work because it is the culturally recognized remedy for possession when carried out by someone believed to be an effective exorcist). Moreover, it is perfectly possible that a healing may help effect a cure through the removal of psychological or emotional distress.

The question remains how far this is a plausible model for the healings reported of Jesus. These healings are very unlike the kind of therapy Kleinman describes a Taiwanese *tâng-ki* performing, which generally involves a number of group sessions over a period of weeks or months. Moreover, Jesus is seldom if ever portrayed as enquiring into the wider social, emotional or family situation of his patients, and each reported healing seems to have been far too rapid for any effective psychotherapy –

---

[10] As Pilch comes close to implying in one or two places, e.g. *Healing*, 34–5, 53.

even folk-psychotherapy – to have taken place.[11] Again, the miracle stories often appear to focus on the cure of the disease: the blind see, the deaf hear, the lame walk, and lepers are cleansed, but we learn very little about other aspects of their life situation. At first sight it may seem like mere special pleading to suppose that the stories in the Gospels are a distortion of a very different historical reality that just happens to conform more closely to a folk-healing model.

But if we probe a little more deeply, another aspect of these stories starts to emerge. If Jesus is not presented as sorting out his patients' life problems, he is not presented as diagnosing and curing diseases either. The symptoms are treated without any attempt to ascertain any underlying biomedical cause, and Jesus is generally represented as accepting the explanatory model of the sufferer. This is more like healing than curing. Moreover, what Jesus achieved was often more than the cure of a disease. In such cases as the cleansing of a leper (Mark 1.40–45), the healing would also have allowed the formerly unclean sufferer back into society, so that in addition to the cure of the disease there would have been a healing of social relations. In four stories (Jairus' daughter, epileptic boy, Syrophoenician woman's daughter and widow of Nain's son; Mark 5.35–43; 9.14–29; 7.24–30; Luke 7.11–17) children are restored to their parents. The cured paralytic returns home, the Gerasene demoniac turns from outcast to missionary, the formerly blind Bartimaeus follows Jesus, and Peter's mother-in-law is restored to her domestic role. In all these stories a healing may be glimpsed as much as a cure. Moreover, Jesus' reply to John the Baptist (Matthew 11.5) includes the preaching of good news to the poor alongside the cures of various diseases, which arguably places these cures in a wider, social, healing context.

Two of these stories are particularly interesting in this regard. In Mark 2.1–12 the healing of the paralytic is preceded by the forgiveness of his sins. Regardless of whether Jesus is portrayed as sharing his contemporaries' belief in the link between sin and illness elsewhere (John 9.1–3), or whether one thinks that in the Markan context the forgiveness of sins is intended to reflect the view of the carping scribes, here Jesus is portrayed as sharing an explanatory model of illness with the wider culture and presumably with the sufferer. Enabling a paralytic to walk through forgiving his sins looks much more like a healing than a cure. The Gerasene demoniac in Mark 5.1–20 is also enmeshed in a web of

---

[11] As noted by Micklem, *Miracles*, 131; cf. Weatherhead, *Psychology*, 38, 47; Hendrick van der Loos, *The Miracles of Jesus* (tr. T. S. Preston; NovTSup, 9; Leiden: Brill, 1965), 106–10.

troublesome social relations. His condition is described as affecting others from the outset: multiple attempts at restraining him had proved futile; his own social relations were badly disrupted, since he lived apart in an unclean place. The expelling of the demons impacts not only the man himself, but the swineherds whose pigs charge into the sea, and all the people in the neighbourhood who are so perturbed by these events that they beg Jesus to go away. There is also the intriguing hint given by the demon's name, Legion, which appears as the Latin word transliterated rather than translated in Mark's Greek text. It is hard not to see this as in some way relating the man's suffering to the actions of Roman troops. However all these details are to be interpreted, there seems to be rather more going on than the cure of an individual sufferer's disease.

To be sure, none of these stories need be read as straightforward transcripts of actual historical happenings. The point is rather that they contain enough elements relating to the healing of illness (as opposed to the curing of disease) not to exclude the illness/healing model as a way of understanding Jesus' healings and exorcisms.

Modelling folk-sainthood

Two problems remain. The first has been mentioned already: for all the healing elements the Gospel stories contain, they still do not look like accounts of someone sorting out sufferers' emotional, psychological or social problems, whether in the manner of a Taiwanese *tâng-ki* or in the manner of the modern Western examples Kleinman gives elsewhere.[12] The second is that the Gospels hardly depict Jesus as just another folk-healer, but rather as a quite extraordinary miracle-worker.

The second problem may be stated thus: given that there were probably many other folk-healers operating in Galilee at the time, what made Jesus stand out as exceptional? One way to address this question might be through an instructive parallel, and one possibly interesting parallel may be that of the Mexican folk-healer (or *curandero*) Don Pedrito Jaramillo, who ministered in south Texas from 1881 until his death in 1907.[13] What makes this folk-healer of particular interest is not so much the details

---

[12] Arthur Kleinman, *The Illness Narratives: Suffering, Healing and the Human Condition* (New York: Basic Books, 1988).

[13] For an account of this folk-healer's ministry see Ruth Dodson, 'Don Pedrito Jaramillo, The Curandero of Los Olmos' in Wilson M. Hudson (ed.), *The Healer of Los Olmos and Other Mexican Lore* (Dallas: Southern Methodist University Press, 1951), 9–70.

of his career as the model developed by Octavio Romano to account for Jaramillo's elevation from folk-healer to folk-saint.[14]

Many of the healing stories told about Pedrito Jaramillo read rather differently from those told of Jesus, since they are often longer and contain rather more circumstantial detail in the form of personal reminiscences, but a few shorter ones will serve to give something of their flavour.

> At times a man suffered from headache until he took to his bed. The remedy for him was that for three mornings he should get up at the same hour and drink a glass of water. He recovered in three days.
>
> For a sick girl, the remedy with which she was cured was that she take a bath every night for nine nights, washing her head well with soap; then that she eat as much as she should want of a can of fruit of whatever kind was available and place the remainder where only the chickens could find it.
>
> The prescription for a certain woman was to dip her head into a bucket of water as she was ready to go to bed. The next morning she was to put half a can of tomatoes into each shoe, then put the shoes on and wear them that way all day, *sin verguenza* – without shame.
>
> A case of particular interest, it was said, was that of a Colonel Toribio Regalo who was brought from the city of Torreón, Mexico. He was so violently insane that he was kept tied. Don Pedrito prescribed a can of tomatoes every morning for nine mornings. The man was confined at Los Olmos while he took the remedy. At the end of nine days he was well, and his friends took him back to Mexico.[15]

These are nowhere as impressive as most of the Gospel healing stories; the healings do not take place instantaneously, and many of the conditions are unspecified or trivial (many of the stories about Pedrito Jaramillo are even vaguer about the nature of the illness than the Gospels are). Nonetheless, the healings described do seem to have been fairly quick, and, more significantly, they no more resemble a form of folk-psychotherapy than do the healings of Jesus. Whatever psycho-social stressors may have been troubling the people Pedrito Jaramillo healed, the stories about him do not recall him enquiring about them or explicitly addressing them, although there is the occasional story that wryly hints at the psychology of the cure, for example:

---

[14] Octavio I. Romano, 'Charismatic Medicine, Folk-Healing and Folk-Sainthood', *American Anthropologist* 67 (1965), 1151–73.

[15] Dodson, 'Don Pedrito', 39.

It appeared that José didn't care to mention the name of a woman in the family who had severe attacks of migraine headaches. When someone went to Don Pedrito to secure a remedy for her, he sent her word to have her head cut off and thrown to the hogs.

When the woman was told what the curandero had prescribed she became violently angry – and didn't have any more headaches.[16]

Many other folk-healers operated in the same area around the same time, but none achieved the reputation of Pedrito Jaramillo, whose shrine was still being visited by pilgrims fifty years after his death. Romano sets out to explain why.

Just as traditional Mediterranean culture tended towards social atomism (a tendency to mutual antagonism between adult males competing for limited goods such as honour),[17] so Romano describes a tendency in nineteenth-century south Texas 'toward individual independence, autonomy, and uncooperativeness'.[18] In other words, among Mexican peasants adult males would generally avoid close relations with people other than relatives. An adult male who maintained both this kind of autonomy and headship of an extended family was likely to gain the respect of others. 'The role definition of male autonomy, therefore, tends towards an atomistic social order which emphasizes mistrust and suspicion as well as general uncooperativeness.'[19]

On the other hand the need for mutual assistance was also recognized. A certain degree of co-operation is necessary if people are going to live together in society, and Catholic Mexican peasants seem to have been aware than the Christian ideal calls for a degree of selflessness. One can envisage a similar tension between the desire for honour maintained at the expense of non-kin and Israelite social ideals in first-century Galilee.

Romano locates the healer role within the context of mutual assistance. If a (male) Mexican peasant adopted the role of healer, he would also have to adopt a co-operative stance, since the healer was expected to be at the service of the public. Moreover, the further up the 'healing hierarchy' he moved, from family, through village, district and internationally renowned healer, the more he would have to renounce himself and dedicate himself solely to the *curandero* role. For a regional healer, 'Renunciation of multiple roles by the healer, along with alternative

---

[16] Dodson, 'Don Pedrito', 36.
[17] For a fuller explanation see Bruce J. Malina, *The New Testament World: Insights from Cultural Anthropology* (London: SCM Press, 1983), 25–50, 71–93.
[18] Romano, 'Charismatic Medicine', 1153.
[19] Romano, 'Charismatic Medicine', 1153–4.

goals, now begins to become a way of life.'[20] Such 'multiple roles' would include family life and earning one's living by normal means. This sounds not unlike the renunciation apparently practised by Jesus and demanded of his followers, but it also characterizes Pedrito Jaramillo.

The question remains what makes Jaramillo stand out from other *curanderos*. Romano suggests a number of factors. First, unlike other *curanderos*, Jaramillo claimed a direct divine mandate for his healing activity, without saintly intermediary. Second, his fame was probably spread round Texas by his extensive travels in the course of his healing ministry and by his providing food for those who came to see him. Third, his healing miracles were strikingly individual, usually involving the instant prescription of the first thing that came into his head, which might vary from coffee to tinned tomatoes, but was most usually water. All these factors were taken up into the cycle of healing stories that began to circulate even in Jaramillo's lifetime.

Yet, in Romano's opinion, none of these factors fully explains why Jaramillo exercised a charisma that other *curanderos* lacked, since many of them were also innovative in their methods. What made Jaramillo stand out in particular was not his innovations, but his 'performing his role in relatively strict accordance with the fundamental and generic definition of healer role as provided by tradition, which relates to the behavioural sector of communality and mutual assistance'.[21] Jaramillo put into practice a dormant ideal of the totally selfless healer, and thereby 'singularly reasserted tradition by making the pre-existent "ideal" into a tangible and recognizable entity'.[22] In Romano's view, Jaramillo is thus to be regarded as a charismatic *renovator* embodying the charisma of conservatism.

An article by Bruce Malina questions whether Jesus should be called a charismatic leader at all (in Weber's sense, in which charismatic author-ity as opposed to traditional or rational-legal authority is power based on the personal qualities of the leader).[23] Malina argues that in Weberian terms Jesus was not a charismatic (revolutionary) leader but a reputational (conservative) one, concerned with the restoration of Israel and its tradi-tional values. His elevation from honourable Galilean healer into revered national Messiah was due to his satisfying some central aspirations of Palestinian society. Jesus' success in defending his honour, together with

---

[20] Romano, 'Charismatic Medicine', 1157.
[21] Romano, 'Charismatic Medicine', 1170.
[22] Romano, 'Charismatic Medicine', 1170.
[23] Bruce J. Malina, 'Jesus as Charismatic Leader?', *BTB* 14 (1984), 55–62.

his healing ability, made him an effective symbol for non-elite persons who saw their own honour being trampled. Jesus repeatedly expressed indifference to personal power over others. In a first-century CE Palestinian context, Malina maintains, it was this refusal to assume power that made him a moral hero, committed to the kingdom of God.

There are clearly important differences between what Romano says about Jaramillo and what Malina says about Jesus. In particular, whereas Jaramillo functioned purely as a folk-healer, Jesus' folk-healing activity is seen as a step to a larger role, that of national Messiah. The important point of convergence is that both Romano and Malina see their subjects as being propelled up the reputational hierarchy by their dedication to their respective roles, and by the fact that these roles matched some key expectation of the societies in which these two healers operated.

An important point to note is that these models concern not just the prowess of an individual healer, but also how that prowess operates within a particular social context. On this understanding charisma is not primarily some innate quality of an extraordinary individual but rather conformity to a pattern which strikes a deep chord with at least some portion of the surrounding society. If no one in the surrounding society recognized that pattern as at all significant, the charisma would fail. This does not mean that the role must be wholly defined in advance, as if Jesus or Jaramillo could gain their reputations only by performing some pre-existing script, but the role needs to be recognizable and to conform to some expectations or aspirations that already exist. Both the anecdotes about Jaramillo and the Gospel portraits of Jesus suggest exceptional dedication to their respective roles, and it may be this that marks them out as extraordinary.

This kind of model also suggests a positive feedback loop: success breeds success. A feature that comes through in several of the healing stories told about both Jesus and Jaramillo is that their cures worked because their patients believed they would work (Mark 5.34; 6.5–6; 10.52), and this would tie in plausibly with a model of healing *illnesses* the causes of which are at root psychological. The more successful healings a person performs, the greater his reputation as a healer will grow, so the more confidence people will have in his ability, and the more successful he will become. One might imagine that this same feedback loop would also affect the individual healer: the more successful he is the more confident he becomes and the more confidence he inspires; at the same time the better he is seen to perform his role, the greater the pressure to conform to that role, and, perhaps, the greater his sense that he *ought* to conform to the role, that it is, indeed, a sacred calling. This would particularly be the case in societies less individualistic than our own.

The model sketched here does not explain everything. We have yet to see why Jesus became renowned not just as an exceptional healer but as a messiah, and we have yet to take the particularities of his situation into account. We shall return to both tasks in Chapter 6, but before we leave cross-cultural anthropology we should look at the light it may be able to shed on one particular kind of healing, namely exorcism.

Spirit possession and exorcism

It would be a mistake to regard demon possession as a primitive way of talking about mental illness. Some people labelled as demon-possessed in antiquity would no doubt be considered as suffering from mental illness today, but mental illness and demon possession are not the same thing. Demon possession is the form of spirit possession that a particular society regards as worrisome, but spirit possession can take forms that are evaluated positively, such as shamanism (or, more generally, spirit control) and spirit-mediumship. Most generally, spirit possession may be defined as '*any altered state of consciousness indigenously interpreted in terms of the influence of an alien spirit*',[24] although some writers prefer to think of it more in terms of the performance of a culturally coded script (i.e. a set of actions that accord with the expectations of a particular culture).[25]

Possession states are by no means necessarily bad. They are more properly understood as the culturally constructed way in which many societies perceive a particular range of trance states.[26] The dissociative mental state that is often labelled 'possession' is neither a form of mental illness nor a peculiarity of primitive savages, but simply an innate capacity of the human brain. Far from regarding them as pathological, some writers see such states as therapeutic.[27]

---

[24] Vincent Crapanzano, 'Introduction' in Vincent Crapanzano and Vivian Garrison (eds), *Case Studies in Spirit Possession* (New York: John Wiley & Sons, 1977), 1–40 (7); emphasis original.

[25] See Janice Boddy, 'Spirit Possession Revisited: Beyond Instrumentality', *Annual Review of Anthropology* 23 (1994), 407–34; Christian Strecker, 'Jesus and the Demoniacs' in Wolfgang Stegemann, Bruce J. Malina and Gerd Theissen (eds), *The Social Setting of Jesus and the Gospels* (Minneapolis: Fortress, 2002), 117–33.

[26] I. M. Lewis, *Ecstatic Religion: A Study of Shamanism and Spirit Possession* (2nd edn; London: Routledge, 1989), 33–41.

[27] e.g. Raymond Prince, 'Foreword' in Vincent Crapanzano and Vivian Garrison (eds), *Case Studies in Spirit Possession* (New York: John Wiley & Sons, 1977), xi–xvi (xii–xiii).

Demon possession is thus quite distinct from the forms of mental illness commonly recognized in modern Western psychiatry. It should not be equated with schizophrenia or even 'hysterical psychosis'.[28] Neither is it the same thing as the condition labelled 'Multiple Personality Disorder' (or more recently relabelled 'Dissociative Identity Disorder'); MPD (assuming it exists at all, which is disputed) is normally the result of a trauma in the past (typically in childhood) whereas possession is frequently a response to stresses in the present. Again, persons suffering from MPD generally have many alternative personalities, whereas the demon-possessed normally have only one.[29] To be sure, a culture will not label something 'demon possession' unless it regards the behaviour of the possessed person as worrying, and it may well be that mentally ill persons who become possessed will exhibit particularly worrying symptoms. One might, therefore, regard the more spectacular manifestations of demon possession as a culturally coded way of expressing and dealing with the social, mental, or emotional stress that is the sufferer's real affliction. In that sense, demonic possession may be symptomatic of an underlying mental disorder, but it is not pathological simply by virtue of being a possession state.

Demonic possession may also occur when there is no underlying mental disease, as a response to domestic, social or political stress. The fact that possessed persons are regarded as demoniacs may be more a cultural evaluation of their protest against oppression than an accurate assessment of their mental health. One approach to understanding this is the structural-function model proposed by I. M. Lewis. Lewis's study of what he calls 'peripheral possession' focuses on situations of domestic stress. On this model, what can often happen is that a downtrodden woman turns the tables on her husband by acquiring a possessing spirit. Since the spirit is understood to be a person quite distinct from the woman, it can make demands that would be ignored if they were thought to come merely from her. In this way peripheral possession functions as an oblique strategy of attack, rather like accusations of sorcery. The difference is that whereas sorcery accusations are generally levelled at equals or inferiors, possession is nearly always employed by inferiors against their social superiors, as a means of redressing the balance of power.[30] In the

---

[28] The latter label is employed by Kleinman, *Patients and Healers*, 168.
[29] Stevan L. Davies, *Jesus the Healer* (London: SCM Press, 1995), 86–9; Erika Bourguignon, *Possession* (San Francisco: Chandler & Sharp, 1976), 38–9.
[30] Cf. Bourguignon, *Possession*, 22–3, 33–41.

main the superiors tolerate this strategy, perhaps because it is seen as a safety valve that does not seriously challenge the status quo. But when possessed persons accommodate themselves to their possessing spirits and advance to becoming spirit mediums or spirit controllers (e.g. shamans or exorcists), they open themselves to charges of sorcery, since they may then be seen as effective leaders of protest against oppression. The suspicion is that someone who can control spirits is probably in league with spirits. Accusing such people of sorcery is a way of discrediting them and limiting their influence.[31] Once again, the Beelzebul Controversy comes to mind.[32]

Such 'peripheral' possession is not limited to cases of domestic stress. It may also be employed for purposes ranging from self-punishment through self-aggrandizement to control of other people.[33] It can also occur in societies under acute stress where the whole society is in danger of becoming marginalized, or in circumstances of radical social change, or as a form of resistance to colonialism and imperialism.[34]

The structural-functional approach is not the only way to understand spirit possession, and has come under criticism from a number of quarters.[35] Part of the problem is that such cross-cultural models risk ignoring the specifics of how spirit possession and demon possession are understood in particular societies, and not least how they relate to other features of those societies' symbolic universes. While Lewis's model offers some insights into the nature of possession, his account of peripheral possession cults (drawn mainly from contemporary African examples) may not be a particularly good fit with first-century Palestine. Spirit possession is not simply a matter of manifesting certain kinds of behaviour, it depends on how that behaviour is interpreted in the culture in which it occurs; behaviour that one culture interprets as possession may be interpreted quite differently in another, and only in the first may we speak of spirit possession at all.[36]

What constituted demonic possession in first-century Palestine will thus in part be determined by the specifics of that time and place, and cannot

---

[31] Lewis, *Ecstatic Religion*, 105–9.
[32] Santiago Guijarro, 'The Politics of Exorcism' in Wolfgang Stegemann, Bruce J. Malina and Gerd Theissen (eds), *The Social Setting of Jesus and the Gospels* (Minneapolis: Fortress, 2002), 159–74.
[33] Crapanzano, 'Introduction', 19–20.
[34] Lewis, *Ecstatic Religion*, 182; Boddy, 'Spirit Possession', 419–20; Paul W. Hollenbach, 'Jesus, Demoniacs, and Public Authorities: A Socio-Historical Study', *JAAR* 49 (1981), 567–88.
[35] e.g. Boddy, 'Spirit Possession', 414.
[36] Bourguignon, *Possession*, 6–10.

simply be read off from cross-cultural models. Erika Bourguignon, for example, points out that possession in Europe has historically been different from that in Africa, and that demonic possession in the Judaeo-Christian tradition is distinctive in representing its victims as suffering from a split consciousness instead of an invading spirit totally displacing the normal personality.[37] She goes on to suggest that among the Jews of Jesus' day demons might reflect the fear of uncleanness, since they tended to be associated with sources of impurity such as corpses and cemeteries.[38] This would certainly tie in with the Markan term 'unclean spirits' but it does not tell the whole story. As we saw in the previous chapter, Second Temple Judaism contained a variety of demonological beliefs. Moreover, spirit possession was a phenomenon attested from Old Testament times, where it might be positively or negatively evaluated in terms of various kinds of prophecy,[39] or else associated with various types of sorcery and illicit spirit-mediumship.[40] Against such a background any type of possession cult was likely to be frowned upon, and any type of spirit possession seen as demonic, especially where it was perceived as socially disruptive. The option to come to terms with the possessing spirit, available in many cultures, would hardly exist (unless the spirit could be perceived as God's Holy Spirit), and exorcism would then seem the only viable option.[41] This situation is not unique to Judaism, and can occur whenever possessing spirits are seen as not just amoral but positively evil, which in turn may be related to social structure, with more structured societies more likely to fear trance-like states. Bourguignon further argues that spirit possession is in any case more likely to occur in complex, rigidly stratified societies such as those that depend on agricultural production.[42] To anticipate what will be said in Chapter 6, first-century Galilee certainly qualifies as such a society.

Being possessed allows someone to say what they could not say in their own persona. They cannot be blamed for what they say when possessed, since it is believed to be not they but the possessing spirit who is saying it. Demon possession may thus be a mechanism for giving vent to

---

[37] Bourguignon, *Possession*, 6.

[38] Bourguignon, *Possession*, 51.

[39] Robert R. Wilson, 'Prophecy and Ecstasy: A Reexamination', *JBL* 98 (1979), 321–37.

[40] See Deuteronomy 18.9–14; Leviticus 20.27; 1 Samuel 28.8–11; and the discussion in S. R. Driver, *A Critical and Exegetical Commentary on Deuteronomy* (ICC; Edinburgh: T. & T. Clark, 1896), 223–6.

[41] Boddy, 'Spirit Possession', 415; Crapanzano, 'Introduction', 15, 18.

[42] Bourguignon, *Possession*, 31, 43; Crapanzano, 'Introduction', 18.

feelings that it would otherwise be socially unacceptable to express.[43] In possession trance such thoughts and emotions are successfully dissociated from a person's normal self, so that he or she is not consciously aware of them at all, and their emergence into consciousness effectively takes the form of a new persona (the possessing spirit or demon), which may totally (though usually only temporally) displace the person's normal conscious self; the person may then be completely unaware of what he or she said or did when possessed.

Exorcism, the process of casting out a possessing spirit, is as much a culturally coded activity as possession. In brief, exorcism is effective when it proceeds according to the expectations of the culture in which it takes place; it works when and because it is believed to work. In some circumstances this may require the performance of an elaborate ritual, but in others it may be sufficient to confront the possessing spirit with a superior spiritual power that can simply order it out, as seems to have been the case in Jesus' exorcisms.[44]

In sum, the anthropology of spirit possession can help us understand what kind of thing demon possession in first-century Galilee may have been, and how it could plausibly be countered by exorcism, but we need to maintain a balance between the generalities of cross-cultural models and the specifics of the particular cultural context. On the one hand, this allows us to regard the accounts of possession and exorcism in the New Testament as describing events of a type that could well occur, without thereby committing ourselves to belief in spirits and demons as entities existing independently of the minds they inhabit (although they could and probably would be as much the product of social circumstances as of individual psychology). On the other hand, it does not allow us to read off a particular theory of the *causes* of the demon possession reported in the Gospels directly from these accounts, both because they do not give sufficiently reliable details of the symptoms, and because, in the abstract, several theories are possible. So, for example, Graham Twelftree may be justified in cautioning against a socio-political reading of the exorcisms in Mark (at the narrative level), but Stevan Davies is too quick to dismiss the possibility that social, economic and political pressures gave rise to the underlying events, and to insist that they can have arisen only in the

---

[43] Bourguignon, *Possession*, 53–4.

[44] Graham H. Twelftree, *Jesus the Exorcist: A Contribution to the Study of the Historical Jesus* (WUNT, 2nd series, 54; Tübingen: Mohr Siebeck, 1993), 22, 51–2.

contexts of domestic stress.[45] In any case, social pressures caused by the oppressive structures of society could well translate into domestic pressures experienced by individuals. In Chapter 6 it will be suggested that political, social and economic pressures were responsible for a significant proportion of the possession encountered by Jesus, but this will be as part of a wider theory. Such a reading is not demanded by the exorcism stories themselves, it is simply compatible with them.

Spirit possession is clearly relevant to Jesus' exorcisms, but it may also be relevant to his other healings as well. For one thing, the Gospels occasionally appear to associate illnesses other than possession with evil spirits (Luke 4.39; 11.14; 13.11; Matthew 9.32–33), and this association can also be found in other texts (e.g. the *Genesis Apocryphon* and the woes blamed on demons in much of the Pseudepigrapha). For another, many of the illnesses Jesus is reported to have healed (such as blindness, deafness and muteness) are of a type that in other cultures could be construed as the onset of a demonic attack.[46] Moreover, if Jesus conceived himself as a spirit-filled prophet overcoming demonic resistance to the reign of God through his healings and exorcisms, then it is plausible that he regarded other illnesses besides possession as being demonically caused too.

Conclusions

This chapter has attempted two tasks. First, by taking a brief look at the anthropology of healing and of spirit possession it has aimed to show the general plausibility of the kind of healing and exorcism ministry attributed to Jesus in the Gospels. Second, it has outlined some theoretical models that will hopefully be of use when we come to discuss how Jesus' healing activity might have fitted the particular circumstances of his ministry.

It is important to be clear about two things this chapter has not attempted. On the one hand it has not proved that Jesus was a healer-

---

[45] Graham H. Twelftree, *In the Name of Jesus: Exorcism among Early Christians* (Grand Rapids, MI: Baker Academic, 2007), 105–11; Davies, *Jesus the Healer*, 78–86.

[46] Crapanzano, 'Introduction', 14; cf. Vincent Crapanzano, 'Mohammed and Dawia: Possession in Morocco', in Vincent Crapanzano and Vivian Garrison (eds), *Case Studies in Spirit Possession* (New York: John Wiley & Sons, 1977), 141–76 (144); Lucie Wood Saunders, 'Variants in Zar Experience in an Egyptian Village' in Crapanzano and Garrison, *Case Studies*, 177–90 (179–80). Cf. the discussion of the continuum of dissociative disorders in peasant Galilee in Davies, *Jesus the Healer*, 73, and of non-trance possession in Bourguignon, *Possession*, 45–6.

exorcist; it has merely helped establish the general plausibility of his having been one. On the other it has not reduced Jesus' miraculous activities to social-scientific explanations; the considerations advanced in this chapter form part of a project to see how Jesus' miracles might fit in with 'ordinary' history, without thereby intending to rule out other kinds of question in other contexts.

The next obvious step in the argument would be to apply the models developed here to the specifics of Jesus' situation, but this can hardly be done without first assessing the sources for Jesus' miracle-working activity, so this is the task that will occupy us for the next two chapters.

4

Sources

Our most detailed portrait of Jesus comes from the canonical Gospels (i.e. the four Gospels in the New Testament). It would be useful if we could discover something outside these Gospels that either confirmed or corrected their portrait, and it would be even better if we could find confirmation in a hostile or neutral source. Unfortunately, material from outside the Gospels that is of any use for investigating the miracles of Jesus is hard to find. This chapter will review the most promising candidates, including some of the sources that are often thought to lie behind the Gospels, but these will be found to provide little more than weak confirmation of the tradition that Jesus was a miracle-worker. For anything more definite, the canonical Gospels will turn out to be by far our most useful sources.

Non-Christian sources

Josephus

The most valuable sources for events in first-century Palestine are the writings of Josephus, so if anyone outside the circle of Jesus' followers made any mention of Jesus' miracles, one might expect it to be him, and indeed *Antiquities* 18.63–4 does contain a paragraph about Jesus, the so-called *Testimonium Flavianum*:

> About this time there lived Jesus, a wise man, if indeed one ought to call him a man. For he was one who wrought surprising feats and was a teacher of such people as accept the truth gladly. He won over many Jews and many of the Greeks. He was the Messiah. When Pilate, upon hearing him accused by men of the highest standing among us, had condemned him to be crucified, those who in the first place had come to love him did not give up their affection for him. On the third day he appeared to them restored to life, for the prophets of God had prophesied these and countless other marvellous things about him. And the tribe of the Christians, so called after him, has still to this day not disappeared.[1]

---
[1] The translation is that of Louis H. Feldman in LCL.

At first sight the notice that Jesus was 'one who wrought surprising feats' (*paradoxōn ergōn poiētēs*) looks like just the kind of independent confirmation we are looking for.[2] Although Christian interpolation in the *Testimonium Flavianum* is widely suspected, the word *paradoxos* (surprising) appears typical of the miracle vocabulary Josephus employs.[3] Moreover, apart from Luke 5.26 it is not a word used of Jesus' miracles in the New Testament. But there are problems with the *Testimonium*. It is uncharacteristic of Josephus to use *poiētēs* in the sense of 'doer', whereas the use of *poieō* with *paradoxos* to refer to the doing of miracles is more characteristic of Eusebius of Caesarea. For this and other reasons it looks suspiciously as if the entire *Testimonium* could be a Eusebian interpolation into the text of Josephus.[4] Even if we could be sure that the *Testimonium* was broadly genuine and did contain a reference to Jesus' performance of miracles, it is not clear how much this would tell us. If Josephus were reporting what was common knowledge among the Palestinian Jews of his day, this might indicate that the miracle traditions concerning Jesus had become widespread, but it would not show how early they are, or whether Josephus was doing any more than reporting Christian claims. It is most unlikely that Josephus would be recording an independent Jewish tradition of a wonder-working Jesus, because virtually everything in *Ant.* 18.63–4 reads like a report of Christian views, and the passage lacks any independent details of (or comment on) what Jesus' *paradoxa erga* were like.

The studied neutrality of this report about Jesus (once obvious Christian interpolations are removed) militates against its authenticity: it is not, as one might expect in its context, either an account of another trouble-maker or an account of another of Pilate's misdeeds. Yet it is unlike Josephus to be quite so detached. That Jesus was a miracle-worker executed by a Roman governor might have led Josephus to portray him more like one of the sign prophets, if the intention had been to discuss another source of trouble under Pilate's governorship. Alternatively, if Josephus had wished to illustrate Pilate's unduly harsh treatment of a righteous man, one would have expected him to lay the blame for Jesus' death far more squarely on Pilate's shoulders. Compare, for example,

---

[2] See, e.g., John P. Meier, *A Marginal Jew: Rethinking the Historical Jesus*, vol. 2: *Mentor, Message, and Miracles* (New York: Doubleday, 1994), 621–2.

[3] Eric Eve, *The Jewish Context of Jesus' Miracles* (JSNTSup, 231; Sheffield: Sheffield Academic Press, 2002), 28–9.

[4] See K. A. Olson, 'Eusebius and the Testimonium Flavianum', *CBQ* 61 (1999), 305–22.

Josephus' account of Onias at *Ant.* 14.22–4, which gives a far more detailed account of the man's death, and makes it perfectly clear that those who killed him were in the wrong. Moreover, Onias is specifically said to have prayed for rain, not to have been a doer of unspecified surprising deeds; elsewhere Josephus is only that vague in connection with some of the sign prophets, who do not perform any miracles, but who do promise unspecified signs and wonders, a promise Josephus clearly regards as deceitful.

It is widely recognized that at the very least *Ant.* 18.63–4 has undergone Christian interpolation. It includes such statements as 'He was the Messiah' and 'On the third day he appeared to them restored to life, for the prophets of God had prophesied these and countless other marvellous things about him.' It is inconceivable that Josephus could have written such things, since he shows absolutely no signs of Christian sympathies anywhere else in his writings. In view of the other considerations outlined here, even if Josephus did write something about Jesus at this point in the *Antiquities*, we should have to conclude that the Christian re-writing of it has made Josephus' original words irrecoverable. Josephus thus cannot be relied upon as an independent witness to Jesus' miracles.

Other Jewish possible sources

Several other (later) Jewish sources contain traces of Jewish polemic to the effect that Jesus was a magician, which is how one might expect a hostile observer to describe a wonder-worker.[5] At first sight, this could be taken as powerful corroboration that Jesus was a wonder-worker, since although his supporters and his enemies label this activity differently, they apparently agree that it took place, and what opposing parties agree on is more likely to be true. But this argument only works if the polemical tradition that Jesus was a magician is independent of the friendly tradition that he was a miracle-worker. The alternative is that the Jewish polemical tradition is simply a reaction to Christian claims. Faced with claims that Jesus was a miracle-worker, an opponent could either deny that Jesus had performed any extraordinary deeds, or else accept that he had but assert that they were not miracles (empowered by God) but magic (empowered by collusion with evil spirits). The problem with the former strategy would be that, by the time the Church's proclamation became a problem, it would be impossible for anyone to prove that Jesus had not performed

---

[5] For details, see Morton Smith, *Jesus the Magician* (London: Victor Gollancz, 1978), 45–67.

any extraordinary deeds. The advantage of the latter strategy would be that it does not just deny the Christians' assertions about Jesus' miracles but turns them against him. Thus, we cannot count on polemical traditions of Jesus as magician as being independent evidence from Jewish sources that Jesus performed extraordinary deeds.

Yet if this polemic does not reflect any independent tradition, it surely presupposes the Christian traditions it seeks to subvert. So if this polemical tradition can be traced back early enough, it may provide independent evidence that the miracle stories predate the Gospels. There are some indications of this within the Gospel of Mark. The Beelzebul Controversy (Mark 3.22–30) has Jesus refute the scribes' accusation that he was casting out demons by the prince of demons; this seems to suggest that this accusation was already being made prior to Mark writing his Gospel, even if the pericope in its present form is substantially due to Markan redaction. The Cursing of the Fig Tree at Mark 11.12–14, 20–25 looks suspiciously like Mark's attempt to domesticate a story earlier told against Jesus. By intercalating the temple incident between the two halves of the story, Mark turns it into a legitimate prophetic sign, and by appending material on prayer and forgiveness he further turns it into the occasion for pious teaching, but without these redactional manoeuvres the story paints a negative picture of a petulant and destructive Jesus.[6] Rather than denying that Jesus ever caused a fig tree to wither, Mark accepts the fact but puts an acceptable spin on it. If this analysis is correct, it assumes the prior hostile use of the fig tree story, which in turn could be part of the polemical tradition set in train to subvert Christian claims about Jesus' miracles. This would imply that traditions of Jesus' miracles existed before Mark's Gospel and were a sufficiently prominent part of Christian proclamation to provoke a polemical response.

Non-canonical sources

The *Gospel of Thomas*

One source that has attracted a good deal of attention as potentially useful for historical-Jesus research is the *Gospel of Thomas*, a collection of sayings of Jesus lacking any narrative framework. Opinions are divided over whether the *Gospel of Thomas* is a relatively early document wholly

---

[6] Eve, *Jewish Context*, 366–7.

independent of the canonical Gospels or whether it is relatively late (second century CE) and dependent upon one or more of the other Gospels. Since the *Gospel of Thomas* is purely a collection of sayings (*Gos. Thom.* 1) we should not expect to find any miracle stories in it. Nevertheless, a sayings collection could contain sayings that alluded to the miracle tradition in some way, as some Synoptic sayings do (e.g. Matthew 11.4–6, 21; Luke 13.32), yet with the possible exceptions of *Gos. Thom.* 14 and 31, the Gospel of Thomas fails to do so. At *Gos. Thom.* 31 Jesus says, 'A prophet is not acceptable in that prophet's own native town. A physician does not heal people who are acquainted with that physician.'[7] But there is nothing to indicate that this is intended as a self-reference, as it is in the similar saying at Matthew 13.57 // Mark 6.4 // Luke 4.24. If *Gos. Thom.* 31 does independently record a genuine saying of Jesus that was originally spoken as a self-reference, then it would provide some corroboration of the tradition that Jesus healed people. But there is too much uncertainty about the original context of this saying to claim that *Gos. Thom.* 31 provides any real support to the traditions of Jesus' healing activities.

At *Gos. Thom.* 14 Jesus says:

> If you (plur.) fast, you will acquire a sin, and if you pray you will be condemned, and if you give alms, it is evil that you will do unto your spirits. And whenever you go into any land and travel in the country places, where they receive you eat whatever they serve you. Heal those among them who are sick. For nothing that enters your mouth will defile you (plur.). Rather it is precisely what comes out of your mouth that will defile you.

Here the injunction to heal the sick looks like an irrelevant aside in a passage that is otherwise concerned with flouting normal Israelite religious practice. Indeed, healing seems so irrelevant here that it is tempting to suppose that *Gos. Thom.* must be dependent on Luke 10.8–9.[8] Even if *Gos. Thom.* 14 could be taken as independent evidence of something Jesus said, then this would only tell us that he commanded his followers to heal, it says nothing about him doing any healing himself. It might be a reasonable inference that Jesus would not command healing if he did not

---

[7] The translations from the Gospel of Thomas used here are those of Bentley Layton, *The Gnostic Scriptures: A New Translation with Annotations and Introductions by Bentley Layton* (London: SCM Press, 1987), 380–99.

[8] So John P. Meier, *A Marginal Jew: Rethinking the Historical Jesus*, vol. 1: *The Roots of the Problem and the Person* (New York: Doubleday, 1991), 137–8; for a contrary view see John Dominic Crossan, *The Birth of Christianity: Discovering What Happened in the Years Immediately After the Execution of Jesus* (San Francisco: Harper, 1998), 327–37.

practise it himself, but it is no more than a reasonable inference, and it certainly constitutes no evidence that Jesus was any better at healing than anyone else. The evidence of this passage is thus extremely weak.

If the *Gospel of Thomas* cannot be pressed into service in support of Jesus' miracles, neither can it be used against them. Synoptic sayings about Jesus' miracles generally occur in some narrative context that provides an occasion for them. No such contexts appear in the *Gospel of Thomas*. The Synoptic sayings frequently make explicit reference to what Jesus is doing in his ministry, and no *Thomas* saying does that. The absence of this kind of material from *Thomas* therefore proves nothing beyond the fact that this was not the kind of material that the compiler of *Thomas* was interested in including. Any argument from silence would thus be perilous. To take a loose parallel, there is nothing in Josephus' *Against Apion* to suggest that Josephus thought that Moses was associated with miracle-working (although *Apion* has quite a bit to say about Moses); but if one were to conclude from this that Josephus knew nothing of miracles associated with Moses one could at once be refuted by Josephus' treatment of them in the *Antiquities*.

We must conclude that whatever date is assigned to the *Gospel of Thomas*, and whatever its relation to the Synoptic Gospels turns out to be, it is a text that has little relevance to determining the authenticity of the Jesus miracle traditions.

Secret Mark

The so-called *Secret Gospel of Mark* is known only from a single surviving copy of a letter purporting to be by Clement of Alexandria, in which Clement apparently gives the text of a pair of passages not found in our canonical Gospel of Mark.[9] It has been argued that *Secret Mark* is in fact an earlier form of the Gospel than our canonical text.[10] If this were the case, its importance for Jesus' miracles would lie in its inclusion of a story, not found in canonical Mark, about Jesus raising a young man from the dead. This story is similar to but apparently independent of the raising of Lazarus in John 11. But the value of this depends on the authenticity of the *Secret Mark* fragment, which may reasonably be called into question. The fragments of *Secret Mark* preserved in the supposed letter of Clement

---

[9] See Morton Smith, *Clement of Alexandria and a Secret Gospel of Mark* (Cambridge, MA: Harvard University Press, 1973).

[10] Helmut Koester, *Ancient Christian Gospels: Their History and Development* (London: SCM Press; Philadelphia: Trinity Press International, 1990), 293–303.

The Healer from Nazareth

look suspiciously like a pastiche of Mark,[11] and it has been argued that the entire letter may be a twentieth-century hoax.[12]

Egerton Papyrus

In 1935 four papyrus fragments of a previously unknown early Christian work dubbed the 'Unknown Gospel' were published. Since the fragments were purchased from a dealer, their precise provenance is unknown, although it is presumably in Egypt. A further fragment, Papyrus Köln 255, was subsequently identified as belonging to the same work. On palaeographical grounds the fragments have been variously dated to probably no later than the middle of the second century CE, or else to the third century, perhaps *c.* 200 CE. Either way, Papyrus Egerton 2 and Papyrus Köln 255 are among the earliest extant Christian papyri, and may represent a copy of a work that is earlier still.[13]

The potential interest of the *Egerton Gospel* (*EG*) for the present enquiry lies in its two miracle stories, for if *EG* should turn out to be independent of the canonical Gospels, we should have independent attestation to the Jesus miracle tradition. Unfortunately, it is far from clear that this is the case. It has been maintained by some scholars that *EG* is independent from, or indeed prior to the canonical Gospels,[14] while others see it as a secondary composition wholly dependent on the canonical Gospels, even though its author may have been to some extent dependent on his memory.[15] A compromise position sees *EG* as dependent upon John but independent of the Synoptics.[16]

---

[11] So, e.g., James D. G. Dunn, *Christianity in the Making*, vol. 1: *Jesus Remembered* (Grand Rapids and Cambridge: Eerdmans, 2003), 169.

[12] See Stephen C. Carlson, *The Gospel Hoax: Morton Smith's Invention of Secret Mark* (Waco, TX: Baylor University Press, 2005). For criticisms of some aspects of Carlson's arguments see Scott G. Brown, 'Reply to Stephen Carlson', *ExpTim* 117 (2006), 144–9, and Allen J. Pantuck and Scott G. Brown, 'Morton Smith as M. Madiotes: Stephen Carlson's Attribution of *Secret Mark* to a Bald Swindler', *JSHJ* 6 (2008), 106–25.

[13] H. Idriss Bell and T. C. Skeat, *Fragments of an Unknown Gospel and Other Early Christian Papyri* (London: Trustees of the British Museum (Oxford University Press), 1935).

[14] See, e.g., John Dominic Crossan, *Four Other Gospels: Shadows on the Contours of Canon* (Minneapolis: Winston Press, 1985), 73–5; Koester, *Ancient Christian Gospels*, 205–16. This is also broadly the position taken in Bell and Skeat, *Fragments of an Unknown Gospel*.

[15] So, e.g., J. Jeremias, 'An Unknown Gospel with Johannine Elements (Pap. Egerton 2)' in E. Hennecke et al. (eds), *New Testament Apocrypha* (tr. G. Ogg et al.; London: Lutterworth, 1963), 1.94–7; Frans Neirynck, *Evangelica II 1982–1991: Collected Essays by Frans Neirynck* (BETL, 99; Leuven: Leuven University Press, 1991), 753–9.

[16] So C. H. Dodd, 'A New Gospel', *BJRL* 20 (1956), 56–92, reprinted in C. H. Dodd, *New Testament Studies* (Manchester: Manchester University Press, 1953), 12–52; John W. Pryor, 'Papyrus Egerton 2 and the Fourth Gospel', *Australian Biblical Review* 37 (1989), 1–13.

76

One of the two miracle stories is an account of the cleansing of a leper that looks similar to but possibly independent of Mark 1.40–44. The text of the other is quite badly damaged, but appears to concern a strange question that baffles some group of people, following which Jesus pauses in his stride along the bank of the River Jordan, stretches out his right hand to sprinkle water on something, so that something or someone brings out fruit.

The account of the cleansing of the leper in *EG* has less in common with the Synoptic accounts than they have with one another. In particular, *EG* lacks the obeisance done to Jesus by the leper at the start of the story, the notice that Jesus stretched out his hand and touched the leper, and the command to silence. So far as we can tell, it also lacks 'as a witness to/against them' as the motive for reporting to the priests. On the other hand, *EG* provides the explanation, lacking in the Synoptics, that the leper contracted the disease while travelling with other lepers and eating with them at an inn, as well as the command to sin no more, which seems more reminiscent of John 5.14 (and 8.11) than of anything in the Synoptics. Finally, while all three Synoptics agree in having the leper say to Jesus, 'if you wish, you can cleanse me', *EG* has him say, 'if you wish, I am cleansed', and while in the Synoptics the leper is ordered to present himself to the priest (singular), in *EG* he is apparently sent to the priests (plural).

Other parts of this fragment contain language sufficiently close to that of John's Gospel to make some form of dependence upon John seem highly probable. The case for and against dependence on one or more of the Synoptic Gospels is more finely balanced, but the balance nevertheless seems to come down on the side of dependence, even though it is more likely to be a dependence mediated by a recollection of the Synoptics than a result of direct copying from a manuscript. Particularly striking is the agreement in wording between the introduction to the healing of the leper in *EG* and Matthew 8.2, given that this is where one would most expect an independent author to say something different (at this point Matthew 8.2 is actually closer to *EG* than to either Mark 1.40 or Luke 5.12). There are also a number of other verbal parallels between *EG* and the Synoptic Gospels both in this pericope and in other parts of *EG*. Cumulatively, these seem to make dependence of *EG* on the canonical Gospels more likely than not, so that *EG* should be seen as a reworking of Gospel material rather than as an independent witness to the Jesus tradition.

The Apostolic Fathers

There are not infrequent references to the Jesus tradition in the Apostolic Fathers, and these references often seem to be independent of the canonical Gospels.[17] But these are nearly all allusions to or quotations of Jesus' sayings; references to Jesus' miracles in the Apostolic Fathers are few and far between. Perhaps the clearest occurs at *Barnabas* 5.8, 'Furthermore, while teaching Israel and doing such great signs and wonders he preached to them and loved them greatly.'[18] Elsewhere references to Jesus' ministry in the Apostolic Fathers tend to restrict themselves to his birth, passion and resurrection. At *Magnesians* 9.2 Ignatius does refer to Jesus raising the dead, but in context the dead who are raised appear to be the prophets of old, perhaps rescued from Sheol after Jesus' resurrection, rather than those allegedly raised during Jesus' earthly ministry. There is a possible allusion to Jesus' miraculous activity at *1 Clement* 16.2, which says that when Jesus came, it was not with pomp and arrogance, 'for all his power', but this is hardly conclusive.

The absence of Jesus miracle tradition from this literature is not so surprising given its nature, which is largely epistolary or homiletic rather than narrative. There is nowhere where the absence of such allusions seems unduly odd, so that one would be unwise to mount an argument from silence. One cannot argue from the Apostolic Fathers that the miracle stories about Jesus were unknown outside the Gospels. Indeed, although the evidence to the contrary is not strong, it is not wholly absent. Ignatius in particular seems to surround Jesus' appearance on earth with a generally miraculous atmosphere, even if he lacks any specific reference to miracles performed by Jesus. The one clear reference to Jesus' miracles, in *Barnabas* 5.8, may be of some significance since it is far from clear from his other use of Jesus material that *Barnabas* knows any of the Gospels.[19]

---

[17] See, e.g., Jonathan Draper, 'The Jesus Tradition in the Didache' in David Wenham (ed.), *Gospel Perspectives*, vol. 5: *The Jesus Tradition Outside the Gospels* (Sheffield: JSOT Press, 1984), 269–87; David A. Hagner, 'The Sayings of Jesus in the Apostolic Fathers and Justin Martyr' in Wenham, *Jesus Tradition*, 233–68; and Oxford Society of Historical Theology, *The New Testament in the Apostolic Fathers* (Oxford: Clarendon Press, 1905).

[18] The translation is that of Kirsopp Lake, *The Apostolic Fathers* (LCL; London: Heinemann, 1912), vol. 1.

[19] See Oxford Society, *Apostolic Fathers*, 17–23, and Hagner, 'Apostolic Fathers', 242–3.

The Apologists

According to Eusebius, *H.E.* 4.3.2, one Quadratus addressed a brief Apology to the Emperor Trajan, in the course of which he wrote:

> But the works of our Saviour were always present, for they were true, those who were cured, those who rose from the dead, who not merely appeared as cured and risen, but were constantly present, not only while the Saviour was living, but even for some time after he had gone; so that some of them survived even until our own time.[20]

If Eusebius can be relied upon in quoting this extract accurately, then Quadratus could well be making a report independent of the Gospel tradition. Whatever one makes of Quadratus' claim that people Jesus had raised from the dead survived until his own time (he was writing in or after 117 CE, but could well have been referring to an earlier period of his life), it at least testifies to a belief that Jesus performed this kind of miracle. And the claim that both healed and revived persons were still around in Quadratus' living memory further suggests that Jesus' healing activity was known about through a living oral tradition independent of any written Gospel accounts.

There is little evidence of such continuing oral tradition in the work of other second-century apologists, but there are sufficient indications of ongoing controversy over Christian miracle claims to show that miracle-working was by then a significant part of the Jesus tradition. Thus, for example, Justin rebuts the charge that Jesus' miracles were worked by magic by arguing that his healings were in accordance with prophecy (Justin, *1 Apol.* 30, 48). Elsewhere he points out that pagans should not regard Jesus' healings as something unprecedented, since similar feats were attributed to Asclepius (Justin, *1 Apol.* 21–2), although pagan myths about Asclepius were based on demonic distortions of Isaiah's prophecy that the Messiah would heal the sick and raise the dead (*1 Apol.* 54.10; *Dial.* 69.3).[21] Justin also shows awareness of Jesus' activity as an exorcist. For example, at *2 Apol.* 6.6 he talks about Jesus being made man in part for the destruction of demons, and cites the contemporary practice of Christian exorcists as evidence of this (see also *Dial.* 30.3; 76.7), and at *Dial.* 85 he compares (effective) Christian exorcism in the name of Jesus

---

[20] The translation is that of Kirsopp Lake, *Eusebius: The Ecclesiastical History* (LCL, 2 vols; London: Heinemann, 1926), 1.309.

[21] See Harold Remus, *Pagan–Christian Conflict over Miracle in the Second Century* (Patristic Monograph Series, 10; Cambridge, MA: Philadelphia Patristic Foundation, 1983), 137–41.

with the more magical practices of Jewish exorcists.[22] It seems highly likely that Justin knew at least some of the canonical Gospels, even if he also had access to other written sources,[23] so none of this can be directly cited as *independent* testimony to Jesus miracle traditions; it does, however, show that Jesus' miracles were a live issue when Justin wrote, and it may indirectly suggest the existence of extra-canonical miracle traditions, since Justin appears to be addressing outsiders who can be expected to know of Jesus' miracle-working reputation, but are unlikely to have learned it from reading the Gospels.

A final point of interest is that Justin and Quadratus both refer to Jesus' activity as a healer, but not to his nature miracles.

The New Testament apocrypha

The Jewish-Christian Gospels identified from patristic citations as the *Gospel of the Hebrews*, the *Gospel of the Ebionites* and the *Gospel of the Nazaraeans* survive only in a few fragments, with few references to miracles. Indeed, the only relevant fragment that survives is one cited by Jerome in his commentary on Matthew 12.13:

> In the Gospel that the Nazarenes and Ebionites use, which I recently translated from the Hebrew into Greek and which most people designate as the authentic text of Matthew, we read that the man with a withered hand was a mason, who asked for help with these words: 'I was a mason, working for my bread with my hands. I pray to you, Jesus, restore me to health so that I do not eat my bread in disgrace.'[24]

In Matthew 12.9–14 the man with the withered hand takes no initiative at all in seeking the healing, he is simply present in the synagogue as an occasion for the Pharisees to try to trap Jesus into healing on the Sabbath and so provide something they can charge him with. The initiative with the healing lies purely with Jesus. Yet although the mason's request thus alters the dynamics of the pericope, some such words could stand between, say, Matthew 12.10a and 12.10b and still result in a coherent story. There is thus no reason to suppose that the words quoted by Jerome are anything other than the novelistic expansion of the Synoptic account that they appear to be.

---

[22] Remus, *Pagan–Christian Conflict*, 151–2.

[23] Hagner, 'Apostolic Fathers', 246–9.

[24] J. K. Elliott (ed.), *The Apocryphal New Testament: A Collection of Apocryphal Christian Literature in an English Translation based on M. R. James* (Oxford: Clarendon Press, 1993), 3–16 (12); P. Vielhauer, 'Jewish-Christian Gospels' in E. Hennecke et al. (eds), *New Testament Apocrypha* (trs. G. Ogg et al.; London, Lutterworth, 1963), 1.117–65 (147–8).

Most apocryphal literature turns out to be surprisingly conservative with the Jesus miracle traditions. Although thousands of apocryphal words are attributed to Jesus, and there are embellishments of the miraculous elements surrounding his infancy and childhood (most notably in the *Infancy Gospel of Thomas*) and his death and resurrection (e.g. in the *Gospel of Peter*), there is very little tendency to elaborate on the miracles Jesus performed in the course of his public ministry.

To take one example, the *Epistula Apostolorum* is probably to be dated to the second century.[25] It takes the form of a letter from the eleven apostles to Christians throughout the world, mainly containing a revelation of things to come vouchsafed them by the risen Christ. This is prefaced by a brief account of Christ's coming, including the miracles wrought in his ministry, and of his resurrection. The summary of the miracles (in *Ep. Apos.* 5) begins with the turning of water into wine at the wedding at Cana, and proceeds through raising the dead, making the lame walk, healing the man with the withered hand and the woman with a haemorrhage, giving hearing to the deaf and sight to the blind, the exorcism of the Legion demon, cleansing lepers, a conflation of the walking on the sea and the calming of the storm, the coin in the fish's mouth, and the feeding of the five thousand. These incidents are handled in a variety of ways, but nowhere is there any suggestion of a miracle that cannot be found in the canonical Gospels, whereas most of the canonical miracles are encompassed in the summary.

Even the fifth-century *Acts of Pilate* exhibits this relative restraint. It is not at all reluctant to introduce further miraculous elements into its story as a whole. Thus, for example, when Jesus is brought before Pilate, the images on the Roman standards all miraculously bow to him (*Acts Pil.* 1.5), and following Jesus' resurrection Joseph of Arimathea is miraculously delivered from execution (*Acts Pil.* 12.1–2; 15.6). But during the course of the trial, where an account of the miracles performed by Jesus during his ministry is given, little is added to the canonical accounts. The fanciful element in the trial scene is rather that two of the people healed by Jesus come forward to testify what has been done for them. There is some novelistic embellishment of events already described in the Gospels, but in essence the miracles attributed to Jesus do not go beyond those reported in the canonical Gospels; indeed, they are restricted to healings and exorcisms without any mention of the nature miracles. Even though

---

[25] Hugo Duensing, 'Epistula Apostolorum' in E. Hennecke et al. (eds), *New Testament Apocrypha* (trs. G. Ogg et al.; London, Lutterworth, 1963), 1.189–227 (190–1).

it may be separated from the *Epistula Apostolorum* by several centuries, the *Acts of Pilate* thus shows a similar restraint in relation to the miracle stories of Jesus' ministry.

An earlier example of Christian literature about Pilate is provided by the fictitious *Letter of Pilate to Claudius*, possibly from the late second century,[26] in which Pilate is made to state that the majority of the Jewish people believed Jesus to be the Son of God on account of his miracles: 'he restored sight to the blind, cleansed lepers, healed paralytics, expelled evil spirits from men, and even raised the dead, and commanded the winds, and walked dry-shod upon the waves of the sea, and did many other miracles'.[27] Given the summary nature of this account, it is perhaps not surprising that no new miracles are attributed to Jesus here, but it once again appears that no miracles beyond those given in the canonical Gospels are known about.

Such restraint is hardly shown towards the miraculous in general in Christian writings of this period, as a comparison both with Infancy Gospels such as that of Thomas and apocryphal acts of various apostles quickly reveals. This restraint thus calls for some comment. It may in part be that the canonical Gospels were thought to furnish a sufficiently impressive set of miracles from Jesus' ministry to render the invention of any further ones redundant; or, especially by the time of composition of the *Acts of Pilate*, the perceived scriptural authority of the canonical accounts may have played a restraining role. Nonetheless, the restraint remains striking; at the very least, one would have thought that if additional miracle stories were being invented after the Evangelists wrote some of them would surface in Christian literature, and their failure to do so would seem to suggest that such additional miracle stories either never existed at all, or at least failed to gain wide circulation.

Paul

The author of the earliest surviving Christian texts is Paul. Paul displays no explicit knowledge of miracle traditions in relation to Jesus, and this could be used as an argument against the authenticity of such traditions in the Gospels; yet Paul does seem to regard the performance of miracles (*dunameis, terata, sēmeia*) as part of Christian mission and ministry (1 Corinthians 12.9–10; Galatians 3.5), and even claims to have performed

---

[26] So Elliott, *Apocryphal New Testament*, 205.
[27] Elliott, *Apocryphal New Testament*, 206.

some himself (Romans 15.19; 2 Corinthians 12.12), so one might argue that in this the early Church was following the practice of its founder.[28]

The negative argument (that Paul is ignorant of any tradition of Jesus' miracles) is considerably weakened both by the genre of Paul's surviving letters and by the overall paucity of any kind of Jesus tradition in what he wrote. Paul's surviving writings are occasional letters written to address specific problems; they are not the entire content of his preaching about Jesus Christ, and, more specifically, they are not narratives. Moreover, Paul is remarkably sparing with his use of the Jesus sayings tradition, even when it might have suited his purpose to appeal to it. At 2 Corinthians 5.16 he famously states that he no longer knows Jesus 'according to the flesh' (whatever exactly he means by that), and at 1 Corinthians 2.2 Paul states his determination to know nothing among the Corinthians apart from Christ and him crucified. These remarks may, of course, simply be rhetorical flourishes aimed at particular people in Corinth; they do not necessarily mean that Paul was determined to be totally ignorant of every aspect of the Jesus tradition apart from the facts of his death and resurrection. So the absence of any explicit trace of Jesus miracle material in Paul tells us nothing.

The argument from Paul's references to apostolic miracles is equally insecure. Paul never appeals to Jesus' miracles as the precedent for apostolic practice. The reason Paul refers to performing the 'signs of a true apostle' at 2 Corinthians 12.12 may simply be that such mighty works demonstrate the power of God's Spirit at work (and hence divine accreditation of Paul's mission). Another problem is that Paul never makes it clear what kind of miracles he was referring to. To be sure, there is a reference at 1 Corinthians 12.9 to healing as a gift of the Spirit, but this appears to be regarded as something separate from the gift of performing mighty works (1 Corinthians 12.10); conceivably these mighty works could be exorcisms, but there is nothing in the text to indicate this. Moreover, the main gift of the Spirit that is in view here is that of speaking in tongues. Since nowhere in the surviving Jesus tradition is Jesus ever credited with speaking in tongues, it is hard to argue that any of the other gifts of the Spirit listed here must reflect the practices of the earthly Jesus.

---

[28] So, e.g., Graham H. Twelftree, *Jesus the Miracle Worker: A Historical and Theological Study* (Downers Grove, IL: InterVarsity Press, 1999), 255–6; and, more cautiously, Twelftree, *In the Name of Jesus: Exorcism among Early Christians* (Grand Rapids, MI: Baker Academic, 2007), 60–4.

In conclusion, the fact that Paul mentions miracles both as signs of a true apostle and as among the gifts of the Spirit (presumably exercised in the Corinthian congregation) is certainly a relevant datum, but it is hard to determine precisely what its relevance is. In isolation it tells us little or nothing about the Jesus tradition at the time of Paul. In combination with other arguments it may at best lend weak corroboration to the existence of miracle stories in the Jesus tradition Paul knew. Perhaps the most we can conclude is that what Paul says in his letters is compatible with there having been miracle stories in the Jesus tradition available to him.

The canonical Gospels and their hypothetical sources

Written sources

In addition to extant texts that may shed some light on the question of Jesus' miracles, there are several putative sources, no longer extant, that can supposedly be reconstructed from the canonical texts. The importance of such sources, if they can be shown to exist, is that they could give us a snapshot of the Jesus tradition at an earlier stage of transmission than we have it in the canonical Gospels. Such sources could also be employed in arguments appealing to the criterion of multiple attestation (the notion that the more independent sources we can find that attest to a particular tradition, the more likely it is to go back to the historical Jesus).

The most widely accepted of these sources is Q (from the German *Quelle*, meaning 'source'), supposedly used by Matthew and Luke for the material they have in common which is not found in Mark. If Q existed, then it would contain the story of the healing of the centurion's servant (Matthew 8.5–13 // Luke 7.1–10) and a number of sayings, such as the woes on Galilean cities (Matthew 11.21–24 // Luke 10.13–15) and Jesus' reply to John the Baptist (Matthew 11.2–6 // Luke 7.19–23), that would indicate that Jesus was a miracle-worker. But the existence of Q is only as secure as one particular solution to the Synoptic Problem (the question of the relationship between Matthew, Mark and Luke), namely the Two Document Hypothesis (2DH, i.e. that Matthew and Luke used both the hypothetical Q source and Mark). Although the 2DH remains the most widely held view of Synoptic relations among New Testament scholars, it has not gone unchallenged. This is not the place to enter into a detailed discussion of the Synoptic Problem, but the Farrer Hypothesis (namely that Matthew used Mark, and Luke used both Matthew and Mark) also has strong arguments in its favour.[29] Moreover, even if the 2DH is correct, it is far from certain that we can be confident of Q's reconstruction.[30] It is thus unclear that a reconstructed Q could give us any information about the Jesus tradition that we could not equally well get directly from Matthew and Luke.

One advantage supposedly conferred by Q is that it offers an independent witness to Jesus' miracle-working activity which can then be used to support the likelihood that Jesus was a miracle-worker through the criterion of multiple attestation.[31] But the criterion of multiple attestation is even more problematic than the existence of Q. The fact that something turns up in a number of sources shows only that it must be older than the sources in which it turns up, not that it goes back to the historical Jesus, and the frequency with which something is narrated may be as much an index of its popularity as its truth.[32] If something were to be found attested in truly independent sources that clearly represent quite different points of view, it might be a different matter, but this would not be the case with Mark and Q, say, for even if there were no literary dependence between them they would both be sources stemming from supporters of Jesus, potentially tapping the same stream of tradition (as the existence of Mark–Q overlaps on the 2DH makes clear).

What applies to Q applies even more to the other written sources that are often postulated behind many of the Gospel miracle stories, including the alleged Signs Source employed by John (principally in Chapters 2—12), the catena (chain or collection) of miracle stories said to have been employed by Mark (in Mark 4—8), and possibly by John as well, and the collection of pre-Markan controversy stories sometimes identified as lying behind Mark 2.1—3.5.[33] The criteria for identifying such sources

---

[29] For arguments against Q, see e.g. A. M. Farrer, 'On Dispensing with Q' in D. E. Nineham (ed.), *Studies in the Gospels: Essays in Memory of R. H. Lightfoot* (Oxford: Blackwell, 1955), 55–88; and Mark Goodacre, *The Case Against Q: Studies in Markan Priority and the Synoptic Problem* (Harrisburg, PA: Trinity Press International, 2002).

[30] See Eric Eve, 'Reconstructing Mark: A Thought Experiment' in Mark S. Goodacre and Nicholas Perrin (eds), *Questioning Q* (London: SPCK, 2004), 89–114, and Nicholas Perrin, 'The Limits of a Reconstructed Q' in the same volume, 71–88.

[31] See Meier, *Marginal Jew*, 2.619–20.

[32] Eric Eve, 'Meier, Miracle and Multiple Attestation', *JSHJ* 3 (2005), 23–45; see also Dale C. Allison, *Jesus of Nazareth: Millenarian Prophet* (Minneapolis: Fortress, 1998), 1–33.

[33] On the Signs Source see Robert Fortna, *The Fourth Gospel and its Predecessor* (Edinburgh: T. & T. Clark, 1989); Fortna, *The Gospel of Signs* (Cambridge: Cambridge University Press, 1970); and W. Nicol, *The Sēmeia in the Fourth Gospel: Tradition and Redaction* (NovTSup, 32; Leiden: Brill, 1972). For the miracle-catenae see Paul J. Achtemeier, 'Toward the Isolation

seem fragile at best, and it seems at least equally plausible to attribute the arrangement of this material to the Evangelists.[34] Even if such sources existed, we could never know that we had reconstructed them correctly, and we could not even know that our reconstructions were even probably correct, since we have no independent means of checking. Conversely, we should not be able to determine the date or provenance of these reconstructed sources, and so would have no means of assessing their value as independent testimony to the historical Jesus.

The point is not to condemn hypothetical sources for being hypothetical, since just about anything we do in studying the New Testament is hypothetical to some extent. Rather, the point is not only that these sources seem to rest on particularly fragile hypotheses, but that they are not even particularly useful hypotheses for the job at hand. Instead of going to the trouble of conjuring conjectural sources out of the text of the Gospels, and then trying to glean historical information out of those conjectural sources, it seems more straightforward to work directly with the Gospels, which in any case contain all the information that any hypothetical sources we could construct out of them would contain.

That said, it is necessary to take some view on the nature of the relationships between the Gospels; we have to work with some source-critical hypothesis. For that purpose I shall assume that the hypothesis of Markan priority is correct, namely that Matthew and Luke both made use of Mark. I shall not assume the existence of Q, but in what follows very little will depend on whether Matthew and Luke independently drew their double-tradition material from Q or whether Luke obtained it from Matthew. Thus, if I argue my case without recourse to Q, it should not be materially damaged should it turn out that the Two Document Hypothesis was correct after all. It would be more damaging should either the Two Gospel (neo-Griesbach) or Augustinian hypothesis (the details of which need not detain us here, suffice it to say that both postulate Matthean priority) prove to be correct, since I should then turn out to have chosen

---

of Pre-Martan Miracle Catenae', *JBL* 89 (1970), 265–91 and 'The Origin and Function of the Pre-Marcan Miracle Catenae', *JBL* 91 (1972), 198–221. On Q see, e.g., John S. Kloppenborg, *The Formation of Q: Trajectories in Ancient Wisdom Collections* (Studies in Antiquity and Christianity; Harrisburg, PA: Trinity Press International, 1999), John S. Kloppenborg Verbin, *Excavating Q: The History and Setting of the Sayings Gospel* (Edinburgh: T. & T. Clark, 2000) and Christopher M. Tuckett, *Q and the History of Early Christianity* (Edinburgh: T. & T. Clark, 1997).

[34] For a composition-critical approach to Mark 4—8, see Robert M. Fowler, *Loaves and Fishes: The Function of the Feeding Stories in the Gospel of Mark* (Chico, CA: Scholars Press, 1981); and Norman R. Petersen, 'The Composition of Mark 4:1—8:26', *HTR* 73 (1980), 185–217.

the wrong Gospel (Mark) to be the chief focus of my analysis; but even that might not be fatal.

Oral tradition

Studies of the Gospels and of the historical Jesus frequently appeal to oral tradition. The oral tradition behind the Gospels is not a source directly available to us, not least because any attempt to reconstruct it is almost bound to be even more speculative than attempts to reconstruct written sources. In any case oral tradition is not a thing that can be reconstructed like a text. Unlike a text, which takes physical form in one or more manuscripts that endure through time, oral tradition is a sequence of speech events, and once speech has been uttered, it is no longer there to be examined; only the memory of it remains.

It is nevertheless worth giving just a little thought to oral tradition, if only because in New Testament Studies it is all too often used as a kind of catch-all term we vaguely gesture to as a supposed non-written means by which Jesus material reached the Evangelists.[35] It is questionable whether we should even talk of 'oral tradition' at all, since in the technical sense this term is used to refer to material that is transmitted orally over several generations,[36] and the normal dating of the Gospels seems too early for this to have occurred by the time the Evangelists wrote; it might thus be better to speak of 'oral transmission'. A further complication is that we have no means of knowing just how purely oral the pre-Gospel tradition actually was. It is fair to assume that orality played an important role in the transmission of traditions about Jesus, but we should not assume that Jesus' followers were all total illiterates on whom writing made no impact at all, so that one can apply models taken from purely oral societies to the transmission of the Jesus tradition. The first-century world was well used to the use of written texts, and although levels of literacy were low, in antiquity texts were primarily scripts for oral performance rather than visual perusal, and persons from all strata of society would be used to hearing texts read aloud. Moreover, if, as seems overwhelmingly likely, the earliest Jesus movement sprang up among Israelites, it would have been transmitted among people familiar

---

[35] For an amplification of this point, see Crossan, *Birth*, 49–89, and contrast Richard Bauckham, *Jesus and the Eyewitnesses: The Gospels as Eyewitness Testimony* (Grand Rapids: Eerdmans, 2006), 319–57.
[36] Jan Vansina, *Oral Tradition as History* (London: James Currey, 1985), 12–13, 27.

with Scripture. That some of Jesus' followers would have committed some material to written form, if only as notes, seems eminently possible, so we cannot be sure that the transmission process was ever purely oral; indeed Paul's first letter to the Corinthians provides several examples of Jesus tradition written down by Paul (1 Corinthians 7.10–11; 11.23–26; 15.3–7).

In any case, there is no one model of oral transmission that must apply in all times and all places, and just about anything is antecedently possible. It is possible for oral transmission to be wildly profligate, distorting the material with each retelling to meet the needs of the moment, and caring nothing for accuracy. It is also possible for oral transmission to be carefully controlled, perhaps by casting the material in memorable poetic form, or by insisting on rote repetition as in much ancient schooling (not least the later rabbinic schools). Both notions of oral transmission, together with variations at all points of the spectrum, have been proposed for the oral transmission of the pre-Gospel Jesus material, and the truth probably lies somewhere in the middle, even if it is hard to formulate a precise model.[37] For we know too little about the primitive Jesus movement to have enough to go on in formulating such a model.

Nevertheless, it is possible to venture a few suggestions about what seems relatively likely. On the one hand, we should expect a number of conservative pressures to operate. The business of narrating material about Jesus was unlikely to be a game of Chinese whispers, in which each person in the transmission chain passed on his or her version without any form of social control. Much of the transmission will have taken place among groups of people some of whom had heard these stories before and would protest if they felt too many liberties were being taken with them. Again, given the nature of the beliefs about Jesus, the traditions about him would not be regarded as trivial, as if they were merely amusing anecdotes or casual gossip; one would expect them to be treated with a certain amount of care and respect, at least among Jesus' most active

---

[37] For a selection of models and critiques of models, see Dunn, *Jesus Remembered*, 192–210; Bauckham, *Eyewitnesses*, 240–318; Werner H. Kelber, *The Oral and the Written Gospel: The Hermeneutics of Speaking and Writing in the Synoptic Tradition, Mark, Paul and Q* (Voices in Performance and Text; Bloomington and Indianapolis: Indiana University Press, 1997); and Øivind Anderson, 'Oral Tradition' in Henry Wansbrough (ed.), *Jesus and the Oral Gospel Tradition* (JSNTSup, 64; Sheffield: Sheffield Academic Press, 1991), 17–58; Dunn, 'Eyewitnesses and the Oral Jesus Tradition', *JSHJ* 6.1 (2008), 85–105; and the various responses to Bauckham in *JSHJ* 6.2 (2008).

followers. Moreover, it seems likely that a certain amount of sheer inertia would operate; there were few prizes for originality in antiquity, so many people who passed on the tradition may well have felt no need to go to the trouble of being innovative when they could simply repeat what they remembered.

On the other hand, we should also expect a number of pressures for innovation and change. As the Jesus tradition came to be narrated in contexts remote from its original setting, certain details might become obscure or irrelevant and so might be dropped or reshaped. Again, many storytellers would naturally adapt and embellish their material and might add narrative touches that felt so appropriate that they were retained; as Jesus' followers struggled to wrestle with his significance, creative imagination might 'improve' on the tradition. In particular, as the conviction grew that Jesus fulfilled the scriptures, so the scriptures could be searched to supply details of what he 'must' have done. Moreover, while social forces might at times be conservative, at other times they might be transformative, reshaping the tradition in accordance with the community's emerging needs and beliefs. At no point need there have been any individual with any intent to deceive for these tendencies to result in a substantial distortion of what we would regard as historical fact.

The outcome of these conflicting pressures cannot be predicted with any precision, nor can it be reverse-engineered to uncover the pristine form of the Jesus tradition at the moment of its inception. One thing that is most unlikely to have occurred as a result of this tug-of-war is a neat division of the tradition into 'authentic' and 'inauthentic' material (particularly when it comes to the miracle stories). There may be some material that we regard as so implausible that it may as well be classified as 'inauthentic', even if it is in fact a gross distortion of some genuine but now irrecoverable historical reminiscence. There could also well be material that does not in fact go back to the historical Jesus even though it now appears plausibly authentic. But the tradition as a whole is likely to be the result of conflicting transformative and conservative tendencies working on the Jesus material in ways often more complex and more subtle than mere accretion.

This does not mean that the tradition is totally unreliable. Nor does it mean that it is totally devoid of clues suggestive of how parts of it may have come about. The point is rather that little is to be gained by trying to reconstruct or reverse-engineer the oral tradition lying behind the Gospels as means of getting at the historical Jesus, beyond a general awareness of the kind of factors that may have shaped it.

The four Gospels

We arrive finally at the main sources we have for Jesus' miracle-working activity: the four canonical Gospels. It might be thought that the next step should be to examine each of them closely in turn, remarking on the redactional/narrative/ideological stance of their authors and the effect this may have had on their use of the miracle material they employed, offer suggestions about the traditions they may have used, and reflect on whether each Evangelist has preserved or distorted the memory of Jesus' miracle-working.[38] Alternatively, we could catalogue and classify all the miracle stories in the four Gospels and work through them all carefully analysing each one in turn.[39] Neither approach will be followed here, however. First, both approaches have been followed elsewhere, so this book would end up repeating what others have already quite thoroughly attempted. Second, there is a danger that the main thread of the argument would become lost in a welter of detail. Third, and most importantly, given that there is no way of neatly dividing the healing and exorcism stories into 'authentic' and 'inauthentic', we will do far better to rely on the overall impression they create (not least, through features they tend to have in common), than on detailed judgements about each and every one, which can never be entirely secure.

On the thesis of Markan priority, much of both Matthew's and Luke's portrait of Jesus as miracle-worker is derived from Mark. If Mark has got it substantially wrong, so have they. Conversely, to the extent that Matthew and Luke diverge from Mark in their presentation of Jesus' miracles, this probably tells us more about their redactional interests than about any miracle-working performed by the historical Jesus. Furthermore, in relation to overall length Mark has the greatest focus on miracle stories of any of the Gospels, and perhaps the most interesting treatment of them. In examining the Gospels as sources we can therefore afford to take Mark as representative, focusing our main attention on that Gospel, and filling out our picture of Jesus' miracle-working from the other Gospels as and when appropriate.

Supporters of the Two Document Hypothesis might protest that Q should be given at least equal attention, since it is also a source for both Matthew and Luke, and may well be more primitive than Mark. Not being convinced of the existence of Q, I shall decline the exercise of subjecting

[38] For an example of this kind of approach see Twelftree, *Miracle Worker*.
[39] Meier, *Marginal Jew*, 2.509–1038 provides probably the most thorough example of this approach.

it to such an examination. In any case, even if Q did exist, Mark and not Q remains the principal source for the Gospels' picture of Jesus as miracle-worker, and any useful Q material can equally well be gleaned from Matthew or Luke.

This leaves the Fourth Gospel. Whether or not John drew upon the Synoptic Gospels is a puzzling question with good arguments on both sides. If John did use one or more of the Synoptics he clearly did not use them in the way Matthew and Luke used Mark, yet there are occasional indications in his Gospel that he is presupposing knowledge of something akin to the Synoptic tradition and, given the overall similarity in shape between John and the Synoptics, it would be strange if John had come up with the Gospel form quite independently of them. On balance, it seems more likely than not that John was familiar with Mark, and maybe one or both of the other Synoptic Gospels as well, even though he does not always seem solely dependent on them for material he shares with them. In any case, John's treatment of Jesus' miracles seems to be so largely shaped in the interests of John's Christology that an examination of the signs in John, interesting though it would be, would probably tell us far more about John's theology than about the historical Jesus.[40] We shall return briefly to some of John's sign stories in Chapter 7, but for the most part, the Fourth Gospel will not be taken much into account.

The next task, then, is to take a close look at how Mark uses his miracle material. This will form the subject of the next chapter.

---

[40] This is effectively conceded by Paul N. Anderson, *The Fourth Gospel and the Quest for Jesus: Modern Foundations Reconsidered* (London: T. & T. Clark, 2006), 147–8 (even though Anderson is otherwise arguing for the rehabilitation of John as a source for the historical Jesus).

5

Miracle in Mark

Mark's Gospel was almost certainly the first of the four canonical Gospels to be written. Its treatment of miracle is arguably both the most complete and most complex of the four. Mark has the highest concentration of miraculous material of any of the Gospels, particularly in the first half of the book (209 out of Mark's 666 verses – 31.38 per cent – are in some way connected with miracle; for the first nine chapters the proportion rises to 181 out of 373 verses – 48.53 per cent).[1] Moreover, Mark's miracle stories are far from being a random selection of stunning deeds; they have been arranged with order and purpose. The problem is determining what precisely that order and purpose is.[2] There seem to be almost as many proposals for the structure of Mark's Gospel as there are scholars proposing them, partly because whatever structure one settles for there are other features of his narrative that stubbornly suggest an alternative pattern. This may be because Mark is attempting to structure his narrative according to several conflicting principles at once: chiastic arrangement (a concentric ABCBA-type pattern), intercalation (sandwiching one story inside another), and cyclic patterns (such as ABCABC) vie with the need to produce a reasonably coherent narrative sequence and the desire to incorporate more material than any neat structure can comfortably hold. The result is a work in which several different structures operate simultaneously within a broad framework that lends coherence to the whole.[3]

---

[1] For the importance of Mark for the Synoptic miracle stories as a whole, see also M. E. Glasswell, 'The Use of Miracles in the Markan Gospel' in C. F. D. Moule (ed.), *Miracles: Cambridge Studies in their Philosophy and History* (London: Mowbray, 1965), 151–62 (153).

[2] Graham H. Twelftree, *Jesus the Miracle Worker: A Historical and Theological Study* (Downers Grove, IL: InterVarsity Press, 1999), 57–8.

[3] The discussion of Mark's narrative techniques in Robert M. Fowler, *Loaves and Fishes: The Function of the Feeding Stories in the Gospel of Mark* (Chico, CA: Scholars Press, 1981), 114, takes a very similar view. Cf. the helpful discussion in Bas M. F. van Iersel, *Mark: A Reader-Response Commentary* (tr. W. H. Bisscheroux; JSNTSup, 164; Sheffield: Sheffield Academic Press, 1998), 68–86; and van Iersel, *Reading Mark* (Collegeville, MN: Liturgical Press, 1988), 18–26.

There also seem to be several layers of meaning in Mark's narrative. At the very least, Mark's Gospel is both a story about Jesus and an address to Christians of Mark's own day. There is also often both a surface and a symbolic meaning, particularly in some of the miracle stories.

In what follows we shall proceed in three stages. First we shall examine how miracle functions in Mark's narrative at the surface level of the text, then we shall explore some of the possible symbolic meanings. After that, we shall see to what extent Mark treats 'nature miracles' differently from healings and exorcisms, before finally stating some conclusions.

Miracle in the surface narrative

The question of authority: Mark 1.16—3.35

The prologue to Mark's Gospel (1.1–15) introduces Jesus as the one who comes from Nazareth, is baptized by John, is driven out into the wilderness by the Spirit to be tempted by Satan, and then returns to Galilee to proclaim the imminent kingdom of God.

This is followed by a longer section (1.16 to 3.35), which is a collection of call stories, miracle stories and controversy stories, plus a number of summaries. There are several ways in which one might describe the structure of this section. One could, for example, see it as containing three cycles structured round the three stories in which Jesus calls people to follow him (1.16–20; 2.13–14; and 3.13–19), but this would cut across other clear structural groupings, not least the sequence of five stories in 2.1— 3.6 in which Jesus comes into controversy with a particular group. This controversy sequence appears to be arranged chiastically (in an ABCBA pattern), with the first and last elements combining controversy with healing. There is also a loose connection between the beginning and end of the section as a whole: in 1.16–20 Jesus calls his first four disciples, as a result of which James and John leave their father behind in the boat, while in 3.31–35 Jesus denies that his mother and siblings have any claims over him and indicates that his true family are those who follow him. In 1.21–28 Jesus performs an exorcism and his teaching astonishes his audience with his authority, which is compared with that of the scribes. In 3.22–30 Jesus clashes with the scribes over the issue of the source of his authority (God or the prince of demons) for his exorcisms.

These structural observations suggest that one major role of miracle in Mark 1.16—3.35 is to bring about Jesus' clash with the Jewish leadership over the issue of his authority. But before we pursue this theme, we should note the others.

To begin with, the prologue sets the scene by having Jesus filled with the Spirit, declared to be God's son, and preach the coming of the kingdom. Jesus' first act, after calling four disciples, is to enter a synagogue where he both casts out an unclean spirit and teaches with authority. The awe-struck response of the crowd at 1.27 closely associates the exorcism and teaching as joint causes for amazement (indeed, in the Greek of this verse it is unclear whether Jesus' amazing authority is associated with his teaching or with his ability to command the obedience of unclean spirits). The unclean spirit also acknowledges Jesus' authority, not only by departing when ordered but by declaring him to be 'the holy one of God'. If 1.14–15 is taken as a summary statement which is exemplified in what follows, then these opening incidents indicate that Jesus' ministry of preaching the kingdom of God consists principally in calling disciples, teaching with authority, and overcoming demonic forces. The next few incidents, however, show that exorcisms are not the only kind of miracle Jesus performs; although he goes on to cast out many more demons (1.32–34, 39) he also heals a variety of other illnesses (1.32), including fever (1.30–31), leprosy (1.40–45) and paralysis (2.1–12). Jesus also teaches and preaches (1.22, 27, 39), but this part of the narrative tells us nothing about the content of his message, so that the focus remains on his miracle-working. The initial reactions to this miracle-working are rapidly spreading fame and the demand for more miracles (1.32–34, 45; 2.2).

Opposition from the authorities first arises in the story of the paralytic (2.1–12), where, however, it is not the cure but Jesus' claim to be able to forgive sins that causes offence (2.7). Jesus' reply presupposes that the authority to cure a paralytic implies the authority to forgive sins (2.9–11). The theme of amazement first mentioned at 1.22 is repeated at 2.12, thereby emphasizing that Jesus' miracles are a cause for astonishment – not simply because he is able to perform extraordinary feats, but because God is perceived to be at work in them.[4]

The story of the paralytic marks the transition from miracle stories to controversy stories, and the next few stories have Jesus clash with the authorities because he does not behave (or insist his disciples behave) as they feel a man of God should: he mixes with the wrong people (2.13–17), and his disciples fail to fast (2.18–22) or observe the Sabbath with sufficient strictness (2.23–28). The final controversy story (3.1–6)

---

[4] The connection between amazement and the perception of God's activity is explored in depth by Timothy Dwyer, *The Motif of Wonder in the Gospel of Mark* (JSNTSup, 128; Sheffield: Sheffield Academic Press, 1996).

involves a further miracle, when Jesus heals a man with a withered hand on the Sabbath. But the reason the Pharisees go out and plot his destruction with the Herodians may be not so much because Jesus has broken the Sabbath law but because his sharp question, 'Is it lawful on the sabbath to do good or to do harm, to save life or to kill?' has made them lose face in public and thereby challenged both their honour and their authority.

The arrival of the scribes from Jerusalem in 3.22 may be the first outcome of the Pharisaic plot. By claiming that Jesus casts out demons by the prince of demons the scribes seek to undermine his claim to authority, and perhaps even arraign him on the capital charge of sorcery. They thus aim to destroy his reputation, if not his life. This episode, known as the Beelzebul Controversy, contains a nice example of Markan irony: the scribes accuse Jesus of casting out the demons by the prince of demons, but the demons know better (1.24, 34; 3.11). Yet it also emphasizes the point of Jesus' exorcisms: Satan is being overcome (3.27).

In this section of Mark's Gospel, then, Jesus' miracles perform a number of functions. They cause amazement among the crowds and rapidly propel Jesus to fame. They provoke opposition from the authorities, who, in their way, prove more obdurate than the demons (who at least recognize who Jesus is and obey him). They meet human need by delivering people from demons and disease, which appears to be an integral part of the proclamation of the kingdom of God, perhaps compelled by the motive of compassion (1.41 – although it is interesting to note that some early manuscripts have the variant reading which has Jesus moved with 'anger' rather than pity or compassion at this point). Above all they raise the question of by what authority Jesus is acting.[5] The demons respond to Jesus by departing at his command, so they already know the answer (presumably due to their status as spiritual beings); the disciples implicitly accept Jesus' authority by accepting his call to follow him; the crowds are amazed at his authority and in the main respond positively by coming to him for healing and by praising God; the Jewish authorities see a challenge to their own authority and so retaliate by attempting to impugn that of Jesus.

All at sea: Mark 4.1—8.26

The next section (4.1—8.26) heightens the issue of Jesus' authority so that it becomes the issue of his identity: the question is thus not just where

---

[5] See also Glaswell, 'Use of Miracles', 156, and van Iersel, *Reading Mark*, 25, 60.

Jesus' power comes from but who he is.[6] This is seen most strikingly in the two sea miracles, the Stilling of the Storm (4.35–41) and the Walking on the Sea (6.45–52), and indeed it is the frequent crossings of the sea in a boat that make this section a unity. Although this boat is first introduced at 3.9, it is first used at 4.1, and it then features frequently until its final employment at 8.13–22a, after which it is never mentioned again.[7] R. M. Fowler suggested that the boat trips can be organized into three pairs of outward and return journeys across the lake; this suggests that the present section is structured around these boat trips. However, not all these boat trips are of equal significance; as Norman Petersen has argued, three of them comprise substantial episodes, while the remainder of them are mere side-trips. On this basis Petersen has proposed that Mark 4.1—8.26 can be divided into three cycles and two intervals as in Table 1 (on the next page).[8]

In each of the three cycles, A concerns Jesus interacting with crowds on one side of the lake, B concerns a significant episode while Jesus and the disciples are crossing the lake, and C concerns healings or exorcisms carried out by Jesus on completion of the boat trip. The two intervals take place entirely on land, with Jesus departing from and then returning to the lake (or 'sea'); this is particularly clear in the second interval with Jesus' excursion up to the region of Tyre and Sidon (7.24) and his explicit return to the Sea of Galilee through the Decapolis (the region situated to the southeast of the Sea of Galilee, taking its name from the ten cities – Greek *deka* ten, *polis* city – it notionally contained) (7.31).

There are also some partial correspondences between the Intervals and the Cycles. Perhaps the clearest of these is the parallelism between the healing of the deaf man (interval 2c) and the blind man (cycle 3C), both of which take place apart from the crowd, both of which appear to require more effort on Jesus' behalf than previous healings, and both of which end with commands to secrecy. Even on the surface level it should be noted that these two stories come either side of Jesus' complaint about the continuing deafness and dumbness of the disciples (8.18). There is also some correspondence between interval 1a and cycles 1C, 2C and 3C, in that the healing of Jairus' daughter and of the woman with a haemorrhage,

---

[6] Not all scholars agree in seeing 4.1—8.26 as a unified section in Mark, but my treatment here is indebted to two scholars that do: Fowler, *Loaves and Fishes*, and Norman R. Petersen, 'The Composition of Mark 4:1—8:26', *HTR* 73 (1980), 185–217.

[7] As Petersen, 'Composition', 194, observes.

[8] Petersen, 'Composition', 188; the suggested structure is his but the descriptions of each unit in the structure are mine; cf. van Iersel, *Reading Mark*, 95–8.

Table 1 Division of Mark 4.1—8.26 according to Petersen

Cycle 1:	A	4.1–34	Jesus teaches in parables by the sea
	B	4.35–41	Stilling of the Storm
	C	5.1–20	Gerasene Demoniac
Interval 1:	a	5.21–43	Jairus' daughter/woman with haemorrhage
	b	6.1–6a	Jesus in his home town marvels at their unbelief
	c	6.6b–29/6b–13	Mission of the Twelve
		/14–16	The response of Herod and Others
		/17–29	Herod's Banquet and the Death of John the Baptist
Cycle 2:	A	6.30–44	Feeding of the Five Thousand (Jesus' Banquet)
	B	6.45–52	Walking on the Sea; disciples astonished because they do not understand about the loaves
	C	6.53–56	Healings at Gennesaret
Interval 2:	a	7.1–23/1–13	Jesus' dispute with the Pharisees on eating bread with unwashed hands
		/14–15	Jesus teaches the crowd that not what goes in but what comes out defiles a person
		/17–23	The disciples ask him privately about this parable (cf. 4.10–13)
	b	7.24–30	Syrophoenician woman's daughter (not fit to give the children's bread to dogs)
	c	7.31–37	Healing of deaf and dumb man
Cycle 3:	A	8.1–12	Feeding of the Four Thousand (and Pharisees demand a sign)
	B	8.13–21	Crossing the sea, disciples fail to understand about the bread
	C	8.22–26	Healing of blind man of Bethsaida

like the C items, takes place immediately upon Jesus' disembarkation from the boat (5.21). Interval 1a also resembles interval 2b in some respects; in each case Jesus is asked by a parent to intervene on behalf of a daughter (he also addresses the woman with a haemorrhage as 'daughter'), and the story creates some tension over whether he will in fact do so. Moreover, there are also parallels between interval 2a and cycle 1A; in both sections Jesus teaches the crowds openly, the disciples subsequently ask him privately about the parable he has just spoken and Jesus is dismayed at their failure to understand (4.10–13; 7.17–18).

Another thing to note is the prominence of bread from the Feeding of the Five Thousand onwards (this is even more prominent in the original Greek in which the word for 'bread' and 'loaf' is the same, namely *artos*; note that some English translations omit the mention of 'loaves' in 7.2 which according to the Greek text are what the disciples are said to be eating with unwashed hands). The juxtaposition of certain incidents may also be significant. For example, Jesus addressed the storm at 4.39 with the same verb (*phimoō*) that he uses to muzzle the demon at 1.25, giving the Stilling of the Storm something of the character of an exorcism; it is immediately followed by the exorcism of the Legion demon from the Gerasene demoniac, which causes a herd of pigs to drown themselves in the very sea Jesus has just crossed and calmed. To take another example, the account of the Feeding of the Five Thousand follows almost immediately on from Mark's flashback to the execution of John the Baptist, thereby providing a stark contrast between Herod's banquet and Jesus' banquet. Such features suggest that the structure of this section is both complex and deliberate.[9]

Miracles play an important part in this structure. We have already noted the paired miracles of Stilling the Storm and Walking on the Sea (more of which below) and of the deaf man and the blind man. The two feeding stories, the Feeding of the Five Thousand (6.33–44) and the Feeding of the Four Thousand (8.1–9), in which Jesus feeds huge crowds from a few loaves and fishes, form another impressive pair, which, like the two sea miracles, go beyond the healings and exorcisms of the previous section. It is also notable how this section, not least through its miracles, emphasizes the disciples' failure to understand. Following the Stilling of the Storm the disciples are terrified, and ask, 'Who is this, then, that even the wind and the sea obey him?', but it seems that it is still only demons who know the answer (4.41; 5.7). When the first hungry crowd gathers, the disciples have no idea how they are to be fed (6.37). This is understandable, even after Jesus' stunning display of power in stilling the storm (since it is the disciples themselves who are commanded to carry

---

[9] John R. Donahue and Daniel J. Harrington, *The Gospel of Mark* (Sacra Pagina, 2; Collegeville: Michael Glazier, 2002), 209.

out the seemingly impossible task of feeding the crowd). It is not so understandable, however, that the disciples still have no idea how a crowd is
to be fed when it comes to the turn of the Four Thousand (8.4); but by
then we have already been told that the disciples failed to understand
about the loaves, and that this was why they were so dumbfounded at Jesus'
walking on the sea (6.52).[10]

This theme of the disciples' failure to understand is first introduced at
4.10–13. There seems to be some irony about it: Jesus tells 'those around
him with the twelve' that they are those to whom the secret of the kingdom of God has been given, in contrast to 'those outside' to whom everything comes 'in parables' so that 'seeing they may see and not perceive,
and hearing they may hear and not understand, lest they should turn again
and be forgiven' (4.11–12). Yet it seems that the disciples have not understood (4.10, 13), and that they still have not understood even after all the
miracles Jesus goes on to perform in front of them over the next four chapters, so that in the final boat trip an exasperated Jesus declares, in words
that echo those he used at 4.12, 'Do you not yet perceive or understand?
Are your hearts hardened? Having ears do you not see, and having eyes
do you not hear?' (8.17b–18a). By this stage, the narrator has already
told us the answer to Jesus' question about the hardening of the disciples'
hearts: 'And they were utterly astounded, for they did not understand about
the loaves, but their hearts were hardened' (6.51b–52).

The function of the miracle stories (particularly the 'nature miracles')
in this section is not solely to emphasize the disciples' hardness of heart
and failure to understand. There is a more positive message as well:
what the disciples fail to grasp is meant to be more apparent to Mark's
readers, and the very fact of the disciples' incomprehension emphasizes
how extraordinary it is. Someone who can still the wind and sea with a
word of command is more than a mere healer and exorcist (even an extra-
ordinarily effective exorcist), for here is someone doing what in the Old
Testament is attributed only to Yahweh himself.[11] The two feeding stories
make a similar point at the surface level, though what precisely they are
meant to teach is something that will need further consideration.

This discussion in the boat takes place immediately after the Pharisees'
request for a sign (8.11–12), which, as Petersen acknowledges, slightly

---

[10] See Fowler, *Loaves and Fishes*, 92–9, and Glaswell, 'Use of Miracles', 158–9.
[11] John Paul Heil, *Jesus Walking on the Sea: Meaning and Gospel Functions of Matt 14:22–33,
Mark 6:45–52 and John 6:15b–21* (Analecta Biblica, 87; Rome: Biblical Institute Press, 1981),
122–7, notes how this raises the question of Jesus' identity in an acute form.

disturbs his proposed structure at 3A. Jesus' reply to the Pharisees is enigmatic: 'Truly, I say to you, no sign shall be given to this generation.' Perhaps 'this generation' refers only to outsiders like the Pharisees (cf. 9.19 where Jesus describes 'this generation' as 'faithless'), so that signs may be offered to those who are meant to be on the inside. Again, the phrase 'from heaven' might either mean 'from God' or 'from the sky'; but given that Mark seldom uses 'heaven' as a reverential circumlocution for 'God' the latter meaning is more likely here.

Apart from this request for a sign, there are no clashes with the authorities over miracles in this section. Instead, Jairus, a ruler of the synagogue, comes to Jesus for help and is in turn encouraged to have faith (5.22–23, 36). Other characters respond to Jesus' miracles in a variety of ways. The woman with a haemorrhage believes that merely touching Jesus will be sufficient to obtain a cure, and her faith is rewarded (5.25–34). The Gerasene demoniac, once cured, wishes to follow Jesus but is instead commanded to proclaim how much the Lord (which in Mark almost certainly means God rather than Jesus) has done for him; instead he goes round proclaiming what Jesus did (5.18–20). Although the (presumably Gentile) people of the Decapolis marvel at the former demoniac's proclamation of Jesus' deeds (5.20), they want him to leave their neighbourhood (5.17). Jesus' fame is nevertheless such that a huge crowd of people flock to him for healing when he lands at Gennesaret (6.53–56), and even a Gentile woman living in the region of Tyre and Sidon has heard enough about him not only to approach him on behalf of her daughter but to persist with a humble yet witty response when he first refuses her request (7.24–30). The healing of the deaf and dumb man that follows immediately after evokes the greatest response yet: those who witnessed it were 'astonished beyond measure' and offer praise in terms that may be intended to echo the praise of God in the Old Testament (7.37). On the other hand, the crowds that benefit from the multiplication of loaves and fishes appear to notice nothing remarkable at all.

Two further themes that emerge are Gentiles and impurity. The Gerasene demoniac is living in the Decapolis, a Gentile region. He is possessed by an unclean spirit and living in an unclean place (among tombs), and his demons are expelled into unclean animals (pigs) (5.1–20). Subsequently, there is a discussion about where true impurity resides (7.1–23), following which Jesus makes a second and deeper foray into Gentile territory, where this time he receives a more positive response (7.24—8.10, assuming that all these episodes are intended to take place in Gentile territory). In between these two trips Jesus has been touched by a menstruating woman and has himself touched a corpse (5.25–27, 41), both actions through which he would contract ritual impurity.

Related to these two themes are the themes of boundary-crossing and faith.[12] The lake itself is a boundary that Jesus crosses several times, and the first crossing is resisted by the demonized storm (4.35–41). Jesus succeeds in overcoming both this opposition and the demons possessing the unfortunate Gerasene, but these actions do not guarantee success at the human level: the disciples display no faith (4.40) and the Gerasenes ask Jesus to depart (5.17). Jesus meets with even less faith in his home town (6.1–6). The haemorrhaging woman does better; she overcomes the barrier of the crowd and her fear of disapproval, believing that Jesus is able to heal her, and Jesus commends her for her faith (5.34). In the episode with the Syrophoenician woman it seems that both parties have barriers to overcome; the Syrophoenician woman has to overcome the barrier of Jesus' initial rejection, while Jesus has to overcome his initial reluctance to give the children's bread to dogs (7.24–30). The one barrier that cannot be overcome, it seems, is that of the disciples' steadfast incomprehension (8.14–21).

Even on the surface level, then, this is a complex section in which miracles perform multiple functions. Jesus continues to minister to the sick and the possessed, and meets with a variety of responses. The opposition from the authorities becomes subdued, and the chief struggle is that with the disciples' failure to understand. This becomes particularly apparent in the two pairs of 'nature miracles', namely the two sea miracles (4.35–41 and 6.45–52) and the two feeding miracles (6.30–44 and 8.1–10), where the focus is on Jesus' interaction with the disciples and their growing fear and puzzlement. But these stories also signal to the reader that something quite extraordinary is happening in Jesus, namely that he is the bearer of God's power and authority in an unprecedented way (as we shall see further on pp. 107–13).

On the way: Mark 8.27—10.52

The third main section runs from 8.27 to 10.52 and is concerned principally with Jesus' journey to Jerusalem and the teaching he gives on the

---

[12] Gerd Theissen, *Miracle Stories of the Early Christian Tradition* (ed. John Riches, tr. Francis McDonagh; Studies of the New Testament and Its World; Edinburgh: T. & T. Clark, 1983), 129–40. Van Iersel, *Mark*, 193, calls this section 'Crossing Boundaries'. Donald H. Juel, *A Master of Surprise: Mark Interpreted* (Minneapolis: Fortress, 1994), esp. 41, 66–7, sees transgressing boundaries as a central theme in Mark's presentation of Jesus throughout.

way, much of it on the cost of discipleship. There is once again a three-fold pattern, this time in Jesus' repeated predictions of his passion and resurrection (8.31; 9.30–31; 10.32–34), each of which is followed by an inappropriate response from one or more disciples (8.32–33; 9.32–34; 10.35–41), which is in turn corrected by Jesus' teaching (8.34—9.1; 9.35–37; 10.42–45). This continues the theme of the disciples' failure to understand, but the area of misunderstanding has moved on. Peter's declaration that Jesus is the Messiah receives a distinctly cool response from Jesus in Mark (8.29–30; according to the Greek of 8.30 Jesus 'rebuked' the disciples to tell no one about him), but it is not wholly incorrect; Peter at least recognizes that Jesus is someone who stands in a special relationship to God. The disciples' difficulty is now accepting the necessity of the cross (8.31–38).

Miracles do not play a large part in this section, but they are not wholly absent. For one thing, the entire section is bracketed by the stories of the healing of blind men (8.22–26; 10.46–52). For another, there is the story of the exorcism of the 'epileptic' boy (9.14–29), although the focus is more on the failure of the disciples and Jesus' dialogue with the boy's father than on the performance of the exorcism (that said, this story does nevertheless show Jesus able to deal readily with a demon that has defeated the best efforts of nine of his disciples, despite their earlier successes against a large number of demons, 6.13).

At the surface level these stories suffice to indicate that Jesus neither loses nor abandons his miraculous powers after Peter's confession, but continues to heal and exorcize when occasion demands, even though the emphasis of the narrative has shifted.

Jesus in Jerusalem: Mark 11.1—16.8

From Chapter 11 onwards the emphasis shifts even more. There are no more healing miracles or exorcisms, and in the passion narrative itself there are no miracles at all, although, as Edwin Broadhead points out, there are miraculous elements throughout the passion narrative (such as Jesus' miraculous foreknowledge, the signs accompanying the crucifixion, and the empty tomb).[13] The only miracle story proper in Mark's final six chapters occurs before the passion narrative, at 11.12–14, 20–21, namely the cursing of the fig tree. This is quite distinctive among Jesus' miracles, not only because it is the only miracle narrated of him in the canonical

---

[13] Edwin K. Broadhead, *Teaching with Authority: Miracles and Christology in the Gospel of Mark* (Sheffield: JSOT Press, 1992), 180–4.

Gospels that has a negative effect, but also because, on the face of it, Jesus appears to behave unreasonably, as the narrator goes out of his way to stress by pointing out that it was unreasonable to expect to find fruit because 'it was not the season for figs' (11.13). The narrative attempts to make sense of this by making it the occasion for teaching on prayer, but at the surface level the effect is highly incongruous; Jesus did not pray about the fig tree, he uttered a curse against it (11.14), which is hardly an auspicious way to introduce teaching on forgiveness (11.25)! Perhaps Mark is attempting to tame a story that was first told to impugn Jesus' reputation by intercalating into it the account of the 'cleansing' of the temple (11.15–19), but this is a point to which we shall need to return when we come to discuss the possible symbolic meanings of the miracles in Mark.

The tailing off of miracle stories in the second half of Mark's Gospel is one factor that has led some scholars (notably T. J. Weeden) to argue that Mark narrates the miracle stories only to repudiate them, thereby correcting a 'divine man' Christology with a theology of the cross.[14] This view is probably not correct, however. It is true that many of the miracles result in the disciples' incomprehension, but so do Jesus' passion predictions and much of his other teaching. Otherwise, there is nothing to indicate that Mark disapproves of the miracle stories he narrates, and they do not cease altogether once the Markan Jesus starts teaching plainly about the cross. As Broadhead again correctly observes, 'the narrative generates an integrated portrait of Jesus as the powerful proclaimer whose teaching leads to his death'.[15]

Summary

On the surface level, then, the miracles in Mark contribute to a portrait of Jesus that proceeds in three main stages. In the first, Jesus bursts on the scene as a healer/exorcist and teacher of extraordinary authority, and this both provokes opposition from the religious authorities and attracts the crowds among whom accounts of Jesus' miracles spread his fame. In the second, Jesus performs the astounding feats of stilling a storm, walking on the sea, and twice feeding huge crowds with a mere handful of loaves and fishes, but these feats only baffle the disciples and apparently remain unknown to everyone else. In the meantime, Jesus continues to perform healings and exorcisms, and this continues to attract both crowds

---

[14] T. J. Weeden, 'The Heresy that Necessitated Mark's Gospel', *ZNW* 59 (1968), 145–58.
[15] Broadhead, *Teaching with Authority*, 184; cf. Theissen, *Miracle Stories*, 220–1; Twelftree, *Miracle Worker*, 92–3.

and individuals. In the third stage, the focus shifts to Jesus' teaching on the cross and the cost of discipleship, although the theme of the disciples' bewilderment continues. A few further miracles are narrated, but by the time we reach Peter's confession in Mark 8.29 the miracle stories have made their main points, and to have continued with large numbers of them would have been a distraction from Mark's main purpose in his travel section (8.31—10.52).

Throughout the first ten chapters of Mark's Gospel, Jesus heals and exorcizes out of compassion (1.41; cf. 6.34; 8.2; 9.22) as part of the work of the kingdom. Although he coerces demons and storms, he never coerces human beings; instead he uses his powers only to serve them (10.45 – up to this point in Mark's Gospel Jesus' main acts of service have been precisely his healings and exorcisms). It is the same powerful healer who performs his greatest act of service by going to the cross (10.45 again, and note the Markan irony at 15.29–30).

A further theme that runs throughout Mark's Gospel in connection with miracles is that of faith. Jesus observes the faith of those who bring the paralytic to be healed (2.5), and frequently comments on the need for faith (5.36; 9.23; 11.23), or berates his disciples for lacking it (4.40; 9.19), or marvels at its absence in his home town (6.6). Conversely, he twice tells those healed that it is their faith that has saved them (5.34; 10.52), and by implication (although the word is not explicitly used), he is impressed by the faith of the Syrophoenician woman (7.27–29). For Mark, faith is never the result of a miracle, but always a precondition, either of receiving healing, or (in the case of the disciples) of perceiving a miracle's significance.[16]

Deeper meanings

In discussing possible symbolic meanings of Mark's miracle stories it will be convenient to start from the end and work backwards, if only because there is relatively wide agreement about the symbolic import of the later miracles.

We left the enigmatic account of the Cursing of the Fig Tree (11.12–14, 20–25) by noting that it did not appear to portray Jesus in a very good light, and suggesting that Mark may have taken over a story told *against* Jesus and attempted to tame it. Nonetheless, the lessons appended at 11.22–25 do not make a very good job of taming it if the narrative is read

---

[16] See further Twelftree, *Miracle Worker*, 99–100.

at the surface level, and this almost compels one to look for a deeper meaning. In this case Mark provides a clear interpretive clue: he sandwiches the account of the 'cleansing' of the temple (perhaps better understood as a symbolic threat of the temple's downfall) between the two halves of the story about the fig tree. The fate of the fig tree then parallels the fate of the temple, just as the fruitlessness of the former symbolizes the fruitlessness of the latter; compare the parable of the tenants at 12.1–11, especially 12.2 which uses the same word for 'fruit' (*karpos*) as 11.14, and the same word for 'time' or 'season' (*kairos*) as 11.13. Seeing that the curse story and the cleansing of the temple are meant to interpret each other helps make more sense of the teaching on prayer and forgiveness at 11.22–25. At 11.17 Jesus declares that the temple is meant to be a 'house of prayer for all nations'; it was also the official institution for mediating atonement (i.e. forgiveness) through animal sacrifice, a process Jesus dramatically interrupted by his demonstration. The lesson Jesus draws from the withered fig tree then moves through an admonition to faith (11.22–23), to an injunction to believing prayer (11.24) and to forgiveness given and received while praying (11.25). The withering of the fig tree is thus made to teach not only the imminent destruction of the fruitless temple, but also its replacement by faith for the purposes of prayer and forgiveness. If using a story about cursing a fig tree still seems an odd way to go about all this, that may lend strength to the suggestion that Mark was also trying to domesticate a well-known story that otherwise made Jesus' character look a little suspect.

It is also widely recognized that there is a symbolic aspect to the placement of Mark's two stories of the healing of blind men (8.22–26; 10.46–52). As mentioned above, the two stories frame the travel section in which Jesus attempts to teach his disciples about the cross and the need for cross-bearing discipleship. Again, as we have noticed, the section running from 4.1 to 8.26 frequently emphasizes the disciples' failure to understand, that is, metaphorically speaking, their almost wilful blindness (8.18). At 8.22–26 the blind man of Bethsaida is restored to sight, but only with difficulty: it takes physical means (spittle) and two attempts to effect a cure. At the first attempt he sees something, but it is men that look like walking trees (8.24). In the episode that immediately follows, Peter rehearses the various misapprehensions about Jesus' identity doing the rounds, then declares that he believes Jesus to be the Messiah (8.27–29). From the ensuing conversation it becomes apparent that though Peter now sees something, it is as distorted as the Bethsaidan's perception of men as walking trees; whatever Peter meant by 'Messiah' his notion of it clearly did not involve suffering many things, being rejected by the authorities and put to death (8.31–33).[17] Jesus' repeated attempts to ram this home apparently make some impression on the disciples; when James and John declare that they can share Jesus' cup and baptism it is unlikely they suppose that Jesus is talking about a drink and a bath, and far more likely that they are now declaring their readiness to suffer with him (as the disciples do again at 14.31). This episode is immediately followed by that of blind Bartimaeus, who seems to symbolize the ideal disciple: he comes to Jesus in persistent faith, receives his sight immediately (unlike his counterpart at Bethsaida), and at once follows Jesus 'on the road' or 'in the way'; the Greek expression *en tē(i) hodō(i)* can bear either meaning, and both are probably intended here: Bartimaeus follows Jesus along the road to Jerusalem, and in so doing follows him in the way of discipleship. Thereafter the theme of the disciples' failure to understand disappears from the story; their final failure at Jesus' arrest is one of nerve, not of cognition (cf. 14.38).

The two stories of the healing of blind men are thus placed to indicate the progressive enlightenment of the disciples. Given that, there is also likely to be a symbolic motive in the placement of the story about healing the deaf and dumb man (7.31–37), so that it and the story of the Blind Man of Bethsaida bracket the complaint about the disciples' deafness and blindness (8.18) and perhaps also their inability to speak properly (8.16–17).[18] It is then ironic that the anonymous 'they' of 7.37 (presumably the people who brought the deaf and dumb man along to Jesus at 7.32) praise Jesus' achievement (despite his command to secrecy) while the disciples say nothing.

The use of spittle in the story of the Blind Man of Bethsaida suggests a further level of symbolism. The closest narrative parallel to this outside the New Testament is the story of Vespasian healing a blind man in Alexandria, also with spittle. If Mark was writing in the early 70s, the Vespasian story would be a piece of current propaganda (as noted in Chapter 3, p. 45); it was one of a series of stories designed to legitimate the new claimant to the imperial throne by presenting him in quasi-messianic terms. Mark may well have borrowed the spittle from the Vespasian story to hint at an ironic contrast between two very different kinds of messiah.[19]

---

[17] See Heil, *Jesus Walking*, 142–3.

[18] Fowler, *Loaves and Fishes*, 112.

[19] Eric Eve, 'Spit in Your Eye: The Blind Man of Bethsaida and the Blind Man of Alexandria', *NTS* 54 (2008), 1–17.

When we come to the two feeding stories and the two sea miracles, the possibilities for symbolic meanings increase, and the interpretation becomes more contentious. For example, the actions Jesus performs with the bread in the feeding stories (6.41; 8.6b) are described in terms that are very similar to those in which Mark describes the institution of the Eucharist at the Last Supper (14.22), and in both feeding stories Jesus distributes the bread, not directly, but through his disciples.[20] Moreover, it has long been argued on the basis of the numbers and locations involved that the first feeding represents a mission to the Jews and the second one to the Gentiles (the twelve baskets at 6.43 representing the twelve tribes of Israel, and the seven baskets at 8.8 the traditional number of seventy Gentile nations; note how these numbers are emphasized again at 8.19–21).[21] Moreover, both feeding stories take place broadly in the context of mission: the Feeding of the Five Thousand takes place following the mission of the Twelve (6.7–13, 30–31), and the Feeding of the Four Thousand follows Jesus' second (and more successful) foray into Gentile territory (7.24–37). One might then see the feeding stories as symbolizing the post-Easter mission of the Church, when the risen Jesus has to minister through his disciples, and the dispensing of the Eucharist might be a metonym for incorporating first Jews and then Gentiles into the Church. Alternatively (or additionally), one might see Jesus as either re-enacting the Mosaic feeding in the wilderness (Exodus 16.4–36) or else anticipating the eschatological Messianic Banquet (the expectation of feasting and plenty in the messianic age) in these stories (clearly these possibilities are not mutually exclusive).[22]

One aspect of the text that offers some control on the symbolic meanings of these stories is the structure of Mark 4—8 noted in the 'surface reading' section above. There it was pointed out that Mark 4—8 contained three cycles (and two intervals) of three elements each. Each of the B elements concerns an episode in the boat while crossing the lake. Elements

---

[20] Donahue and Harrington, *Mark*, 210–11; Gerd Theissen and Annette Merz, *The Historical Jesus: A Comprehensive Guide* (tr. John Bowden; London: SCM Press, 1998), 302–3. Against seeing any eucharistic significance in the feeding stories see Fowler, *Loaves and Fishes*, pp. 139–45 and G. H. Boobyer, 'The Eucharistic Interpretation of the Miracles of the Loaves in Mark's Gospel', *JTS* 3 (1952), 161–71.

[21] Twelftree, *Miracle Worker*, 69–70, 81–2; Werner H. Kelber, *Mark's Story of Jesus* (Philadelphia: Fortress, 1979), 35–41; van Iersel, *Reading Mark*, 110–11.

[22] Barry L. Blackburn, *Theios Anēr and the Markan Miracle Traditions: A Critique of the Theios Anēr Concept as an Interpretative Background of the Miracle Traditions Used by Mark* (WUNT, 2; Tübingen: Mohr Siebeck, 1991), 195.

1B and 2B are both sea miracles (the Stilling of the Storm and the Walking on the Sea), while 3B is a discussion about bread that refers back to the two feeding stories (2A and 3A). Each of the A elements concerns Jesus interacting with a crowd by the lake: 2A and 3A are the two feeding stories, while 1A is the sequence of parables (the sower, the seed growing secretly, and the mustard seed). 1A makes it clear that the disciples fail to understand the parables; both 2B and 3B refer to the disciples' inability to understand the preceding feeding miracles (2A and 3A). This pattern is surely significant, and suggests that the two feeding stories are in some way meant to be related to the parable section.[23]

Further elements of the text point in this direction. As we have already seen, the account of Jesus' first miracle, an exorcism, at 1.21–28 closely associates Jesus' teaching and miracle-working as joint causes of astonishment. The first feeding story (2B) is introduced by the notice that when Jesus went ashore, 'he saw a great throng, and he had compassion on them, because they were like sheep without a shepherd; and he began to teach them many things' (6.34); it is only after this teaching that he also feeds them with bread. The explanation of the parable of the sower given at 4.14–20 begins with the words, 'The sower sows the word.' The parable thus becomes a parable about the reception of parables, but it is also a parable of growth; the farmer unexpectedly obtains a bumper crop (thus enabling the production of much bread, if it is a wheat crop), the seed is multiplied to an extraordinary extent (4.8, 20). This suggests that the bread of the feeding miracles could also represent the word, and the feeding miracles themselves could represent the spread of the word. It might be impossible to multiply a few loaves and fishes to feed five thousand people, but it is perfectly possible for the preached word to spread in such a way.[24]

The fact that it is spread through the disciples may indicate that the post-Easter mission of the Church is in view. In other words, the structure of the text supports the missionary reading of the feeding stories. Two further features of the text lend further support to this reading. The first is the use of the bread motif elsewhere in the section. In particular Jesus at first refuses to give the Syrophoenician woman the children's bread (7.27), but relents when she says that even the dogs are entitled to the leftovers (7.28; cf. the leftovers mentioned in the feeding stories at 6.43; 8.8,

[23] So also, although on partially different lines, van Iersel, *Reading Mark*, 118–20.
[24] Morna D. Hooker, *The Gospel According to St Mark* (BNTC; London: A. & C. Black, 1991), 164–5; Donahue and Harrington, *Mark*, 207–10; Broadhead, *Teaching with Authority*, 118–23; see also Proverbs 9.1–5; Isaiah 55.1–3, 10–11; Sirach 15.3; 24.19–22.

19–21). The second is the report of the mission of the Twelve at 6.7–13. This includes preaching, healing and exorcism, just like Jesus' mission; but unlike Jesus' mission, the healings are accomplished through anointing with oil, a practice that seems more characteristic of the early Church (cf. James 5.14).

If this is correct, then *bread* may be a symbol with several resonances in Mark. First, it is the basic staple of physical life, and hence appropriate as a symbol for what provides eternal life or entry into the kingdom of God (admittedly this sounds more Johannine, and John indeed uses bread in this way, but note the parallel between entering life and entering the kingdom of God implied at Mark 9.43, 45, 47). For Mark what provides this life/entry into the kingdom is partly the proclamation of the word (Mark 4.1–20) together with a ministry of healing and exorcism, but also Jesus' giving himself as a ransom for many (10.45), which he does by allowing his body to be broken on the cross, which is in turn symbolized by the breaking of *bread* at the Last Supper (14.22).[25]

This line of interpretation suggests that, while at the surface level, the text is telling the story of Jesus' ministry on and around the Sea of Galilee, at the symbolic level, it is also talking about the mission of the post-Easter Church.[26] This may also be indicated by tensions in the narrative's presentation of the disciples. On the one hand, the narrative (not least Chapters 4—8) underlines the disciples' failure to understand at nearly every point. On the other hand, the symbolic interpretation proposed for the feeding stories suggests that they *successfully* fulfil their role as ministers of the 'bread' to the crowds (i.e. as missionaries to the Jews and Gentiles), just as they apparently know how to preach and exorcize perfectly well in 6.7–13 despite their inability elsewhere to understand what Jesus is about, let alone to perform a successful exorcism (9.14–29). This tension may arise because Mark is trying to make the disciples symbolize two different things at different levels of his narrative.[27]

It would seem odd, however, if the missionary-eucharistic reading were the only symbolic meaning intended by Mark's feeding stories. Given the role of Peter's confession at 8.29 following the healing of the blind man of Bethsaida we should expect there to be some Christological meaning (i.e. something about the significance of Christ's work and person) as well.

[25] See also van Iersel, *Reading Mark*, 193–6.
[26] Austin Farrer, *A Study in St. Mark* (London: Dacre, 1951), 142–4.
[27] As Heikki Räisänen, *The 'Messianic Secret' in Mark's Gospel* (Edinburgh: T. & T. Clark, 1990), 118, 197, points out.

This is in any case indicated by 6.52; the disciples were astounded by Jesus walking on the sea because they did not understand about the loaves. What they failed to understand about the loaves cannot be simply that the feeding stories symbolize the post-Easter mission of the Church. It must first of all be something they failed to understand about *Jesus* that would otherwise have made his watery walk far less surprising. The question then is whether what they failed to understand is meant to be subtle or obvious.

The obvious understanding would be that at the surface level of the text. Feeding 5,000 people with five loaves and two fishes is an impossible feat. If someone can perform one impossible feat, it should be no surprise that he can perform another. Put more theologically, if the Feeding of the Five Thousand already shows Jesus to be the bearer of divine powers, then the Walking on the Sea should have occasioned no surprise. But can this be all that Mark meant? Probably not, for Jesus' despairing question on the last boat trip, 'do you not yet understand?', is followed by the healing of the blind man of Bethsaida, which is in turn followed by Peter's confession of Jesus as Messiah.[28] The implication is that the disciples ought to have seen something messianic in the feedings. The prophecy that most clearly links a messianic figure with acts of feeding would be that of the Davidic shepherd at Ezekiel 34.23, which occurs in a chapter that berates the existing shepherds of Israel for failing to feed the sheep, strengthen the weak, heal the sick, bind up the crippled, bring back the strays and seek the lost (Ezekiel 34.2–4), with the result that the sheep 'were scattered, because there was no shepherd' (Ezekiel 34.5). Just before Jesus feeds the five thousand, Mark states that 'he had compassion on them, because they were like sheep without a shepherd' (Mark 6.34); there are several Old Testament passages this could be an echo of, but Ezekiel 34 best fits the context of a messianic feeder.[29] It seems likely, therefore, that Ezekiel 34 provides the lens through which the Markan disciples should have viewed the feedings had their hearts not been hardened.

Mark also relates the hardening of the disciples' hearts to their astonishment at Jesus' walking on the sea. By that point the question of Jesus' identity has already been raised for the disciples at the Stilling of the Storm, when they ask in baffled amazement, 'Who then is this, that wind and sea

---

[28] See also Theissen, *Miracle Stories*, 213–14.

[29] Other possible Old Testament allusions include Numbers 27.17; 1 Kings 22.17; 2 Chronicles 18.16; and Judith 11.19. See van Iersel, *Mark*, 225; Hooker, *Mark*, 165–6; Donahue and Harrington, *Mark*, 205; Twelftree, *Miracle Worker*, 76.

obey him?' In the corresponding element of the next cycle, the Walking on the Sea, the disciples are terrified and, thinking they have seen a ghost, they cry out. Jesus' response to them is ambiguous: the Greek of Mark 6.50c could be translated either 'Buck up, it's only me; nothing to be afraid of' or 'Take heart, I AM (*egō eimi*); fear not!' The latter is probably to be preferred, however, in which case it echoes the language of divine reassurance in the Old Testament, notably Isaiah 43.1b–2a, 'Fear not, for I have redeemed you; I have called you by name, you are mine. When you pass through the waters I will be with you; and through the rivers, they shall not overwhelm you.' That Mark may have this passage in mind is also indicated by Isaiah 43.8, which so aptly describes the Markan disciples: 'Bring forth the people who are blind, yet have eyes, who are deaf, yet have ears!', and 43.10b, 'that you may know and believe me and understand that I am He (LXX *egō eimi*)'. The way the imagery of storm-tossed ships is taken up in intertestamental literature such as 1QH 11.6, 12–18; 15.4–5; 14.23–4 (cf. Isaiah 43.16) and *T. Naph.* 6 would suggest that the sea-rescue motif could function as a metaphor for rescue from eschatological distress (the expectation that the time immediately preceding the end would be one of intensified suffering and turmoil).[30]

The Stilling of the Storm also employs the language of exorcism. The verb with which Jesus calms the sea at 4.39 (*pephimōso*) is the same with which he silences the unclean spirit at 1.25 (*phimōthēte* – also from *phimoun*, to silence); and just as Jesus 'rebukes' (*epitimēsen*) the wind at 4.39 so he 'rebukes' (*epitimēsen*) the unclean spirit at 1.25 (and also at 3.12 and 9.25); Howard Clark Kee has argued that in such contexts 'rebuke' does not mean 'reproach' but rather signifies bringing hostile powers into submission to God.[31] This suggests that Mark does not see the Stilling of the Storm as a 'nature miracle' but as a type of exorcism, overcoming the forces of evil threatening the disciples. Conversely, applying the language of exorcism to this miracle may indicate the significance of all Jesus' exorcisms for Mark. To the extent that the sea-rescue motif functions as a metaphor for eschatological salvation, so Jesus' exorcisms are also to be understood in this way (as 3.23–27 likewise suggests); in casting out unclean spirits Jesus does not merely deliver individuals from demonic

---

[30] Heil, *Jesus Walking*, 17–30. Note that the numbering of the columns of 1QH has changed, so that Heil cites column numbers that are eight less than those used here, which follow the numbering in Geza Vermes, *The Complete Dead Sea Scrolls in English* (Harmondsworth: Penguin Books, 1998), 259–74.
[31] Howard Clark Kee, 'The Terminology of Mark's Exorcism Stories', *NTS* 14 (1967–8), 232–46.

possession, he enacts the subjection of demonic forces to God's eschatological reign.

Although the two sea miracles are different, they are clearly related, and seem intended to be understood as a pair. Every verse but two (6.46 and 6.49) of the Walking on the Sea pericope contains some echo of the Stilling of the Storm. Both stories contain the motifs of crossing to the other side (4.35 and 6.45), the departure from or dismissal of a crowd (4.36 and 6.45), the arrival of evening (4.35 and 6.47), the separation of Jesus from the disciples (by sleep at 4.38 or physical distance at 6.46), the adverse wind (4.37 and 6.48), the disciples' fear (4.38, 40 and 6.49–50), Jesus addressing that fear (4.40 and 6.50), and the dropping of the wind (4.39 and 6.51).

The two sea miracles also share an epiphanic quality. They both seem designed to recall not just particular Old Testament passages but the recurring Old Testament theme of Yahweh's triumph over the hostile waters of chaos, including passages where he stills storms or tramples on the waves (e.g. Jonah 1; Psalm 77.16–20; Psalm 107.23–32; Job 9.8; 38.8–16; Habakkuk 3.15; Sirach 24.5–6).[32] Mark's seemingly odd remark that when Jesus walked on the water he wanted to pass the disciples by (Mark 6.48) echoes the language of certain Old Testament epiphanies (notably those involving Moses and Elijah, Exodus 33.18—34.6; 1 Kings 19.11).[33] We shall consider some of these echoes more closely in Chapter 7. In any case, Mark appears to be telling both sea-miracle stories in such a way as to emphasize that Jesus can do what in the Old Testament only Yahweh, the God of Israel, could do. In addition to emphasizing the disciples' failure to understand, their intent thus seems primarily Christological and soteriological (i.e. concerned with salvation). Jesus not only reveals his power, but uses his power to save his disciples from the hostile elements, symbolizing his embodiment of Yahweh's power to save his people.[34] Finally, the disciples' fear and astonishment, and even their failure to understand, which come particularly to the fore in these sea miracles, may be part of the wider theme of numinous awe in Mark. Such reactions of wonder at Jesus' deeds and words could be intended not merely to portray him as acting in surprising ways, but to show that the

---

[32] For reservations about the relevance of Job 9.8 here, see Patrick J. Madden, *Jesus' Walking on the Sea: An Investigation of the Origin of the Narrative Account* (BZNW, 81; Berlin: Walter de Gruyter, 1997), 63–5.

[33] For more details see John P. Meier, *A Marginal Jew: Rethinking the Historical Jesus*, vol. 2: *Mentor, Message, and Miracles* (New York: Doubleday, 1994), 914–19; 930–2; Blackburn, *Theios Anēr*, 145–8; Heil, *Jesus Walking*, 69–72; Dwyer, *Motif of Wonder*, 109–12, 128–30.

[34] Heil, *Jesus Walking*, 172–3.

kingdom of God was breaking in through him, since God was expected to astound his people in the last days.[35]

Healings and 'nature miracles' in Mark

Given that Mark's Gospel contains a number of miracle stories (the so-called 'nature miracles') that look both incredible historically and symbolic in intent, one may wonder if the same might apply to all the miracle stories in Mark, so that, for example, stories of healing the deaf and blind have nothing to do with any healing ministry performed by the historical Jesus and everything to do with Mark's narrative portrayal of Jesus' struggle to make the disciples understand. This suspicion would be eased if Mark treats healings and nature miracles in significantly different ways.

It would thus be helpful to determine whether there is any basis in Mark's text for distinguishing healing miracles and exorcisms from nature miracles. Even if one suspects that the latter are more purely symbolic, this cannot be made the basis for the distinction, since many of the healings (e.g. those of blind men) also contain symbolic elements. Neither will it do to suggest that the nature miracles are presented as more astounding, so that the disciples are more amazed by the Stilling of the Storm than by anything that has gone before. All sorts of people are amazed at all sorts of things Jesus says and does in Mark, and a reaction of astonishment would not in itself distinguish the Stilling of the Storm from (say) the Healing of the Deaf and Dumb Man at 7.32–37. But we may follow Heil's suggestion that it is the Stilling of the Storm that first raises the question of Jesus' *identity* (or 'deeper significance') for the disciples.[36] The question is then whether this distinguishing feature can be extended to the other nature miracles.

It can arguably be extended to most of them. The question of Christology is not explicitly raised in the feeding stories, yet their Christological potential is underlined by Mark at 6.52. Had the disciples understood about the loaves they would not have been so dumbfounded by Jesus' walking on the sea. Mark thus signals that although the Feeding of the Five Thousand did not raise the question of Jesus' identity in the disciples' minds, it certainly should have done. In this way we can include all the nature miracles apart from the Cursing of the Fig Tree in a category of 'miracle of special Christological significance'.

---

[35] Dwyer, *Motif of Wonder*, esp. 53, 66, 109–12, 128–34, 198–9.
[36] Heil, *Jesus Walking*, 124–5.

The phrase 'special Christological significance' needs qualification, since it can hardly be argued that the other miracles are wholly devoid of Christological significance. The distinction is that while the healing and exorcism stories raise the question of Jesus' *authority* (e.g. 1.27; 2.10), it is the Stilling of the Storm that first raises the question of his *identity*. Thus the nature miracles seem more focused on Jesus' person than his mission, while with the exorcisms and healings it tends to be the other way about. If this distinction can be sustained, it will allow a basis in the text for seeing the nature miracles as theological reflection on Jesus' person in contrast to a straightforward portrayal of his ministry (though this contrast is far from totally sharp). Such a distinction may require further support, but such support can be provided on broadly narrative-critical grounds.

Other people in Mark heal and exorcize, but the nature miracles are associated with Jesus alone: Jesus gives his disciples authority to cast out demons and they also heal, but such feats as walking on water and stilling storms appear to be non-transferable. Again, when Jesus heals, the person healed or exorcized appears only for the occasion, whereas the 'nature miracles' are always performed for the benefit of recurring characters, such as the crowd or the disciples. Furthermore, Jesus' mighty works of healing operate as an integral part of his ministry of proclaiming the kingdom, and give rise to a twofold response: the adulation of the crowds and the opposition of the authorities. Moreover, in the summary accounts of Jesus' activity he is said to perform many healings and exorcisms, but not to make a habit of walking on water, stilling storms, or feeding multitudes. Jesus' healings and exorcisms are represented as typical, but the so-called 'nature miracles' as exceptional.

The sea and feeding stories particularly emphasize the interaction between Jesus and his disciples. In the two feeding stories, far more prominence is given to the disciples than to the crowds: at Mark 6.34 the crowd are likened to sheep without a shepherd, and for all the reaction they display they might as well be sheep; unlike the crowd in John, and unlike the crowds in Mark's healing stories, they show no signs of having witnessed anything odd at all.

The fact that the nature miracles are performed principally in front of disciples who are baffled by them suggests another distinction between the narrative functions of the nature miracles and the healing stories. Only the latter serve to further the plot. Apart from portraying the disciples as almost unbelievably dense, neither the feeding stories nor the sea stories nor the Cursing of the Fig Tree achieve anything by way of advancing the plot action of Mark's Gospel. They contribute neither to Jesus' fame nor to the growing opposition against him. And like the threefold prediction of Jesus' passion and resurrection they contribute little to the disciples' understanding. In so far as Mark uses the disciples as a rhetorical foil, one might say that while his stories of healing and exorcism advance the plot of his story, the nature miracles function mainly as part of his address to the reader. Mark's insistence on the failure of the disciples to understand is a challenge to his readers to do better.

The structure of Mark 4.1—8.26 affords a further argument for distinguishing between the nature miracles and healings in Mark's text. The nature miracles help to define the three cycles in such a way as to suggest a correspondence between miracles and parables. The parables are represented as something which the disciples ought to understand but which needs explaining to them. In the final boat trip (corresponding to the sea miracles in previous cycles), the two feeding stories are represented in the same way. In this way, Mark drops a hint that these particular miracles share the same riddling character as the parables. In Chapter 11 the one (nature) miracle (the Cursing of the Fig Tree, vv. 12–14, 20–25) almost demands to be read at a symbolic level and is interpreted, not only by Jesus' actions in the temple, but by another parable, the Tenants in the Vineyard (12.1–11). All of this indicates that the nature miracles have a particularly parabolic character not necessarily shared by the miracles of healing and exorcism.[37] This is not to deny that at one level Mark presents both the healing and the nature miracles equally as things Jesus actually did, it is rather to suggest that Mark's narrative invites the more discerning reader to attend to the symbolic rather than the surface meaning especially in the case of the nature miracles.

The argument that Mark's text supports a distinction between nature miracles and healings is thus cumulative. Although no one criterion absolutely distinguishes the two, when they are taken jointly, sufficiently clear distinctions do emerge. The nature miracles tend to have a highly symbolic character, they tend to be built into the structure of the narrative in a particular way, the disciples are the only witnesses to them, they tend to focus attention on Jesus' person, they operate more at the level of discourse than of plot, and they are more overtly Christological. In contrast the healings and exorcisms tend to be public, to be performed for a variety of characters in front of a number of audiences, and to further the plot

---

[37] For the miracles as 'parabolic communication' see further Christopher D. Marshall, *Faith as a Theme in Mark's Narrative* (Cambridge: Cambridge University Press, 1989), 60–72.

by promoting Jesus' fame, provoking opposition from the authorities, and advancing the earthly work of the kingdom. These distinctions are not watertight. The Stilling of the Storm, for example, has elements of an exorcism story which could make it part of Jesus' work of subduing elements hostile to the reign of God; conversely there are symbolic elements in both stories of the healing of blind men, which also serve a structural function in demarcating their respective sections. The distinction we wish to draw is not as neat as we might like it to be. Mark's employment of traditional stories, now adapted to different purposes, may well have blurred it. Nonetheless, the distinction is there.[38]

Conclusions

We have seen that there is a great deal more to Mark's use of miracle stories than a straightforward catalogue of Jesus' miraculous deeds. Mark uses his miracle stories in a skilful way to further his narrative and theological purposes. Jesus' healings and exorcisms underline Jesus' authority, spread his fame, and provoke opposition from the authorities. His so-called 'nature miracles' both underline the disciples' failure to understand and raise the Christological stakes from the issue of Jesus' extraordinary authority to that of his messianic identity. Although Mark's narrative does not make this as explicit as we might wish, all this seems to be tied into Jesus' work of proclaiming the kingdom, by restoring the lost, feeding the hungry, healing the sick, and overcoming the forces of evil. Jesus' miracles are both a demonstration and a foretaste of the kingdom 'come in power'.

It would be a dull historian who merely gave a catalogue of facts without putting any kind of interpretive construction on them, but it should by now have become clear that Mark's primary interpretive categories are theological rather than those of modern historiography. History in any modern sense was not Mark's prime concern. The same applies to Matthew, Luke and John;[39] conducting a similar exercise with these three Gospels would tell us a great deal about their theology but would not give us many more clues about the miracles of the historical Jesus, beyond a few potentially relevant sayings. In any case, on the thesis of Markan

---

[38] For an alternative route to a similar conclusion, see Theissen and Merz, *Historical Jesus*, 301–4.

[39] For a discussion of the presentation of Jesus' miracles in all four Gospels, see Twelftree, *Miracle Worker*, 57–238. For Matthew, see also G. Bornkamm, G. Barth and H. J. Held, *Tradition and Interpretation in Matthew* (London: SCM Press, 1963); on John see, e.g., W. Nicol, *The Sēmeia in the Fourth Gospel: Tradition and Redaction* (NovTSup, 32; Leiden: Brill, 1972).

priority it remains the case that Mark provides the basis for the picture of Jesus as miracle-worker in Matthew and Luke, and that if anything the presentation of Jesus' signs in John looks even more removed from historical concerns than Mark.

On the one hand, then, we risk being beguiled by the picture Mark paints. On the other, however, we should not assume that Mark has totally falsified his portrait just because he has a particular point of view (as any writer must have); even if Mark's primary concern was theological rather than historical, he may still have intended his narrative to reflect a real figure from the past, and there may be aspects of his portrait that in fact do so quite well. In the next chapter we shall explore how we may be able to use Mark, and to a lesser extent the other three Gospels, to develop our own model of Jesus as healer and exorcist in the light of what else we know.

6

Healing and exorcism in the ministry of Jesus

In the last chapter we saw that Mark's portrayal of Jesus' miracle-working was anything but a naive historical account. If we had the space to conduct a similar analysis of the other three Gospels we should find much the same thing, and in any case the picture of Jesus' miracles that emerges from Matthew and Luke is to a considerable extent dependent on that established by Mark. This might make us wonder whether we can use the Gospels to say much about the miracles of the historical Jesus. The issue is not so much whether or not Jesus healed people and cast out demons, since that much is being assumed as part of our working hypothesis. The issue is rather whether we can use any of the details of the Gospel accounts to go beyond the bare fact of Jesus' miracle-working and the likelihood that it contributed to his fame.

Several considerations suggest that we should be able to go further than this. The first is that there is no reason to suppose that Mark invented all the material he used, and the indications are that he employed a considerable amount of material taken from his tradition. The same could also apply to some of the non-Markan material found in the other Gospels.

The second is that however theological Mark's portrait is, it apparently does intend to refer to a specific individual, Jesus of Nazareth, who was a contemporary of a specific Roman governor, Pontius Pilate, and who operated in a specific geographical area. If Mark and the other Gospels intend to refer to this figure there are both social and logical limits to what they can get away with. Socially, the Evangelists would have been constrained by how much their target audiences would tolerate deviances from what they already knew or believed about Jesus of Nazareth. The logical limits are on how far deviations from what is known or believed can be taken before the intended reference to Jesus of Nazareth simply fails. If I set out to write a historical novel about Horatio Nelson, there are limits to the liberties I can take if my central character is to be recognizable as the famous admiral rather than someone who just happens to share his name. I cannot make Nelson an American; I cannot allow him to survive the Battle of Trafalgar; I cannot depict him as a cavalry officer, or make him inno-cent of any relationship with Lady Hamilton. Likewise, there are limits to the liberties any writer could take with the figure of Jesus while leaving him recognizable as Jesus of Nazareth.[1]

The third consideration is that being theological, symbolic and mytho-logical does not automatically disqualify Mark's account (or any of the other Gospel accounts) from historical consideration, in so far as Jesus' miracles may have been perceived in similar categories by his contem-poraries. It is not the case that Mark has added a theological gloss to events that Jesus and those who witnessed him would have understood in purely naturalistic terms. To the extent that Jesus and his closest followers under-stood healing and exorcism to be part of the work of proclaiming the king-dom, these deeds would have been perceived theologically from the start by people who held a mythological worldview not wholly unlike that of the Evangelists (and certainly much more like it than our modern Western worldview).[2] To be sure, this does not guarantee that the Evangelists put the same theological construction on Jesus' miracles as Jesus' contempor-aries did, but it at least opens up the possibility of some continuity.

Finally, and perhaps most importantly in terms of method, it may be that the memory of the sort of things Jesus did is more reliable than the accounts of individual incidents.[3] This assumes that the tradition would be more tolerant of stories that seemed in character with what was be-lieved about Jesus than those that did not, so that even purely fictitious incidents might succeed in portraying the sort of things Jesus typically did. It also assumes that recurring or typical features of the miracle stories may be a guide to how Jesus was remembered.[4]

Our next step is thus to see if all the threads reviewed so far can be drawn together into an account of Jesus as healer-exorcist that fits both what we know of his particular context and what the Gospels recount. This is not the same as assessing each and every miracle story on an indi-vidual basis and grading its historical plausibility.[5] It is in any case unwise

---

[1] A similar point is made by Bas M. F. van Iersel, *Reading Mark* (Collegeville, MN: Liturgical Press, 1988), 5–6.

[2] Cf. Morton Smith, *Jesus the Magician* (London: Victor Gollancz, 1978), 4–5.

[3] See Peter Carnley, *The Structure of Resurrection Belief* (Oxford: Clarendon Press, 1987), 266–96, for this distinction between episodic and dispositional memory.

[4] Compare the more global use of this technique in Dale C. Allison, *Jesus of Nazareth: Millenar-ian Prophet* (Minneapolis: Fortress, 1998), 39–69.

[5] For a thorough example of that kind of exercise, see John P. Meier, *A Marginal Jew: Rethink-ing the Historical Jesus*, vol. 2: *Mentor, Message, and Miracles* (New York: Doubleday, 1994), 646–1038.

to rely too much on the details of any individual miracle story given that there is no way of reverse-engineering the transformation such stories undoubtedly underwent in the course of oral transmission (as well as Mark's literary deployment of them). It will be safer to work from the general impression the stories create, not in a totally vague sense, but rather in the sense of the generalizations that can be drawn from what they have in common. It will also be safer to treat such generalizations as being, at least in the first instance, not so much direct evidence of what Jesus actually did, but evidence of the impression he made and how he was perceived. We can then go on to enquire what sort of figure may have lain behind such impressions.

General impressions

For the moment we are concerned with Jesus only as healer and exorcist, so stories of raising the dead or performing 'nature miracles' can be left aside till the next chapter. The Gospel of Mark contains four stories of Jesus casting out demons (Mark 1.21–28; 5.1–20; 7.24–30; 9.14–29), together with a number of summary statements indicating that he cast out demons on other occasions (1.32–39; 3.11–12) and two incidents that presuppose Jesus' reputation as an exorcist (3.22–30; 9.38–39). There is also one healing of a fever (Mark 1.29–31), one healing of 'leprosy' (1.40–45), one healing of a paralytic (2.1–12), one healing of a man with a withered hand (3.1–6), one healing of a woman with a haemorrhage (5.25–34), one healing of a deaf and dumb man (7.31–37), two healings of blind men (8.22–26; 10.46–52), a number of summaries of multiple healings (1.32–34; 3.10; 6.5, 53–56), and one or two other sayings and incidents that arguably presuppose Jesus' reputation as a healer (6.1–6; 6.14; 8.11; 15.31). Notably absent from this list are any stories of Jesus mending broken bones or miraculously curing cuts, severed limbs or other such injuries, or indeed of performing any cure of what is clearly a disease with an organic, biomedical cause (for the difference between disease and illness see pp. 52–3). The list creates a slight impression of a particular emphasis on exorcism, otherwise the only repeated category is that of the healing of blindness, which could well be due to Mark's redactional interest in the metaphorical blindness of the disciples. Apart from that, the list looks a little as if it has been designed to illustrate the range of conditions Jesus was reputed to have healed. If so, this maps nicely onto a range of conditions that could be due to the somatization of psychological or social stress (conversion disorders).

Matthew and Luke add few healing stories not already in this list, but those they do add tend to confirm rather than contradict this picture, indicating that it is not purely a Markan idiosyncrasy. Matthew and Luke both narrate the story of the Capernaum centurion's boy, in which the illness is not specified. Luke also adds a healing of dropsy (Luke 14.1–6), the crippled woman healed on the Sabbath (13.10–17), the exorcism of a dumb demon (11.14) and a healing of ten lepers (17.11–19), as well as a single anomalous case, the healing of the high priest's slave's severed ear (Luke 22.50–51), which does not appear in any of the parallel accounts of the arrest scene, and so is suspect as probable Lukan invention.[6]

Again in Mark, the impression given is that Jesus' healings and exorcisms helped both to spread his fame and to provoke the opposition of the authorities. It seems likely that these were the two sides of the same coin: were Jesus not attracting a measure of popular support the authorities might not have considered him a threat worth countering. This is illustrated in particular by the Beelzebul Controversy (Mark 3.22–30), which represents the authorities trying to discredit Jesus by claiming that he used Satanic power to cast out demons. Such an accusation presupposes that Jesus has gained a reputation as an exorcist that needed to be undermined. Meanwhile Jesus' spreading fame is not only explicitly indicated by the narrator (e.g. Mark 1.28, 37, 45; 3.9–10; 6.14–16, 54–56; 7.24, 36–37) but is presupposed in virtually every story where people come to Jesus for healing (for they would have no reason to do this unless Jesus had acquired a reputation as a healer). Once again, the other Gospels broadly support this picture, but it must be added that only the Fourth Gospel suggests that Jesus' miracle-working provoked the decision to have him executed (John 11.45–53).

When it comes to the purpose of these healing miracles, in terms of their role in Jesus' overall mission, the picture is less clear. By emphasizing their role in spreading Jesus' fame Mark could be taken as implying that they were a means of securing attention for Jesus' teaching, but the commands to secrecy after a number of healings (Mark 1.44; 5.43; 7.36; 8.26) seem designed to counteract this impression, a lead Matthew partly follows (Matthew 12.15–21) and partly contradicts (e.g. Matthew 4.23–25, where Jesus' healing tour appears to attract the crowd who at 7.28–29 are said to have been astonished at his teaching in the Sermon on the Mount). Such commands to secrecy are problematic for a number of

---

[6] Meier, *Marginal Jew*, 2.714–18.

reasons, as Wrede pointed out.[7] For example, the command to secrecy after the raising of Jairus' daughter (Mark 5.43) would have been utterly point-less unless Jesus intended the girl to be locked away in secret for the rest of her life, which hardly seems likely. Moreover, it is simply incoherent to suppose that Jesus was attempting to conduct a public ministry in secret. The commands to secrecy thus look suspiciously like artificial construc-tions, perhaps designed to counter accusations that Jesus' healings were the acts of someone seeking fame for himself. The idea that Jesus' mira-cles were intended to attract publicity is therefore not excluded.

A seemingly obvious purpose for Jesus' healing and teaching ministry might be to demonstrate compassion in action, so that his deeds matched his teaching, but this is suggested comparatively rarely in the text (Mark 1.41 perhaps, depending on the textual reading; Mark 3.5 by implication perhaps; Matthew 9.35–36 perhaps); at Mark 6.34 Jesus' compassionate reaction is not said to be to heal but to teach; the parallel at Matthew 14.14 changes the response from teaching to healing thus creating an explicit connection between healing and compassion. It might be argued that since Jesus is represented as healing all and sundry without apparently asking anything in return, the link is too obvious to need pointing out. But this may be to read the Gospels through modern spectacles. In antiquity some form of reciprocity may have been taken for granted; at the very least Jesus probably gained in honour and reputation; it may well be that he earned hospitality and sustenance as well.[8] Moreover, the Gospels nowhere state that Jesus' healing ministry was intended as a practical demonstration of the command to love one's neighbour; in Jesus' preaching the practical examples of that command seem to take the form of generosity with possessions rather than healing the sick. And again, linking healing with compassion does not adequately select between, say, healing as exemplify-ing a timeless ethic and healing as demonstrating the nature of the com-ing kingdom. This is not to deny that Jesus may have been motivated by compassion, it is rather to suggest that this explanation may not take us very far.

Mark also stresses the connection between teaching and miracle-working, but this looks suspiciously like a Markan construction. For example at Mark 1.21–22, 27, Jesus is said to teach in the synagogue and to cause astonishment at his teaching, but what is narrated in the

---

[7] William Wrede, *The Messianic Secret* (tr. James C. G. Greig; Cambridge: James Clarke, 1971).

[8] Jerome H. Neyrey, 'Miracles, in Other Words: Social Science Perspectives on Healings' in John C. Cavadini (ed.), *Miracles in Jewish and Christian Antiquity* (Notre Dame, IN: University of Notre Dame Press, 1999), 19–55.

intervening verses is not teaching but an exorcism. The ambiguous verse 27 (in which 'with authority' could go either with 'a new teaching' or 'he commands even the unclean spirits') creates the impression that Jesus' authority to teach is intimately connected with (or demonstrated by) his ability to cast out demons. Although this looks suspiciously like literary artifice on Mark's part, it is not necessarily misrepresentation. Other things being equal someone who performs impressive deeds is more likely to get a hearing for his words, and given the connection between miracle-working and prophecy that was already established in Israelite tradition (as we have seen, p. 20), someone performing miracles might more readily be accepted as a prophet (a connection explicitly made at Mark 6.15; Luke 7.16; 13.32–33; 24.19). It would be fair to say, then, that the Gospels create the impression that Jesus' miracles served to enhance his prophetic authority.

A direct connection between miracles and the coming kingdom of God is comparatively uncommon. At Mark 1.24 the unclean spirit is made to cry out, 'have you come to destroy us?', and although the question is left unanswered the implication may be that destroying unclean spirits is an aspect of the work of announcing the coming kingdom. There is a similar implication in the Matthean account of the Gadarene demoniacs, where the demons ask if Jesus has come to torment them 'before the time' (Matthew 8.29). If Mark 3.27 is meant to imply that Jesus is the plunderer who has bound Satan (the strong man), then this would be a further indication that Jesus' exorcisms are intended as part of the eschatological overthrow of demonic powers, but the logic is confused by the previous verses (3.23–26), which seem to presuppose that Satan is *not* coming to an end in order to demonstrate the absurdity of the charge that Jesus is casting out demons by the power of demons. The connection between exorcism and the coming of the kingdom is made far clearer in Matthew's version of the Beelzebul Controversy at Matthew 12.28, 'if it is by the Spirit of God that I cast out demons, then the kingdom of God has come upon you'; Matthew often tries to clarify Mark and this may be the case here.[9] A connection between casting out unclean spirits, healing, and the preaching of repentance seems to be implicit in the account of the mission of the Twelve in Mark 6.7–13, and once again the connection between healing, casting out demons and proclaiming the kingdom is made clearer in the Matthean parallel at Matthew 10.5–15. It is also implied in

---

[9] See Eric Eve, *The Jewish Context of Jesus' Miracles* (JSNTSup, 231; Sheffield: Sheffield Academic Press, 2002), 330–3.

the woes against Galilean cities at Matthew 11.20–24, where Jesus says that his mighty works ought to have provoked repentance.

For the most part, though, the precise connection between Jesus' ministry of healing and exorcism and his proclamation of the coming kingdom (and other teaching) is left vague. The impression that there *is* a connection is created more by the juxtaposition of these activities than by many explicit attempts to relate the two. The so-called 'nature miracles' (which we shall look at in the next chapter) may be more Christologically explicit, but most of the healing and exorcism stories contain little or no attempt to draw any deeper lessons, so much so that Gerd Theissen has suggested that they must originally have circulated in a non-Christian context.[10] But even if that were so it does not explain why the Evangelists were apparently so content to allow these miracle stories to speak for themselves.

One possibility is that the miracle stories are an extraneous import into the story of a figure who was simply a teacher or teller of parables, so that there is no intrinsic connection to make.[11] So far, however, the evidence has tended to favour the hypothesis that Jesus was a healer/exorcist, so this explanation should only be adopted if none better can be found.

The most obvious alternative is that the healings and exorcisms never had any deeper meaning. Jesus performed them because he found he could, or because they were expected of him, and because they helped authenticate his message, but they were never intended to have any deeper significance in relation to the coming kingdom of God.

A third possibility is that Jesus never preached a coming kingdom of God in the first place, at least not in the sense of an apocalyptic eschatology that expected a catastrophic intervention in the normal course of history, and that this emphasis is due to later interpretations of his life. The lack of much explicit connection between miracles and kingdom would then be explained by the lack of any original emphasis on the kingdom, so that if Jesus' healings and exorcisms ever had any deeper significance, one must look elsewhere than eschatology to discover it.

A fourth possibility is that the tradition contained little that spelt out a connection between miracles and eschatology because no one saw the need to be more explicit, the hints given in the text being regarded as sufficient for their target audience. The final possibility is that the failure

---

[10] Gerd Theissen, *The Gospels in Context: Social and Political History in the Synoptic Tradition* (Edinburgh: T. & T. Clark, 1992), 97–112; cf. Gerd Theissen and Annette Merz, *The Historical Jesus: A Comprehensive Guide* (tr. John Bowden, London: SCM Press, 1998), 301–2.

[11] See, e.g., Burton L. Mack, *A Myth of Innocence: Mark and Christian Origins* (Philadelphia: Fortress, 1988), 208–45.

of the eschaton to arrive by the time the Evangelists wrote discouraged them from emphasizing any connection between miracles and eschatology.

Before trying to decide whether Jesus' miracles had any eschatological import we should take a look at the particularities of Jesus' situation. We can then go on to explore the connection between miracle and eschatology in more detail before attempting a synthesis of the various approaches covered so far.

Contextual considerations

Jesus was not a generic folk-healer operating in a generic context. He was not even a generic Jewish folk-healer operating in a generic first-century context. He was specifically a northern Israelite (apparently from the village of Nazareth) with a role yet to be determined operating mainly in rural Galilee somewhere around 30 CE. It is necessary to sketch in some of the particularities of this situation before trying to construct a more specific theory of Jesus' healing activities.

We should begin by clarifying the term 'rural Galilee'. In an agrarian society (such as the Roman empire), the bulk of the population (perhaps about 90 per cent) would be directly or indirectly engaged in working the land. These peasant farmers would typically be living at subsistence level, any surpluses being siphoned off to enrich the tiny elite (about 1 per cent of the population) and to support their retainers (soldiers, bureaucrats, tax-collectors and the like), who were necessary to keep the system of ex-action going. Galilee was well suited to agricultural production, as well as to fishing in the area round the lake (known in the Gospels as the Sea of Galilee). Traditional peasants generally aimed at self-sufficiency, pro-ducing nearly all of what they consumed in individual households and vil-lages, with the possible exception of some specialist items such as pottery (which might depend on the availability of suitable clay). The interests and values of smallholding farmers are expressed as Israelite ideals in much of the Old Testament, with every man secure 'under his vine and under his fig tree' (1 Kings 4.25; Micah 4.4). Such ideals were threatened first by the institution of the monarchy (as symbolized, for example, in the story of Naboth's vineyard at 1 Kings 21.1–19), and then by the succession of empires under whose sway Israel fell. During Jesus' lifetime the current imperial power was, of course, Rome.[12]

---

[12] See, e.g., Marcus J. Borg, *Jesus in Contemporary Scholarship* (Valley Forge, PA: Trinity Press International, 1994), 101–17.

Although Palestine had been taken into the Roman empire by Pompey in 63 BCE, Galilee was not under direct Roman rule at the time of Jesus. During the time immediately preceding the birth of Jesus, much of Palestine had been ruled by Herod the Great, a client king acting on behalf of Rome (i.e. keeping the peace and ensuring the payment of tribute). When Herod died in 4 BCE his kingdom was divided between his three sons, with Judaea and Samaria going to Archelaeus and Galilee to Antipas (often called 'Herod' in the Gospels). Archelaeus proved a poor ruler and was deposed by the Romans in 6 CE, at which point Judaea and Samaria came under direct Roman rule with a Roman governor (or 'prefect') normally resident at Caesarea Maritima. As is well known, the prefect at the time of Jesus was Pontius Pilate.

Although Galilee was ruled by Herod Antipas, it was not immune from the effects of Roman imperialism. While no Roman troops were stationed there on a regular basis, they could be sent in to intervene if the situation demanded, and a Roman legion had attacked and allegedly destroyed the Galilean city of Sepphoris in living memory (4 BCE), although the archaeological remains suggest that Josephus' claim of total destruction may be exaggerated.[13] Galilee was not crawling with Roman legionaries, but the threat of Roman violence remained in the background (and would become a reality once more during the Jewish Revolt of 66–70 CE).

In the meanwhile, indirect Romanization was having an economic impact in Galilee. Prior to the time of Jesus the land was well able to support a population of independent smallholders in what could have counted as moderate prosperity.[14] The programme of urbanization begun by Herod Antipas (in accordance with Roman policy if not under direct Roman orders) would have put pressure on the rural population. Antipas rebuilt Sepphoris in 4 BCE and founded the new city of Tiberias in 18 CE. New urban populations would have needed feeding, ancient cities being centres of consumption rather than production, and this would have been achieved through exactions on the peasantry in the surrounding country-side (through a combination of rents and taxes, and by appropriating land for some of the people settled in Tiberias).[15] Antipas also had to collect

---

[13] *Ant.* 17.288–9; *J.W.* 2.68–9; Jonathan L. Reed, *Archaeology and the Galilean Jesus* (Harrisburg, PA: Trinity Press International, 2000), 117.

[14] Sean Freyne, *Jesus, a Jewish Galilean: A New Reading of the Jesus-Story* (London: T. & T. Clark, 2004), 44.

[15] Freyne, *Jewish Galilean*, 45–6; Reed, *Archaeology*, 66–8, 83–9; John S. Kloppenborg Verbin, *Excavating Q: The History and Setting of the Sayings Gospel* (Edinburgh: T. & T. Clark, 2000), 234–42; William E. Arnal, *Jesus and the Village Scribes: Galilean Conflicts and the Setting of Q* (Minneapolis: Fortress, 2001), 101, 127–55; Richard A. Horsley, *Archaeology, History,*

tribute on behalf of Rome, and this too would be in the form of taxation imposed on the population (probably in kind rather than cash). The result of these changes was that many peasants would have found themselves having to hand over more of their produce to the authorities, with less left over to feed themselves and their families. They would thus become more vulnerable to the vagaries of poor harvests, and might find themselves forced to sell their land to make ends meet, becoming tenants on land they had previously owned. In the worst case they might find themselves obliged to borrow money at ruinous rates of interest and become forced off their land altogether when they became unable to repay. In such a situation a former peasant might have little option but to resort to banditry. Estimates vary on how widespread such a dire fate actually was, and on how onerous the burden of taxation actually would have been, but it does appear that Jesus was ministering in Galilee at a time when things had recently become worse (Jesus would have been about twenty when Tiberias was founded), and in which resentment against the relatively new cities and their inhabitants might well have been growing. In such a situation a message proclaiming the reversal of fortunes of rich and poor, or the coming of a kingdom that restored an older Israelite ideal, might well find a ready hearing among those who perceived themselves as (and who indeed were) oppressed under the present order.

In addition to the effect of Romanization there is the issue of the relation of Galilee to Jerusalem and Judaea. So far as the ethnic identity of the first-century population of Galilee is concerned, the archaeological evidence (in conjunction with what Josephus says about Galilee) strongly supports the view that the population of Galilee was predominantly Judaean in origin, both in the towns and villages, and in the cities of Tiberias and Sepphoris. This is indicated both by the presence of Jewish identity markers such as stone vessels, stepped pools or *mikvaoth* used for ritual bathing, and secondary burial, and by the rarity of pork bones, remains of pagan temples or other objects obviously used in connection with a pagan cult. This is all the more striking when contrasted with the much more frequent remains of pagan culture in neighbouring locations such as Caesarea Maritima or Scythopolis.[16] Had there been a substantial

---

and Society in Galilee (Valley Forge: Trinity Press International, 1996), 12, 28–34, 60, 79–85, 118–24, 177–81; John Dominic Crossan, *The Birth of Christianity: Discovering What Happened in the Years Immediately After the Execution of Jesus* (San Francisco: Harper, 1998), 146–59, 215–35.

[16] Mark A. Chancey, *The Myth of a Gentile Galilee* (SNTSMS, 118; Cambridge: Cambridge University Press, 2002), 140–8; Reed, *Archaeology*, 51–2.

pagan population in Galilee, one would have expected such physical remains of pagan culture to be far more evident. Conversely, the presence of distinctive stone vessels and *mikvaoth*, reflecting peculiarly Jewish purity concerns, the absence of pork bones, indicating observance of Jewish dietary laws, and evidence for the distinctively Jewish custom of the secondary burial of bones are strong indicators of a Jewish population.[17] It is unclear whether the use of ossuaries for secondary burial was mostly confined to Judaea.[18] But the practice of secondary burial was carried out by Jews throughout Roman Palestine, as was the location of tombs well away from human habitation, presumably out of concern for purity.[19] The most natural conclusion is that the majority population of first-century Galilee was Jewish.[20]

There is very little evidence of much settlement in the region after the time of the Assyrian conquest in the late eighth century BCE, when the region seems to have become largely depopulated.[21] Although there appears to have been a modest resettlement in the Persian and early Hellenistic periods,[22] there seems to have been no large increase of population until the late Hellenistic period, around the time of the Hasmonean expansion into the area at the end of the second century BCE and on into the early Roman period.[23] At the same time there is some evidence of some of the existing, probably pagan, population abandoning their settlements in and around Galilee at around this time (which may be related to the Hasmonean policy of demanding conversion to Judaism of any who remained, if that is how Josephus, *Ant.* 13.318–19 is to be taken).[24] The introduction of Hasmonean (alongside Tyrian) coinage in Galilee from this time indicates that the region came under Hasmonean political control and had economic links with Jerusalem.[25] Overall this evidence suggests that the bulk of the population of first-century Galilee were the descendants of

---

[17] Reed, *Archaeology*, 43–51; but see Kloppenborg Verbin, *Excavating Q*, 231, and Horsley, *Archaeology*, 110, for reservations about the significance of some of this evidence.

[18] Contrast Byron R. McCane, *Roll Back the Stone: Death and Burial in the World of Jesus* (Harrisburg: Trinity Press International, 2003), 39–47, 54, with Reed, *Archaeology*, 44–51.

[19] McCane, *Roll Back the Stone*, 55–6.

[20] Chancey, *Myth*, 66–8, 117–19; Reed, *Archaeology*, 49–53.

[21] Chancey, *Myth*, 31–4; Reed, *Archaeology*, 27–34; Freyne, *Jewish Galilean*, 15, 62. For the alternative view that the Galileans were the descendants of northern Israelites who had remained since the Assyrian conquest, see Horsley, *Archaeology*, 23, 94.

[22] Chancey, *Myth*, 43–7; Reed, *Archaeology*, 34–9.

[23] Reed, *Archaeology*, 39–43; Freyne, *Jewish Galilean*, 81–2.

[24] Reed, *Archaeology*, 42–3; Chancey, *Myth*, 112–13.

[25] Chancey, *Myth*, 46; Reed, *Archaeology*, 41–2.

immigrants from Judaea, a conclusion further borne out by the similarity of the material culture of Judaea and Galilee in contrast to other parts of Palestine.[26]

This suggests that one can assume some reasonable similarity of traditions and beliefs between Judaeans and Galileans, and that what we can learn from Jewish belief and practice from Judaean sources may also be relevant to Galilee. At the most general level this implies that Galileans would be broadly familiar with and loyal to the traditions contained in Israel's scriptures. On the other hand, among Galilean (and indeed Judaean) peasantry this familiarity would be mediated by the 'little tradition', that is by the largely oral appropriation and adaptation of the written traditions of the elite (the so-called 'great tradition'). We can legitimately use Second Temple literature to help illuminate how ordinary Galileans may have understood the sacred traditions of Israel, but in doing so we also need to allow for the differences in social and geographical location between (mainly illiterate) rural Galileans and the people who wrote Second Temple Jewish texts (the literate elite and their scribal retainers).

Miracle and eschatology

This book is principally about Jesus' miracles, not about every aspect of the historical Jesus, but before we can get much further with establishing the significance of Jesus' miracles, we need to take a view on some wider aspects of Jesus' ministry. In particular, we need to decide whether Jesus' healings and exorcisms should be interpreted in the context of some kind of imminent eschatological expectation (as scholars such as Sanders and Allison argue) or whether Jesus is better understood in a non-eschatological framework (as others such as Borg, Crossan and Horsley propose, in somewhat different ways). Before we can do this we need to be clear what we mean by eschatology since, as Borg has rightly complained, the term has become alarmingly elastic in much New Testament scholarship.[27]

Defining eschatology as involving an imminent expectation of the end of the world would be a little too narrow. On the other hand, Crossan's proposal to extend eschatology to cover all forms of world-denial, so that 'ethical eschatology' and 'ascetic eschatology' (linked to present behaviour rather than imminent future expectation) stand alongside 'apocalyptic

[26] Reed, *Archaeology*, 49.
[27] Borg, *Jesus in Contemporary Scholarship*, 8–9, 30–1, 70–4.

eschatology' as three species of the same genus, broadens the term too far to be useful.[28] 'Eschatology' derives from the Greek *eschatos*, meaning 'last', and it seems reasonable to insist on some link between eschatology and finality. This does not have to mean the end of the entire space-time universe, however; although belief in such a final destruction can be found in some ancient eschatologies, it does not appear to be the dominant view in biblical and other Jewish texts. Again, while the term 'eschatology' certainly could include an otherworldly consummation, it need not, and in the first-century Jewish context often did not. More positively, an eschatological expectation is one which expects a radical transformation of the existing world order so that evil is overcome, all is put right, and divine rule is fully manifested. While this does not necessarily entail the end of history, it implies finality in the sense that, to put it crudely, one could then end one's account of human history with 'and they all lived happily ever after' (where 'they' would not, of course, include those who fell under eschatological condemnation). Apocalyptic eschatology is then the expectation that this consummation will be brought about by a dramatic or even catastrophic divine intervention. An imminent apocalyptic eschatology is one that expects this to happen soon.

These definitions do not draw completely sharp boundaries. A strictly eschatological expectation could shade into a merely salvation-historical one (the hope that things will get dramatically better, without the expectation that this will be final).[29] Moreover, what one person or culture views as dramatic divine intervention another may see as the results of natural causes or a turbulent period of otherwise ordinary historical process, and what counts as 'soon' can often become highly elastic. Nonetheless, people who want things to become dramatically better are likely to want them to stay better, and for the change to occur as soon as possible, and the greater the gap between the presently perceived evils and the hoped-for ideal state, the more likely it is that a dramatic divine intervention will appear necessary to bring the latter into being. If things seem bad enough, eschatological hopes are likely to take the form of imminent apocalyptic eschatology, and other Jewish texts from around the time of Jesus suggest that such hopes were fairly widespread.[30] The previous section suggests some reasons why they may also have existed among

---

[28] Crossan, *Birth*, 273–89.
[29] The latter seems to be Horsley's view of Jesus' position; see Richard A. Horsley, *Jesus and the Spiral of Violence* (Minneapolis: Fortress, 1993), 157–60, 167–71.
[30] Allison, *Jesus of Nazareth*, 33–69, 95–129.

Galilean peasants suffering a relatively rapid decline in living standards with concomitant threats to their traditional values. In what follows, 'eschatology' will therefore mainly function as shorthand for 'imminent apocalyptic eschatology'.

Whether or not Jesus' miracles are best understood in an eschatological framework can hardly be determined from the miracle tradition alone.[31] As noted above, few of the healing and exorcism stories carry any explicit eschatological interpretation, and even if they did, we should then have to decide whether such an interpretation was traditional or redactional. The main apparent exception is Jesus' statement at Matthew 12.28 // Luke 11.20, 'But if it is by the Spirit of God that I cast out demons, then the kingdom of God has come upon you.' But anyone who doubts that there ever was such a document as Q cannot be sure that this verse is not due to Matthean redaction,[32] and even if it is not, the interpretation of the verse is questionable.[33] Among other things, it depends what is meant by that much-debated term 'kingdom of God'. The work of Johannes Weiss and Albert Schweitzer persuaded scholars in the first half of the twentieth century to see Jesus' preaching of the 'kingdom of God' as eschatological, but over the last few decades this has come under increasing challenge, especially from the view that what Jesus proclaimed was a 'sapiential' kingdom (God's rule manifested by living in accordance with the subversive wisdom Jesus preached, rather than by dramatically irrupting into history in apocalyptic intervention),[34] or else the kingdom of God as a symbol of a renewed social order.[35]

The notion of a sapiential kingdom is by no means self-evidently absurd, since the term 'kingdom of God' certainly could be applied to the reign of God manifested by obedience to God's will,[36] but it is not perhaps the most obvious resonance of the term in a context of resistance to the pressures of imperial domination, in which 'the good news of the kingdom of God' is more likely to be heard as an assurance that God's rule is about to replace Caesar's. There are several other reasons for supposing that Jesus' ministry took place in the context of eschatological expectation. So far as we can tell, John the Baptist proclaimed an imminent

---

[31] As E. P. Sanders, *Jesus and Judaism* (London: SCM Press, 1985), 170–3, argues.

[32] Eve, *Jewish Context*, 330–3.

[33] Sanders, *Jesus and Judaism*, 133–6.

[34] So, e.g., John Dominic Crossan, *The Historical Jesus: The Life of a Mediterranean Jewish Peasant* (San Francisco: HarperCollins, 1992), 265–302.

[35] Horsley, *Spiral*, 167–208.

[36] See Crossan, *Historical Jesus*, 248–91, for examples.

judgement, and eschatological expectations seem to have been rife among many of those members of the primitive Jesus-movement whose writings found their way into the New Testament. Prima facie, one would thus expect Jesus, who stands between John the Baptist and the early Church, to share the eschatological orientation common to both. Dale Allison has made a persuasive case for seeing the early Jesus-movement as matching the sociological pattern of millenarian movements documented across history. For example, in common with many other millenarian movements, that associated with Jesus addressed the disaffected in a period of social change that threatened traditional ways, saw the present and near future as times of suffering and catastrophe, envisaged a comprehensive redemption through an imminent reversal of current circumstances, divided the world into the saved and unsaved, broke hallowed taboos, replaced traditional family bonds with fictive kin, demanded intense commitment and unconditional loyalty, and focused upon a charismatic leader.[37] On this understanding, Jesus should be seen as a millenarian prophet (and performing miracles is the sort of things millenarian prophets are expected to do).[38]

The claim is sometimes made that the eschatological expectations of the early Church were created by Jesus' resurrection,[39] but this seems to put things back to front; the fact that the appearances of Jesus to his followers after his death were interpreted in terms of resurrection (an end-time expectation in Jewish thought) implies that they were experienced in the framework of lively eschatological expectations that were already in place.[40] A similar point may be made about the application of the title 'Messiah' to Jesus, which is already taken so much for granted by Paul that it can be used by him virtually as a proper name. Even allowing for the fact that 'messiah' was a fluid term in Second Temple Judaism, Jesus' career as described in the Gospels does not look conventionally messianic, but it is again hard to see why the resurrection appearances could by themselves have given rise to calling Jesus 'Messiah' unless he was already seen as a potentially messianic figure, such as a millenarian prophet acting as the focus for intense eschatological expectations.

To enter into an extended debate with non-eschatological views would take us too far away from our main topic, but a few points may be made in brief. First, the non-eschatological understanding often rests on

[37] Allison, *Jesus of Nazareth*, 61–4, 78–94.
[38] Allison, *Jesus of Nazareth*, 91.
[39] e.g. Borg, *Jesus in Contemporary Scholarship*, 58.
[40] Allison, *Jesus of Nazareth*, 112.

detecting a purely sapiential layer in the earliest stage of the redaction of Q and then (often by taking this in conjunction with parallel material in the *Gospel of Thomas*) assuming that this best represents the authentic teaching of the historical Jesus. Quite apart from the question of whether Q ever existed at all, this in turn depends on: a stratification of Q which not all supporters of Q would accept;[41] a dubious identification of the earliest redactional layer of Q with the earliest Jesus tradition, contrary to what is stated by one of the leading proponents of its analysis into redactional layers;[42] the unproven assumption that Q should be privileged above Mark; and the methodologically dubious procedure of isolating a collection of sayings and taking these to be most indicative of what the historical Jesus was about, as if it were possible to isolate authentic material independently of some overarching view of Jesus.[43]

This is not to say that the identification of sapiential material in the Jesus tradition is worthless, but rather to cast doubt on whether it alone can be taken as determinative for understanding him. There is no reason why sapiential and apocalyptic concerns should not be combined in the same individual or group.[44] In this combination, the sapiential material may be advising how life should be lived in the light of the kingdom's advent; this might suggest that Jesus' eschatology has a strong this-worldly orientation (that is, that he was expecting a dramatic change of circumstances in this world rather than translation to another, a 'political' rather than a 'cosmic' eschatology), but it does not prevent its being an imminent apocalyptic eschatology. To the extent that the sapiential material can be seen as advocating a return to Israelite ideals (or at least, Israelite peasant ideals) to bring about the renewal of Galilean society in the face of the commercializing pressures of Roman imperialism, it is also compatible with the understanding of Jesus as an eschatological prophet of Israelite renewal.

Although a prophet of renewal espousing a counter-cultural return to Israelite ideals under the symbol 'kingdom of God' need not be eschatological,[45] removing the eschatological dimension creates more problems than it solves. For one thing, it is unclear how a programme of social

---

[41] e.g. Christopher M. Tuckett, *Q and the History of Early Christianity* (Edinburgh: T. & T. Clark, 1997), 64–82, 325–54.

[42] John S. Kloppenborg, *The Formation of Q: Trajectories in Ancient Wisdom Collections* (Studies in Antiquity and Christianity; Harrisburg, PA: Trinity Press International, 1999), 244–5.

[43] For a fuller critique, see Allison, *Jesus of Nazareth*, 10–39 (against Crossan), 97–129 (against Marcus Borg and Stephen Patterson).

[44] Freyne, *Jewish Galilean*, 136–41; Allison, *Jesus of Nazareth*, 113–15.

[45] So Horsley, *Spiral*, 167–9, and Borg, *Jesus in Contemporary Scholarship*, 53–7.

renewal in Galilean villages (such as Crossan's suggestion of open table-fellowship in the service of a brokerless kingdom, a society without the intermediaries who brokered power and privilege) could ever give rise to something like primitive Christianity; the cause does not seem commensurate with the effect. For another, it is unclear how the purely sapiential Jesus' counter-cultural espousal of village renewal could aspire to be an effective response to the problem it was supposedly addressing; it would be like urging better table manners on passengers aboard a ship sailing in the wrong direction. Richard Horsley spots this problem nicely, and suggests that Jesus proposed a programme of social reform while leaving the political revolution to God (which seems to bring him quite close to an eschatological viewpoint, albeit more akin to political than to cosmic eschatology).[46] Finally, the model of Jesus the social reformer that often seems to emerge from non-eschatological views risks looking anachronistic. The problem is not that ancient peasants could not envisage equality as an ideal, indeed, egalitarianism is characteristic of millenarian movements in many times and places,[47] it is rather that these proposals make Jesus into someone who analyses his society's ills in social, economic and political terms and then proposes remedies based on his reading of the Israelite tradition. This makes Jesus too much like a modern calculating rationalist employing modern social-scientific categories, and the religious dimension becomes underplayed. This objection is not adequately answered by the perfectly correct observation that religion and politics were closely intertwined in antiquity, since the point is not to deny the validity of the political dimension, but to insist on the spiritual, theological and mythological elements that also contributed to the conceptual, emotional and imaginative mindset of most people in antiquity. For such people, God and the spirit-world of angels and demons were likely to have been much more of a lived reality than they are for most people in the modern West.[48]

This does not mean that the political and social dimensions of Jesus' activity should be ignored. On the contrary, they can usefully be integrated into an eschatological understanding. In so far as eschatological expectations challenge the status quo they have both political and social implications, and a useful way into exploring the eschatological significance of Jesus' healings and exorcisms may be to look at the ways in which they brought him into conflict with the authorities.

---

[46] Horsley, *Spiral*, 321–2.

[47] Allison, *Jesus of Nazareth*, 108–10.

[48] Borg, *Jesus in Contemporary Scholarship*, 56, 127–39; Freyne, *Jewish Galilean*, 137–8.

There is little to suggest that Jesus' miracles contributed directly to his death; at least, little in the Synoptic Gospels suggests this (with the possible exception of Mark 3.1–6), and while John makes the raising of Lazarus the occasion for the Jewish authorities' decision to get rid of Jesus, this almost certainly owes more to John's theology than to historical reminiscence. In the first place, then, the conflict caused by Jesus' healings must be sought in the context of his Galilean ministry. There are several reports of Jesus being criticized by his opponents for healing on the Sabbath (Mark 3.1–6; Luke 13.10–17; 14.1–6; John 5.1–18), but the theme is not as extensive as it is sometimes made out to be. The story of the scribes inwardly fuming at Jesus pronouncing forgiveness to the paralytic he goes on to heal (Mark 2.1–12) may not be historically accurate (how, for example, could Mark know what the scribes were saying in their hearts?), but is nonetheless suggestive for what may have been at stake: the temple establishment tended to regard mediating forgiveness of sins (and hence healing of the conditions that resulted as a 'punishment' for those sins) as their priestly prerogative, and it is this that Jesus is shown usurping here. Whether or not Mark 2.1–12 narrates an incident that actually occurred, it does help point out why Jesus' healing ministry may have offended those who wished to claim a monopoly on mediating divine benefits (not least because the temple's claim to be the source of such benefits would constitute a large part of the legitimation for its demands for support from the hard-pressed peasantry). To put it at its simplest, a successful charismatic healing ministry carried out in God's name could be seen as a rival claim to authority, and hence as a challenge to the institutional authority of the elite.

This may in part explain why reports of Jesus' miracles alarmed Herod Antipas, if Mark 6.14–16 and Luke 13.31–32 can be taken as suggesting they did so. Josephus reports that Antipas had John the Baptist executed because he attracted a following, and that attracting a popular following might all too easily lead to sedition (*Ant.* 18.116–19). To the extent that Jesus' miracles helped attract a popular following, they may have led Antipas (and other Jewish leaders) to see Jesus in the same light.[49]

Perhaps the single most telling incident is the Beelzebul Controversy (Mark 3.22–30 // Matthew 12.22–32 // Luke 11.15–22) in which the authorities accuse Jesus of casting out demons by the prince of demons. Whatever the precise tradition history of this story, the accusation it contains is unlikely to have been invented by the early Church. Its main point

---

[49] Ellis Rivkin, *What Crucified Jesus?* (London: SCM Press, 1984), 14–15, 37–8, 49–55.

is clear enough: Jesus' ability to cast out demons is not being denied, but being attributed to demonic rather than divine power and thereby denied legitimacy. This can be seen as a form of sorcery accusation commonly used to put upstart charismatics in their place, particularly when their abilities run to spirit control. It can also be understood in terms of the politics of name-calling as a means of controlling social deviance.[50] Either way it suggests that the authorities regarded Jesus as a sufficient threat on account of his exorcisms that they needed to discredit him.

This raises the question why they should have seen an exorcist as such a threat. Perhaps one of the most influential attempts to answer that question has been an article by Paul Hollenbach.[51] Hollenbach attempts to draw analogies between Jesus' exorcisms in the context of Roman imperialism and the rising incidence of mental illness in twentieth-century postcolonial situations. This approach is suggestive in general, if problematic in detail (for example by trying to extract more historical information from stories such as the Gerasene demoniac than due caution might justify). That the social and economic pressures of first-century Galilean urbanization could have led to a rise in demonic possession among the Galilean peasantry is plausible. But even if this is the case, it is not immediately obvious why reversing possession should have been seen as a challenge to the political elites. The fact that *we* have a social-scientific theory that relates social pressures to a rise in mental illness or demonic possession does not mean that anyone in the first century can be expected to share the same insight; it is unlikely that anyone among the first-century elites would have thought 'we caused all this demon possession by imposing additional stress on the peasantry, so by casting out demons Jesus is making a subversive protest against our exploitation'. Yet the fact that such a link between exorcism and protest was unlikely to have been seen in those terms does not mean it could not have been perceived at all.

A further element is the symbolism provided by an apocalyptic imagination, in which events in heaven among God, angels, and demons run in parallel with political events on earth.[52] Thus, for example, in the book of Daniel the various nations have angelic representatives with Michael (and perhaps also the one like a son of man in Daniel 7.13) representing

---

[50] Santiago Guijarro, 'The Politics of Exorcism' in Wolfgang Stegemann, Bruce J. Malina and Gerd Theissen (eds), *The Social Setting of Jesus and the Gospels* (Minneapolis: Fortress, 2002), 159–74.

[51] Paul Hollenbach, 'Jesus, Demoniacs and Public Authorities: A Socio-Historical Study', *JAAR* 49 (1981), 567–88; cf. Horsley, *Spiral*, 32–3, 154–5, 184–90, 319.

[52] See, e.g., Horsley, *Spiral*, 129–45.

Israel, and in the Qumran *War Scroll* heavenly battles rage in parallel with earthly ones. It might be possible to see apocalyptic language as thus a veiled, symbolic or metaphorical way of talking about social and political realities; it is probably more accurate to think of apocalyptic symbolism as a mythological way of conceiving what we would talk about in social and political terms. For many of the people who used such language angels and demons were no less real than Caesar and his legions, but at the same time hostile alien spirits might be seen as symbolizing hostile alien political influences:

> Within a society which can express its problems and intentions in mythical language, social and political pressure can be expressed as the rule of demons. Or, to put it more carefully, political control by a foreign power and the resulting socio-cultural pressure can intensify the experience expressed in belief in demons and lead to the spread of possession on the vast scale which we must assume existed in the world of primitive Christianity.[53]

Be that as it may, apocalyptic language typically saw a close linkage between heavenly and earthly events, so that, for example, if Jesus did indeed say something like 'I saw Satan fall like lightning from heaven' (Luke 10.18), then he would most likely have expected this to have earthly consequences; in particular his hearers would expect the defeat of evil in heaven to be quickly followed by the defeat of evil on earth. Luke places this saying in the context of the Seventy's success in casting out demons, thereby making a link between individual exorcisms and the final defeat of evil. If Jesus saw existing power structures as part of the problem, then he would not intend Satan's fall to be good news for existing human elites.

Thus, although it would be anachronistic to credit Jesus' contemporaries with an analytical awareness of sociological theories that link oppressive conditions and mental or physical ill-health, the link might nevertheless have been made at a more mythological level. From the peasant perspective, illness and unjust power structures were both part of what was wrong with the world. It would thus be open to anyone dissatisfied with such conditions to attribute them to demonic powers, and a prophet who proclaimed the good news that God was about to change things might well reinforce this viewpoint: 'a cult of exorcism would be an act of liberation transposed into the mythical realm'.[54] While an exorcist who attracted too

---

[53] Gerd Theissen, *Miracle Stories of the Early Christian Tradition* (ed. John Riches, tr. Francis McDonagh; Studies of the New Testament and Its World; Edinburgh: T. & T. Clark, 1983), 256; cf. I. M. Lewis, *Ecstatic Religion: A Study of Shamanism and Spirit Possession* (2nd edn; London: Routledge, 1989), 182.

[54] Theissen, *Miracle Stories*, 256.

much attention to himself might be seen as a threat in any case, simply by virtue of exhibiting a rival authority, an exorcist who interpreted his exorcisms in the framework of eschatological expectations that denied the ongoing legitimacy of the current elite was likely to be seen as doubly dangerous.

The danger would have been real. Although Josephus attempts to blame the Jewish Revolt on fringe Jewish fanatics and bad Roman governors, his account can be and has been read as one of a lower-class revolt against the Jewish aristocracy. A revolt against the Jewish aristocracy and a revolt against Rome would not be two different things, since the former had been co-opted into the system imposed by the latter: the Jewish leaders were meant to keep order and collect tribute on Rome's behalf, and in turn benefited from playing their part in the system, so that their interests and Rome's interests would tend to be aligned. This in itself may have undermined their credibility in the eyes of ordinary Israelites. Even if Josephus is right that bad Roman governors were partly to blame, the outbreak of an open revolt suggests that the Jewish aristocracy had lost legitimacy in the eyes of the people. Moreover, in one place Josephus appears to blame the Jewish Revolt on messianic expectations (*J.W.* 6.312–13), perhaps another indication of widespread dissatisfaction with the current leadership. The point is not that Jesus intended the Jewish Revolt that occurred forty years after his death, or that he should be blamed for causing it by inflaming messianic hopes; the point is rather that the manipulation of legitimating symbols could have serious political repercussions, so that neither the Galilean nor the Jerusalem elites should be accused of being unduly paranoid in seeing an eschatological prophet as a threat to their position.

Rome and its client rulers could and did impose their will by force if necessary, but this is never the ideal way to rule. As Theissen observes, 'Governance or ruling is the exercise of power not only by force, but also by legitimacy and symbols. The more that power is based on legitimacy and the more that it is supported by convincing symbols, the less this rule has to be gained and maintained by physical coercion.'[55] Theissen goes on to argue that it was precisely the politics of symbols that Jesus was engaged in: 'Jesus refused the use of force, but he was probably a master

---

[55] Gerd Theissen, 'The Political Dimension of Jesus' Activities' in Wolfgang Stegemann, Bruce J. Malina and Gerd Theissen (eds), *The Social Setting of Jesus and the Gospels* (Minneapolis: Fortress, 2002), 225–50 (237).

of symbolic actions in the political arena.'[56] To possess any potency, symbols must clearly resonate with already existing hopes, aspirations and beliefs, and we have just seen how Jesus' exorcisms may have done so. Similar considerations can be extended to his healings.

It is not at all clear why any member of the elite should object to a folk-healer as such. Healthy peasants are more productive than sick ones and it was presumably in the interests of the elite that peasants be productive. The problem comes when the folk-healer's prowess gains him too much honour and reputation, so that he comes to be seen as a rival source of authority. This problem is greatly exacerbated if his healings are seen as having symbolic import. The notion that Jesus healed people purely out of compassion is inadequate. However much compassion may have motivated him, there is nothing to suggest that Jesus programmatically attempted to eliminate disease from the entire Israelite population as part of some grand humanitarian initiative. His healing activity, like his exorcisms, is better seen as having symbolic import within his preaching of the coming kingdom. Of course this has a compassionate aspect, in that if healings are associated with the kingdom of God they become symbols of God's compassionate will, but that is only part of the point.

We have already seen that healing could be used as a metaphor for national revival, which would be highly pertinent to a prophet of Israelite renewal. Jesus' healings also raise issues of purity and social inclusion. It is often observed that in some healing accounts Jesus touches or is touched by people who would have been regarded as unclean: a leper (Mark 1.40–44), a menstruating woman (Mark 5.25–34) and a dead girl (Mark 5.35–43). Mark's account suggests that instead of contracting impurity from such contact, Jesus imparted purity to the sufferer: the leper was cleansed, the woman healed, and the girl raised from the dead. At the very least this brings about the inclusion of formerly excluded people back into full social life. Whether it also directly challenges the purity system is debatable; nothing Jesus is reported to have said or done in these stories indicates that he is disagreeing with the prevailing definitions of what counts as pure and impure. The challenge is rather at the level of how purity (and social acceptability) is conferred; Jesus' healings symbolically wrest control of such matters from priest and temple by acting as a conduit for God's healing (and cleansing) power.

Again, we need not assume that Jesus' contemporaries had any intellectual grasp of medical anthropology in order to suppose that Kleinman's

---

[56] Theissen, 'Political Dimension', 239; cf. Horsley, *Spiral*, 121–45.

reflections on the nature of illness may have some relevance here. As we saw in Chapter 3 (pp. 52–3), illness, as distinct from disease, is socially embedded, sickness as viewed in the context of social relations. If, as we have suggested, conditions were becoming worse for Galilean peasants, it seems likely that illness would increase as a result.[57] As for demon possession, so also for other forms of illness, this connection could be mythologically perceived in terms of demonic forces being responsible for both illness and social oppression. This does not at all mean that peasants would blame demons instead of the local elites who were exacting rents and taxes, but rather that demonic forces might be invoked as part of an explanation for why God allowed the rich to ride roughshod over the poor, alongside the perception that demons were responsible for at least some illnesses. Within the context of apocalyptic expectation, the defeat of such demonic forces would be seen as a necessary prelude to a dramatic change in social conditions, and healing could be seen as part of (or as symbolic of) that defeat.

Within Israelite tradition healings could also function as a more direct social critique. As we saw in Chapter 1, the most plausible way to link a healing ministry with messianic expectation would be through the eschatological Davidic shepherd tradition most clearly articulated in Ezekiel 34. This chapter not only promises that the Davidic shepherd will feed and care for his flock, but roundly condemns the existing shepherds of Israel for failing to do so. The description of these bad shepherds might well look like an excellent description of the urban elite as seen from the peasant perspective; instead of caring for their people, the rulers tax them, exact rent from them, lend money to them, and foreclose on the debts: 'You eat the fat, you clothe yourselves with the wool, you slaughter the fatlings; but you do not feed the sheep' (Ezekiel 34.3). To the extent that Jesus' healings could be interpreted as symbolically enacting the role of the ideal Davidic shepherd, they would also constitute an implicit symbolic critique of the existing rulers: 'the weak you have not strengthened, the sick you have not healed' (Ezekiel 34.4).

None of this *proves* that Jesus' healings and exorcisms have to be seen in an eschatological context, but it does suggest that such a context would help to explain their symbolic potency. The purely sapiential Jesus effectively says, 'Things are bad, but God wants you to live like this to make them a bit more tolerable.' The eschatological Jesus says, 'Things

---

[57] Horsley, *Spiral*, 181–4; Crossan, *Birth*, 293–302.

are bad, but God is about to change them; this is how you should live in the light of that.' Given a choice between the two, the eschatological Jesus would appear to have the more compelling message, and can thus be expected to make the greater impact. This greater impact would seem to be needed to explain the birth of the Church that wrote the Gospels.

Towards a synthesis

We have now covered what some may consider a bewildering variety of approaches. Chapters 1, 2, 4 and 5 were primarily concerned with the interpretation of texts, often at the level of the theological ideas they contain. Chapter 3 discussed a number of social-scientific approaches to healing and exorcism, including phenomena such as folk-healing and the cross-cultural anthropology of spirit possession, and the current chapter has combined elements of all these approaches, literary, theological, and social-scientific. The question may be asked whether this results in a convincing synthesis or simply an eclectic mess. To encourage the former of these two answers it may be useful to offer a brief review of how the salient points fit together.

The religious background gleaned from the texts surveyed in Chapters 1 and 2 suggests an association of miracle-working with prophets, healing as symbolizing national restoration (and in that context, as an element of eschatological hope), and the end-time expectation of the final defeat of demonic powers. The social-scientific approaches examined in Chapter 3 show not only how someone could plausibly be a successful healer-exorcist, but how that success might relate to the healer's social situation. On the one hand social stress could be a contributory factor to various kinds of illness, demonic possession included. On the other, dedication to the healer role in a manner that resonates with key aspirations of society at large could greatly enhance a healer's reputation (and thus his success); indeed, it may be a large part of what contributes to the healer's charisma. The particular historical circumstances in which Jesus operated were ones of increasing social and economic pressures in which illness could well be linked with oppression, and demonic possession be on the increase. These factors, together with the threat to traditional values, would make the Galilee of Jesus' day ripe for the appearance of millenarian movements, and the Jesus-movement seems to have had many of the characteristics of one. Against this background, coupled with that of the apocalyptic imagination exhibited in several Jewish texts, the symbolic import of Jesus' healings and exorcisms explains both their relevance to the eschatological preaching of the kingdom and the opposition they apparently provoked from the authorities.

It is important to bear in mind that we are seeking answers to two different but related questions here. On the one hand we are trying to understand what happened and why in terms that make sense to us. On the other hand we are trying to understand what people at the time made of Jesus' miracles. To use the jargon of social science, we are seeking both an *etic* explanation (how to make sense of Jesus' miracles on our terms) and an *emic* one (how Jesus' contemporaries may have made sense of them). These explanations are inevitably related, however, not only because they concern the same phenomena, but because even an emic explanation can only end up being *our* understanding of their understanding.

The distinction may become clearer with a relevant example. On an etic level we are describing Jesus as the leader of a millenarian sect. Since we are discussing healing we may want to combine this with Romano's model of how a folk-healer becomes a folk-saint. On both models Jesus' reputation could be expected to increase with his dedication to his role and his ability to focus existing expectations.[58] As we saw earlier in the chapter, several scholars see much of the content of Jesus' teaching as an attempt to defend traditional Israelite rural values in the face of urban pressure, and this would tie in nicely with how a millenarian prophet could be expected to behave. Malina's model (also mentioned in Chapter 3, pp. 61–2) of Jesus as conservative renovator also fits well here. To this mix we can add the model of a positive feedback loop (as already suggested in Chapter 3). The more Jesus healed, the greater his reputation became; the greater his reputation became, the more people had confidence in his ability to heal; the more confidence people had in his ability to heal, the more effective he became as a healer, and the higher up the healing hierarchy he was propelled. We may also expect such a positive feedback loop to have an effect on Jesus' own self-understanding; the more successful a healer he was, the more he might be persuaded that God's power was operative in him, and the more confident he might become; and the more confident he became, the more he would inspire confidence in others, and the more effective he would be.

An emic explanation of all this would look rather different. Presumably Jesus saw himself as called by God to carry out his prophetic ministry. It is clear that his ministry met with opposition in some quarters,

---

[58] Allison, *Jesus of Nazareth*, 170; Octavio I. Romano, 'Charismatic Medicine, Folk-Healing and Folk-Sainthood', *American Anthropologist* 67 (1965), 1151–73 (1170).

but Israel's tradition was familiar with prophets meeting with stubborn blindness and hardness of heart (e.g. Isaiah 6.9–10), so such opposition could just as easily confirm as undermine Jesus' sense of divine calling. On the other hand his success as healer-exorcist would tend to confirm, both to him and to others sympathetic to him, that God was with him, and the more powerful a healer-exorcist he became, the more he would feel God's power at work acting through him.

Again, despite the impression created by the Gospels and subsequent Christian piety, we do not need to suppose that Jesus started out with a clear plan of action, a consistently thought-out message, and an unshakeable sense of his own place in God's plan, and then set out to heal, preach, and cast out demons on the basis of all three. Quite apart from anything else, such notions may make Jesus too much of a modern Western individual instead of an ancient charismatic dyadic personality.[59] Both 'charismatic' and 'dyadic' are relational terms. In brief, a dyadic personality (as ancient Mediterranean persons are taken to be) judged their self-worth not through introspection, but on the basis of how others rated them. Thus, when Jesus asked Peter, 'Who do you say I am?' (Mark 8.29) he was not necessarily conducting an oral examination to see if Peter could at last get the right answer (although this is admittedly how it is made to appear in its Markan context), he could rather have been trying to gauge his standing among his closest followers in order to help define his own identity. That people came to believe Jesus was the Messiah does not at all require Jesus to have been the first person to think he was; it is by no means impossible that he came to think he was because other people told him so.

Much the same could be said of the term 'charismatic'. In social-scientific terms 'charisma' does not refer to the innate quality of an individual, but to the status accorded a leader by his followers. To be sure, such a leader must be able to strike some kind of chord in his potential followers in the first place, but from a social-scientific perspective it may be as true to say that the following creates its charismatic leader as to say that the charismatic leader creates his following.

It is fruitless to get into a chicken-and-egg speculation about whether Jesus first found he could heal because he was accorded a charismatic reputation, or whether he first gained a charismatic reputation because he

[59] For a fuller explanation of the concept of dyadic personality, Bruce J. Malina, *The New Testament World: Insights from Cultural Anthropology* (London: SCM Press, 1983), 51–70.

could heal. Whichever came first, both would quickly become mutually reinforcing in the kind of positive feedback loop already described.

To summarize: the proposal here is that Jesus' healings and exorcisms served both to authenticate Jesus' standing as an eschatological prophet (to others and to himself) and as a symbolic enactment of the eschatological kingdom of God he proclaimed, a kingdom that would replace existing power structures, such that proclaiming it challenged the legitimacy of those structures. To be sure, Jesus proclaimed the kingdom more as a promise to the poor than as a threat to the powerful (who seem not to have been his primary target audience), and within the context of that promise healings and exorcisms would have demonstrated God's liberating power in action. The combination of eschatological proclamation with healings and exorcisms performed in the context of that proclamation best explains how Jesus came to make the impact he did, and the various types of theory and evidence considered up to this point combine very well in support of this proposal.

7

Anomalous miracles

The problem of anomaly

The previous chapter discussed Jesus as a healer and exorcist but took no account of the so-called 'nature miracles', such as the feeding stories or the Stilling of the Storm. Yet these other miracles are arguably just as central to the Gospel portraits of Jesus. If they are simply dismissed as obviously unhistorical, this might cast doubt on all the miracle stories, for if the Evangelists or their tradition were capable of inventing fantastic accounts of Jesus performing impossible deeds, then perhaps the healing stories were equally fantastic inventions. Conversely, if Jesus was an exceptionally gifted healer, then perhaps he possessed other unusual abilities too, or if all the stories of Jesus' miracles have grown in the telling, then perhaps the seemingly impossible 'nature miracles' grew out of events that were rather more mundane. If we are to give a complete account of Jesus' miracles based on the evidence of the Gospels, some account must therefore be given of how the nature miracles entered the tradition.

'Nature miracle' is the traditional term for those miracles of Jesus that do not involve exorcism or healing. These include the Feeding of the Five Thousand (Mark 6.34–44 // Matthew 14.13–21 // Luke 9.11–17 // John 6.5–13), the Feeding of the Four Thousand (Mark 8.1–9 // Matthew 15.32–39), the Stilling of the Storm (Mark 4.35–41 // Matthew 8.18, 23–27 // Luke 8.22–25), the Walking on the Sea (Mark 6.45–52 // Matthew 14.22–33 // John 6.15–21), the Cursing of the Fig Tree (Mark 11.12–14, 20–21 // Matthew 21.18–22), the Wedding at Cana (John 2.1–11), and the Miraculous Catch of Fish (Luke 5.1–11; cf. John 21.4–8). The term 'nature miracle' is not ideal, not least because 'nature' is not a biblical category, but it continues to be used for want of a better term. The term 'anomalous miracle' may serve better, since the purpose of the present chapter is to consider those miracles that are problematic precisely because they involve seemingly anomalous events.

The category of 'anomalous miracles' is not identical to that of 'nature miracles', both because not all the 'nature miracles' are equally anomalous and also because there is another class of purported miracle that also seems anomalous, namely accounts of Jesus raising people from the dead (Mark 5.35–43; Luke 7.11–17; John 11). Even if the raising of Jairus' daughter (Mark 5.35–43) and the Widow's Son at Nain (Luke 7.11–17) leave open the possibility that the resuscitated persons were not really dead, Jesus' ability to revive them from a coma would still be remarkable, and the story of the Raising of Lazarus (John 11) seems to have been written in such a way as to exclude even that possibility.

Many of these stories narrate events that would constitute scientific anomalies had they occurred. Crowds of four or five thousand cannot be fed with a few loaves and fishes. To miraculously multiply loaves and fishes would require a breach either of the Law of Conservation of Matter/Energy (if we imagine the additional loaves being created out of nothing) or the Second Law of Thermodynamics (if we imagine them being spontaneously formed from inert matter that lay to hand). These laws are so fundamental to our modern scientific understanding of the world that we can be certain that a miraculous multiplication of the loaves and fishes would be physically impossible (the notices about the baskets full of leftovers at Mark 6.43 and 8.8 make it clear that some such multiplication is envisaged). Moreover, the feeding stories slide over important steps in the sequence of events. Mark 6.41 states that the disciples distributed the broken bread to the people and that Jesus divided the fish among everyone, while Mark 6.42 states that they all ate and were satisfied. So at what stage did the multiplication of loaves and fishes take place? What would it have looked like? Did fragments of bread swell like balloons as they were passed round? Did people suddenly find bits of bread and fish popping into their laps from nowhere?[1] If you were going to recreate the scene for the cinema, how would you shoot it without making the scene look grotesque? You would probably do the cinematic equivalent of what Mark does, by cutting from a picture of Jesus breaking the loaves to a picture of the crowds eating their fill; but this leaves a worrying discontinuity: the feeding stories are not just scientifically anomalous, they are hard to imagine as an actual sequence of events.

The other anomalous miracles are reasonably easy to imagine, but some are just as impossible as anomalies. Water cannot spontaneously be turned into wine. People cannot walk across a lake unless it is frozen, and

---

[1] Cf. David Friedrich Strauss, *The Life of Jesus Critically Examined* (4th edn, ed. Peter C. Hodgson, tr. George Eliot; London: SCM Press, 1973), 512–13, partially cited in E. Keller and M. L. Keller, *Miracles in Dispute* (London: SCM Press, 1969), 83.

the way the story of Jesus walking on the water is told clearly rules out that possibility. In other cases the anomaly is less clear-cut. It is conceivable that a storm just happened to abate at the moment Jesus rebuked the wind and waves; that, after all, is all anyone present could actually have observed; that the storm stopped *because* Jesus told it to would have been an interpretation of the event, not a direct observation. It would have been a highly striking coincidence, but highly striking coincidences do sometimes happen, so there is no scientific anomaly here, unless Mark's notice (4.39) that there was a 'great calm' is taken to mean that the Sea of Galilee instantly became as flat as a millpond. Again it is possible that Jesus cursed a fig tree that was found to be withered not long afterwards, or that he helped Peter locate a bumper catch of fish. The problem with such explanations is not that they are inherently implausible, but that the more they are invoked the more the point of the Gospel text is undermined. They would end up implying that Jesus gained a reputation as spectacular miracle-worker through a series of happy accidents.[2]

The same objections apply to attempts to rationalize the harder anomalous miracles. It could be, for example, that what actually happened at the Feeding of the Five Thousand was that Jesus' sharing of loaves and fishes encouraged everyone else present to share, so that it turned out that there was enough for all. The problem with such an explanation is that it is entirely speculative; there is no way of determining whether the alleged sharing took place or not. A further problem is that this type of explanation fails to do justice to the text, since Mark's story clearly presupposes that the crowd do not have any provisions with them and Jesus has to do something utterly extraordinary to feed them.[3] If the historical reality behind Mark's story of the Five Thousand was a bring-and-share picnic we are left with the problem of how such a mundane event became transmogrified into such a spectacular miracle.

Some may wish to suggest that there is no need for any rationalizing explanations, on the grounds that even the most anomalous miracles took place just as narrated, and it is only an irrational modern prejudice against the miraculous that prevents us from accepting them. It may also be urged that we should expect extraordinary things to happen when God is present on earth. Since this type of argument is sometimes encountered,

---

[2] See also Keller and Keller, *Miracles in Dispute*, 67–79.
[3] Morna D. Hooker, *The Gospel According to St Mark* (BNTC; London: A. & C. Black, 1991), 164.

we should pause to consider why it is incompatible with critical historical enquiry.

To count as critical a historical enquiry must be open to the possibility that things did not happen the way any given text narrates. It must also have some means of judging the historical plausibility of the events described. To do that, the critical enquirer needs some kind of notion of what counts as more or less plausible. No human enquirer has the benefit of knowing what is ultimately impossible from the perspective of Absolute Truth (whatever that might mean); we instead have to work with our best currently available understanding of the way things are. In our time and culture, such an understanding of the way the world works inevitably includes the best-grounded scientific theories. If we regularly use such an understanding of the world to make judgements about plausibility in everyday affairs and secular historical enquiry, then it is inconsistent to stop using them when investigating the historical Jesus. That does not mean that these fundamental scientific principles cannot be challenged; but rather that such a challenge would be an exercise in revising our conceptual framework, which is a different exercise from working within it, as critical historical enquiry generally has to do. A scientific anomaly is, by definition, a physically impossible event (according to our best current understanding). The occurrence of a physically impossible event must necessarily be less plausible than any competing explanation. To allow the possibility of physically impossible events is to undercut any means of sifting sense from nonsense, and so to nullify any attempt at historical explanation. This does not mean that anomalies cannot occur, but it does mean that the occurrence of an anomaly would defeat any attempt to reason historically about what had taken place, since an anomaly would sunder cause and effect and so negate our ability to reason from evidence to event. To entertain the possibility of anomaly (which is, it should be recalled, a concept distinct from that of miracle, see pp. xv–xvi) is to cut off the epistemological branch on which we need to sit into order to conduct a critical historical enquiry.

Moreover, historical enquiry should proceed in accordance with the criterion of the level playing field. This means applying the same standards of judgement to all texts, regardless of whether they happen to stem from a religion we believe in. If I am willing to entertain the historical reliability of a miracle story in the Gospels when I would not entertain anything similar if it appeared anywhere else, then I am not engaged in critical history. For example, Josephus reports a series of portents foretelling the downfall of Jerusalem, including chariots hurtling through the sky, the temple doors opening of their own accord, and a cow giving birth to a lamb in the temple courts (*J.W.* 6.288–300).[4] Perhaps some of these omens could be regarded as fanciful ways of construing natural phenomena, but we should surely draw the line at a cow giving birth to a lamb. Josephus ought to be an excellent source, since he was in a position to have witnessed many of these portents himself, and could have drawn on eyewitness accounts for the rest; yet most modern readers would probably view his reports with a certain amount of scepticism. But in that case, we should be equally sceptical about fantastic events reported in the Gospels, or else we are guilty of applying double standards.

The objection is sometimes made that denying the possibility of anomalies presupposes an atheistic worldview. But it is far from clear why the existence of God should make anomalies (as opposed to miracles) more likely. On atheistic assumptions the universe just happens to exist, and there is no particular reason for it to exhibit regular behaviour; it is just our good fortune that it seems to do so (but that might change and there could always be exceptions, since if there is no reason for regularity in the first place then there is no reason why irregularities should not occur). On the assumption of a Creator God, on the other hand, there is a possible reason for its regular behaviour, namely that God designed the order and maintains its existence. The existence of God is thus arguably a better guarantee of the impossibility of anomaly than the non-existence of God. Of course this does not necessarily follow, but as arguments go it is no less cogent than the assumption that the existence of God makes anomalies more probable. The assumption that belief in God makes anomalies more likely only works if we have prior reason to believe that God intervenes to cause anomalous events, and the only reason most people have for supposing that is that God is sometimes portrayed that way in the Bible. But if the purpose of the exercise is to make a critical assessment of the Gospel miracle stories, then to rely on the biblical portrayal of God in this way is to argue in a circle.

Some people may nevertheless claim that applying the methods of secular historical enquiry to the Gospels is wrong-headed. The argument will then be framed not in terms of presupposing the non-existence of God but of presupposing the falsity of the Bible, with the rider that the Bible should be the criterion by which other things are judged, and not something that should be judged by alien criteria. But this move is a retreat

---

[4] For a fuller discussion of these portents see S. V. McCasland, 'Portents in Josephus and in the Gospels', *JBL* 51 (1932), 323–35.

from critical historical enquiry into fideism (the doctrine that knowledge depends on faith or revelation). Any results based on such a move can have currency only among people willing to share its presuppositions. To count as historical in the wider public arena the method of enquiry must be the same as that for any other historical enquiry conducted in that arena.

Old Testament echoes

The anomalous nature of some Gospel miracle stories is not the only reason for regarding them with historical suspicion. There are also literary considerations. As we have already seen, many of the anomalous miracles are particularly replete with Old Testament allusions which point to deeper meanings beneath the surface of the narrative. This does not of itself prove that they are unhistorical, but it does offer a more plausible alternative to seeing them as accounts of actual historical happenings.

The deployment of the sea-crossing stories and feeding stories in Mark seems in part designed to echo the great exodus miracles of the crossing of the Red Sea (Exodus 14) and the manna in the wilderness (Exodus 16). Taken in isolation the Markan stories are not as obviously Exodus-like as they are sometimes taken to be. The feedings take place in the wilderness, but they take place through the multiplication of ordinary bread, not through the collection of manna, and the Gospel feeding stories show few of the features that retellings of the manna story frequently contain, such as the manna being supernatural food come down from heaven. Likewise the Walking on the Sea and the Stilling of the Storm lack the most distinctive features of the Crossing of the Red Sea, such as the parting of the waters and the drowning of the Egyptians. But the pairing of a feeding story with a water-crossing story in Mark 6.30–52 surely strengthens the Exodus allusion. The same is true of having the Stilling of the Storm (Mark 4.35–41) followed immediately by the Gerasene Demoniac (Mark 5.1–20), for although no pursuing Egyptian army is drowned in the first story, a demonized herd of pigs is drowned in the second. Neither is this allusion confined to Mark; the bread of life discourse in John 6.22–71 shows that the Fourth Evangelist also interpreted his version of the feeding story (John 6.1–14) in the light of the manna story, and like Mark, John also follows the feeding story with an account of Jesus walking across the lake (John 6.16–21); here the mention of a strong wind at John 6.18 is a possible allusion to Exodus 14.21 (the strong wind that drove back the Red Sea).

We have already seen (in Chapter 1) that Moses was the most significant miracle-working figure in Israelite tradition, and that he may have been seen as a type of the messianic deliverer, presumably in connection with the expectation of a prophet like Moses (Deuteronomy 18). A tendency to make Jesus' miracles more Moses-like is thus much what we might expect. Apart from the sea stories and feedings Jesus' miracles are not at all Moses-like. Although several miracles are associated with Moses in the Pentateuch and subsequent retellings of it (such as Philo's *Life of Moses* and Josephus' *Jewish Antiquities*), none of them make Moses remotely resemble the healer-exorcist depicted by the bulk of the Gospel miracle stories. The Gospels thus appear in part to be using the feeding stories and sea stories to make Jesus look more like Moses than he actually was.[5]

A closer look at these stories suggests that this is unlikely to have been their original purpose, however. The structure of the Markan story of the Feeding of the Five Thousand is not particularly similar to that of the manna story in Exodus 16, but is remarkably similar to the story about Elisha at 2 Kings 4.42–44. In this story the prophet Elisha feeds 100 men with 20 barley loaves. The Markan story is fuller, and the numbers are more impressive, but the basic story is the same: in each story the man of God (Jesus or Elisha) is given a quantity of loaves insufficient to feed the crowd before him; in each case his assistant or assistants protest that there is not enough food to feed everyone; in each case the food is given to the crowd, everyone is fed, and some food is left over. The two main details present in the Markan story but absent from the story about Elisha are (a) the breaking and blessing of the bread, and (b) the seating of the crowd in hundreds and fifties on the green grass. The language of (a) is quite close to the language of Jesus' breaking and blessing the bread in Mark's account of the Last Supper (Mark 14.22), while the details in (b) may be intended to overlay the story with allusions to the exodus. Calling attention to the fact that the grass was green, which on the face of it seems superfluous, may be intended to indicate that the feeding took place in the spring, around Passover time (John 6.4 explicitly dates the feeding at Passover), or else to suggest a pastoral motif (and hence Jesus as shepherd). Passover was the commemoration of the flight from Egypt. Moreover many commentators have suggested that dividing the crowd into

---

[5] On Jesus seen as the prophet like Moses and its relation to miracle stories see Barry L. Blackburn, *Theios Anēr and the Markan Miracle Traditions: A Critique of the Theios Anēr Concept as an Interpretative Background of the Miracle Traditions Used by Mark* (WUNT, 2; Tübingen: Mohr Siebeck, 1991), 251–6.

hundreds and fifties might be intended as a recollection of the division of
Israel into hundreds and fifties at the time of the exodus (Exodus 18.21,
25; Deuteronomy 1.15).[6]

Whether or not the alleged exodus overtones appear over-subtle, the
similarity of the Markan feeding story to the Elisha feeding story is unmistakable. Mark himself, however, shows little interest in the figure of
Elisha, and, as we have seen, his redaction of the story appears to give it
eucharistic and exodus overtones. It rather looks, then, as if an earlier version of the story was intended to draw the parallel with Elisha, before Mark
or his tradition gave it a more Mosaic twist. This suspicion is supported
by a detail in the Johannine version of the Feeding of the Five Thousand.
According to John 6.9 the five loaves Jesus was supplied with were *barley*
loaves, as in 2 Kings 4.42. This might not seem all that significant but for
the fact that *krithinous artous* (the Greek expression for 'barley loaves')
appears nowhere else in the New Testament and only in a handful of
places in the Septuagint, 2 Kings (or rather, as the Septuagint calls it, 4
Kingdoms) 4.42 being one of them. Given the similarity in structure between the two stories it is hard to resist the conclusion that the mention
of barley loaves at John 6.9 was designed to strengthen the allusion to
Elisha's Feeding of the One Hundred. But it is most unlikely to be John
who created this allusion, since he shows no interest in the Elisha
parallel, with the ensuing bread of life discourse (John 6.22–71) instead
presupposing a parallel with the manna story. This therefore suggests
that the Elisha parallel was created prior to John's use of the story.

We have already seen that in Israelite tradition prophets were the human figures most commonly associated with miracles. Of all the prophets
described in the Old Testament, it is Elijah and Elisha who come closest
to performing healing miracles of the sort Jesus performed. The Gospels
also portray Jesus as acting as spokesman for God. Within Israel someone
performing miracles and claiming to act as God's spokesman was likely
to be seen as a prophet, and according to Mark 6.15; 8.28, one popular
opinion about Jesus was indeed that he was 'Elijah, or one of the prophets'.
Mark evidently does not think Jesus was Elijah or one of the prophets, so
if he is citing this opinion only to correct it, it seems likely that the opinion already existed to correct.

Apart from healing and preaching, Jesus also seems to have been remembered for eating with people. His eating with 'tax-collectors and

---

[6] e.g. Robert H. Gundry, *Mark: A Commentary on His Apology for the Cross* (Grand Rapids:
Eerdmans, 1993), 325; Hugh Anderson, *The Gospel of Mark* (softback edn; NCB; London:
Marshall, Morgan & Scott, 1981), 175; Hooker, *Mark*, 166–7.

sinners' seems to have been a cause of offence (Mark 2.15–17). Moreover, whatever the historical value of the Last Supper accounts, it seems clear that Jesus was remembered as having broken bread and shared it on the night he was arrested, and that this soon became the basis of a rite performed in his honour (1 Corinthians 11.23–26). So if Jesus was already remembered as an Elijah-like prophet, performing miraculous healings, including the Elisha-like healing of lepers (Mark 1.40–45; 2 Kings 5) and eating with outcasts, and if he was remembered in the breaking and distribution of bread, it is not too hard to see how an Elisha-like feeding miracle involving the breaking and distribution of bread might come to be attributed to him.[7] It is possible that this was triggered by the memory of some particular large gathering at which Jesus ate with the crowds, but such a conjecture is not a necessary component of the trajectory sketched here. It is perhaps more likely that the attribution of this miracle to Jesus grew out of his followers' conviction that he fulfilled the scriptures, and so *must* have performed a miracle whose biblical prototype fitted so well. In any case, enough elements already existed in the Jesus tradition to make his performance of such a miracle seem plausible, and once accepted as plausible, the plausibility could quickly harden into 'fact'. This might happen even more easily in circles where Jesus' messiahship was interpreted in terms of the Davidic shepherd figure of Ezekiel 34, part of whose remit was to feed the flock (Ezekiel 34.23; cf. Mark 6.34).

The Feeding of the Five Thousand is not the only Gospel miracle story with a possible Old Testament prototype. As has already been noted, in itself the Stilling of the Storm (Mark 4.35–41 and parallels) is not particularly similar to the story of the crossing of the Red Sea. It is rather more similar to the story of a storm-stilling that occurs at Jonah 1.1–16. The Jonah story is fuller, but the Markan story shares with it a life-threatening storm at sea, the fact that the central character is asleep during the storm and is woken with a rebuke telling him to do something about it to avoid everyone perishing, the fear of the other people in the vessel, the sudden calming of the storm, and the awe-struck response of the other passengers. There is also a significant contrast: the other travellers aboard Jonah's ship obtain safety by throwing Jonah overboard, whereas the disciples are kept safe by Jesus' presence among them.[8]

---

[7] See also Blackburn, *Theios Anēr*, 242–3; Gerd Theissen and Annette Merz, *The Historical Jesus: A Comprehensive Guide* (tr. John Bowden; London: SCM Press, 1998), 294–5.

[8] See further John P. Meier, *A Marginal Jew: Rethinking the Historical Jesus*, vol. 2: *Mentor, Message, and Miracles* (New York: Doubleday, 1994), 931–2; Bas M. F. van Iersel, *Reading Mark* (Collegeville, MN: Liturgical Press, 1988), 112–14.

Pointing out the similarities between these two accounts does not automatically explain how something like the Jonah story became attached to Jesus. But there are other elements in the tradition that may help. For one thing, Jonah is the only Israelite prophet explicitly said to have come from Galilee (2 Kings 14.25), so that if Jesus had already gained a reputation as a miracle-working prophet, it might be that comparisons would be attempted with this other famous Galilean prophet. Comparisons of Jesus with Jonah are explicitly made in the Gospels: Matthew 12.41 // Luke 11.32 has Jesus say 'something greater than Jonah is here', while both Matthew 12.39 and Luke 11.29 contain an enigmatic saying about no sign being given to this generation except the sign of Jonah, which Matthew and Luke go on to interpret in different ways. If this reflects the presence of an enigmatic saying about the sign of Jonah floating around in the Jesus tradition, then it is understandable that people keen on attributing prophet-like miracles to Jesus might hit upon the storm-stilling incident of Jonah 1. This would be all the more plausible if Jesus was known to have made boat trips across the Sea of Galilee, which would have been a convenient mode of transport if his entourage included fishermen as the Gospels state (and there is no particular reason to doubt this).[9] Sudden storms could occur on the lake, and if Jesus and his disciples did make frequent boat trips it is entirely plausible that they encountered one, and that the encounter subsequently became retold and remembered in the light of the story about Galilee's most famous prophet (coupled with theological reflection about the significance of Jesus).

A further possibility is that the Stilling of the Storm is a variant of the Walking on the Sea, developed in the light of the Jonah story and other Old Testament texts. We have already discussed the points of resemblance between the Markan versions of these two stories (see p. 112). Many of them may be the product of Markan redaction introducing elements of the Stilling of the Storm into the Walking on the Sea.[10] That the Walking on the Sea developed entirely out of the Stilling of the Storm seems unlikely, however, since the Johannine version of the Walking on the Sea (John 6.16–21) looks both independent of and prior to the Synoptic version.[11] This is hard to prove conclusively, since arguments that John did not have Mark or Matthew before him when he wrote do not show that he could not have based his version on a recollection of having pre-

---

[9] Theissen and Merz, *Historical Jesus*, 295.

[10] Patrick J. Madden, *Jesus' Walking on the Sea: An Investigation of the Origin of the Narrative Account* (BZNW, 81; Berlin: Walter de Gruyter, 1997), 99.

[11] Madden, *Jesus' Walking*, 71–3, 90–5.

viously seen or heard the Synoptic version, but there are few obvious signs of dependence of the Johannine account on the Synoptic one, and in many respects the Markan version seems more developed, especially in the richness of its Old Testament allusions.

As Mark tells it, the Walking on the Sea is made to parallel the Stilling of the Storm in both structure and phrasing at several points, and the detail that the disciples were having trouble making headway against the wind (Mark 6.48) might conceivably be an echo of Jonah 1.13 (a strong wind is also mentioned at John 6.18 but it is not said to cause the disciples any difficulty). Although the story is replete with Old Testament allusions, they suggest a far higher Christology than Jesus as miracle-working prophet. Mysteriously, Mark states that Jesus meant to pass the disciples by. The language would appear to be that of divine epiphany, recalling Yahweh passing by Moses and Elijah (Exodus 33.21–23; 34.5–7; 1 Kings 19.11) and trampling the waves (Job 9.8; Psalm 77.19; Isaiah 43.1–16, see pp. 111–12). Given the high Christology that this tissue of Old Testament allusion creates, it seems unlikely that John would have passed over most of it had he obtained the story from Mark.

The Johannine version still appears to be an epiphany story, in that its main point is that the disciples start separated from Jesus (John 6.16–18), they encounter Jesus under sufficiently unusual circumstances to cause fear (6.19), and he then identifies himself to them in the language of divine self-revelation (6.20). Elsewhere in the Gospels this kind of sequence is characteristic of resurrection appearances, suggesting that the Walking on the Sea may have started out as a displaced resurrection appearance story. Similarities to the resurrection appearance story of John 21.1–8 strengthen this possibility. In the latter story the disciples again encounter Jesus *epi tēs thalassēs* ('by the sea', 21.1) while they are in a boat, there is again a delayed recognition (21.4) and, as in Matthew 14.29, Peter again leaves the boat to meet Jesus (John 21.7). At John 6.19 and Mark 6.49 the phrase *epi tēs thalassēs* is used to denote Jesus walking *on* the sea, whereas at John 21.1 it is used to denote Jesus standing *by* the sea. This suggests the possibility that John 21.1–8 represents an earlier form of a resurrection appearance story set *by* the sea which was transformed into a story of Jesus walking *on* the sea under the influence of the Old Testament motifs we have already explored.[12]

This is admittedly speculative, but it does seem preferable to most of the alternatives that have been suggested. It is most unlikely that the

---

[12] Madden, *Jesus' Walking*, 116–17; cf. Theissen and Merz, *Historical Jesus*, 303.

Walking on the Sea originated in some event in Jesus' ministry with a rational explanation, such as Jesus wading in the shallows, or walking along a concealed sandbar or log, since there would be little reason for such a mundane event to be remembered.[13] It is conceivable that the Walking on the Sea originated in some kind of mystical or paranormal experience of the disciples,[14] but this seems more speculative than an origin in a displaced resurrection appearance. It is also conceivable that the story is a purely symbolic creation, but the difficulty is then finding a sufficient basis in either Jewish or pagan ideas to give rise to a story of Jesus walking on the sea as an appropriate expression of theological conviction.[15]

Certainty is impossible, especially in a case like this where the tradition history seems to be of considerable complexity. The two sea miracles look as if they have become intertwined to some extent in Markan redaction, and it is conceivable that one helped give rise to the other some time before. Behind them may lie historical recollections of boat trips and storms on the lake, and a resurrection appearance on or by the lake, all reshaped by post-resurrection beliefs about Jesus and numerous Old Testament motifs.

Raising the dead

A separate class of anomalous miracle attributed to Jesus is raising people from the dead. In one sense this is impossible by definition: if we succeed in resuscitating someone who appears to be dead we normally conclude that they were not really dead after all: irreversibility is part of our concept of death. It could be, of course, that the ancient concept was more elastic, so that in some instances Jesus succeeded in reviving people who merely appeared to be dead. This could be argued with some plausibility in the case of the raising of Jairus' daughter (Mark 5.21–24, 35–43), particularly since the child was apparently not long dead and Mark has Jesus declare that she 'is not dead but sleeping'. Although John 11.11–14 has Jesus use sleep as a euphemism for death ('our friend Lazarus has fallen asleep'), the formula 'not dead but sleeping' at Mark 5.39 implies a contrast between the two states. Even if Mark supposed that the girl had really died, it is conceivable that he took over the story from a tradition that

---

[13] Madden, *Jesus' Walking*, 48–9; Keller and Keller, *Miracles in Dispute*, 69–71.

[14] Bruce J. Malina, 'Assessing the Historicity of Jesus' Walking on the Sea: Insights from Cross-Cultural Social Psychology' in Bruce Chilton and Craig A. Evans (eds), *Authenticating the Activities of Jesus* (Leiden: Brill, 1999), 351–71; Hugh Montefiore, *The Miracles of Jesus* (London: SPCK, 2005), 87–92.

[15] Madden, *Jesus' Walking*, 49–73.

told of Jesus reviving a girl mistakenly thought to be dead. Such a tradition would not be without its problems, since it is unclear how Jesus would have known the girl was not dead, or how he could have revived her from a coma (say). Nonetheless, it is not inconceivable that this story has a historical nucleus in some such incident.

If that were the case, it would help explain how stories of Jesus raising the dead entered the tradition. It may be, however, that such stories grew from no more than a conviction that since Jesus was at least as great a prophet as Elijah and Elisha, he should be able to equal or better their miraculous feats, which included raising dead children (1 Kings 17.17–24; 2 Kings 4.18–37). This seems to have been an influence on the raising of the widow's son at Nain (Luke 7.11–17), but it is also possible that the Elijah and Elisha stories helped other stories of Jesus healing near-dead or apparently dead people to grow in the telling. There is in any case no possible means of recovering the original incident or incidents behind such stories (assuming there were any), and it seems overwhelmingly probable that they have been shaped in the light of these Old Testament stories and post-Easter faith. At the very least it would have seemed appropriate that the one raised from the dead should have the power to conquer death in others, and stories of raising people from the dead would serve to symbolize the eschatological salvation Jesus was believed to bring.

This is particularly so of John's account of the Raising of Lazarus (John 11), where John makes it abundantly clear that Lazarus was really dead. Not only does Jesus himself say so quite bluntly (11.14), but we are told that Lazarus has been in the tomb for four days (11.17), which should probably be understood in light of the Jewish belief that the soul lingered by the corpse for only three. Moreover Lazarus' sister Martha is concerned that after four days the body will stench (11.39) and both his body and face had been wrapped (11.44). While it may be barely possible that this story grew out of an incident in which Jesus rescued someone who had been prematurely entombed, it hardly seems probable, and if the story of the raising of Lazarus did grow out of such an incident, then it has grown out of all recognition.

In any case, the Synoptic Evangelists show no knowledge of the Lazarus story, which is particularly telling since John makes it the occasion for the authorities' decision to do away with Jesus. In the Synoptics this function is performed by the 'cleansing' of the temple. John and the Synoptics cannot both be right, and in view of the difficulty posed by the scientific anomaly involved in John's story, it is best to view this story as effectively unhistorical.

It may be that the raising of Lazarus is but one example of John's tendency to heighten the anomalous nature of Jesus' miracles. The Synoptic Jesus heals blind men; the Johannine Jesus performs the much more difficult feat of healing a man blind from birth (John 9.1–7). The Synoptic Jesus heals a paralytic (Mark 2.1–12); the Johannine Jesus performs the harder feat of healing a man who has been unable to walk for 38 years (John 5.1–9). In all four Gospels Jesus feeds a vast crowd with a few loaves and fishes, but in John he also turns gallons of water into wine (John 2.1–12). It is hard to avoid the suspicion that such heightening of the miraculous is in the interests of John's heightened Christology, such seemingly impossible deeds being designed to manifest the glory of the Word made flesh (John 1.14; 2.11). It is not arbitrary to regard such stories as non-historical (at least in the form they have reached us).

It may be asked where such a judgement leaves the resurrection, since at first sight what applies to the raising of Lazarus would seem also to apply to the raising of Jesus. But while John's accounts of these two raisings contain parallels, they also contain important contrasts. Lazarus emerges from his tomb bound in bandages, presumably to return to normal life and die again within a few decades. Jesus leaves his bandages behind (John 20.7), is not instantly recognizable (20.14–16), appears suddenly in a room with locked doors (20.19–23) and returns not to normal earthly life, but in order to ascend to the Father (20.17). John himself does not regard the resurrection simply as the resuscitation of a corpse, and neither should we. In any case the primary witness to the resurrection in the New Testament is not the Gospels but Paul, particularly at 1 Corinthians 15.3–8. Not only is Paul the earliest writer to mention the resurrection, but he is the only one who claims to have encountered the risen Jesus himself. Admittedly, what Paul means by 'he appeared also to me' is notoriously unclear; Paul gives scarcely any clue concerning the nature of the experience, being more concerned to describe its effects (e.g. Galatians 1.11–17). It is clear that Paul believed he had encountered the risen Jesus and that the encounter was life-changing. Presumably the same applies to many others of Jesus' first followers.

What lies behind this belief is beyond the reach of historical investigation (we can speculate, but we cannot test our speculations beyond a general sense of their relative plausibility), but one or two more things can be said. First, whatever it was that Paul and the others experienced, it did not simply convince them that Jesus was risen from the dead, but that he was Lord and God's Messiah. If you met your recently deceased Uncle Fred and had a chat with him, you might be convinced that he was back from the dead, but you would be unlikely to jump to the conclusion that he was the Messiah, so something else must have been at work in the case of Jesus. Second, both messiahship and resurrection were eschatological concepts in first-century Israelite circles: the Messiah would be God's agent to usher in the age to come, and the end-time would be the time of general resurrection. This suggests that belief in Jesus' resurrection would have occurred within some framework of eschatological expectation. Whatever Paul and the others encountered, it could not have been merely a revived corpse, and since a revived corpse would constitute a scientific anomaly it can probably be dispensed with as a component of the resurrection; it is neither a necessary nor a sufficient condition of the New Testament witness. It seems clear that *something* happened to convince Paul and other early followers of Jesus that Jesus was not only raised from the dead by God but vindicated and exalted by God, but what precisely that something was is far from easy to determine, and would require a whole book in itself to discuss.[16]

Conclusion

This chapter has attempted to provide a plausible account of how miracle stories that narrate apparent scientific anomalies may have entered the Jesus tradition. In the previous chapter it was argued that Jesus gained a reputation as a healer-exorcist of exceptional prowess. Given that he also claimed to speak for God, he would probably have been seen by many as a prophet like some of the famous Old Testament prophets. This would have encouraged people to attribute some more prophet-like miracles to him, such as stilling the storm (a little like Jonah), feeding a crowd with a few loaves (like Elisha) and raising people from the dead (like both Elijah and Elisha). It is possible, but by no means certain, that some of these stories had a historical nucleus in rather more mundane events, but most of these stories owe their present form to being reworked, first in the light of the conviction that Jesus must have performed deeds at least as impressive as the great prophets of old, then in order to make him more closely resemble Moses, the greatest founder and redeemer figure in Israelite tradition, and also in the light of post-Easter beliefs about Jesus. We do

---

[16] For a range of views on the resurrection see Dale C. Allison, *Resurrecting Jesus: The Earliest Christian Tradition and its Interpreters* (New York: T. & T. Clark, 2005); Peter Carnley, *The Structure of Resurrection Belief* (Oxford: Clarendon Press, 1987); N. T. Wright, *The Resurrection of the Son of God* (London: SPCK, 2003); A. J. M. Wedderburn, *Beyond Resurrection* (London: SCM Press, 1999); Theissen and Merz, *Historical Jesus*, 474–511.

not need to assume that all this necessarily had to take a long time, or that it necessarily represents a series of stages within the same circle of believers. Exaggerated tales of Jesus' prophet-like deeds could have originated during his Galilean ministry, and have been taken up and developed among his closest followers soon after his resurrection in the light of resurrection belief.[17]

If at one level this makes the anomalous miracles essentially unhistorical, at another level they may still shed light on how the healings and exorcisms of the historical Jesus were understood. We have already seen this in relation to the Stilling of the Storm, where in Chapter 5 it was argued that Mark's assimilation of this story to an exorcism could well indicate how Mark understood the significance of all Jesus' exorcisms. Moreover, in Chapter 6 it was suggested that in his healings and exorcisms Jesus was engaged in the manipulation of symbols. The anomalous miracles continue that tradition by broadening and intensifying the range of symbols employed.

---

[17] A salutary example of how even the most fictitious tall story can gain rapid currency is provided by Arthur Machen, *The Angels of Mons: The Bowmen and Other Legends of the War* (2nd edn; London: Simpkin, Marshall, Hamilton, Kent & Co., 1915); the significance of this example for the Jesus miracle traditions is discussed briefly at Eric Eve, 'Meier, Miracle and Multiple Attestation', *JSHJ* 3.1 (2005), 29–30.

8

Conclusions

Summary

The argument of this book has progressed in several stages. We began by making a distinction between *miracle* (a strikingly surprising event with apparent religious significance attributed directly or indirectly to an act of God) and *anomaly* (an event which would contradict some fundamental scientific principle and which thus would appear to be ruled out as impossible on our current best understanding of the way the world works). Some purported miracles may also be anomalous in this sense, but not all are, any more than all anomalies would necessarily be miraculous. It was subsequently argued that we could not accept the possibility that an anomalous event had actually occurred without undermining the principles of historical criticism. This leaves the possibility of miracle open, provided the alleged miracle is not also anomalous in the strict (and fairly narrow) sense defined here. In particular it does not demand that we can only accept those miracles for which we can provide a natural explanation; it may be that all sorts of things happen which we cannot explain, and there is a gap between 'we cannot explain this' and 'this is contradicted by some fundamental principle of our best current scientific theories'.

The second major step was to survey what miracles would have meant to Jesus' contemporaries. We found that there was a variety of views, but that there was a tendency in Israelite tradition to associate miracles with prophets (although not specifically with the Messiah, except perhaps for the shepherd-prophecy of Ezekiel 34). We also found a considerable range of views on demonology and exorcism; belief both in demons and in the ability to cast them out seems to have been widespread, but interest in casting out individual demons and expectations of a final overthrow of demonic powers seem to have belonged to different strands of thought, only coming together in the Jesus tradition. In any case, the Gospel portrait of Jesus turns out to be quite distinctive in depicting him as a figure who performs multiple healings and exorcisms.

We then turned to the anthropology of healing and spirit possession. Several important conclusions emerged from this part of our study: first, that healing the kind of illnesses Jesus mainly seems to have healed, including casting out invasive spirits, is a reasonably well attested phenomenon, so that there is no particular problem in attributing such deeds to Jesus; second, that some healers may nevertheless be quite exceptional, and it may be that a peculiar dedication to their role helps explain their success; and third, that both illness in general and possession in particular may be the consequence of various forms of stress (whether domestic or political), so that there is often a wider, social dimension to healing. This does not, however, reduce healing to a form of folk-psychotherapy; successful healing will often result in the alleviation of symptoms and even the cure of the underlying disease. Moreover, the speed with which Jesus is reported to have effected his healings remains remarkable.

The fourth step was to examine the sources for Jesus' miracle-working activity. We surveyed a range of material, but while we found that all of it was compatible with Jesus' having been a renowned miracle-worker, the only material that offered any strong evidence of his miracle-working activity turned out to be the canonical Gospels. Rather than trawl through all four of them we next took a closer look at Mark, on the grounds, first that Mark's treatment of Jesus' miracles is in many respects the most interesting and second, that on the thesis of Markan priority, Mark's portrayal of a miracle-working Jesus is likely to be the main source for that of Matthew and Luke, and possibly John as well. We found that Mark was by no means a naive transmitter of tradition, simply recording Jesus' miraculous deeds for posterity, but an author of some sophistication, often deploying his miracle stories for particular narrative, theological and symbolic purposes. Mark's account therefore cannot be read as a straightforward record of Jesus' ministry. It is nonetheless noteworthy that Mark's narrative creates an implicit distinction in function between the healing miracles and the so-called 'nature miracles', with only the former forming part of Jesus' public ministry. There is thus an implicit recognition in Mark that the anomalous miracles need not be taken literally (even though they are presented that way at the surface level of the narrative). Conversely, the healing miracles and exorcisms are so pervasive in Mark's account of Jesus' public ministry that they could not be excised without doing terminal damage to Mark's portrait of him. This allows us to suppose that Mark (and the other Gospels) may preserve a general memory of Jesus' reputation as a healer-exorcist which can be used with due caution to gain a general notion of Jesus' healing ministry.

The fifth step was to gather up the insights gleaned from the previous four to propose a model of Jesus' healing ministry in its particular time and place. We saw that Galilean peasants at the time of Jesus were suffering a decline in their already marginal standard of living due to the pressures of recent urbanization. Feeling their traditional values threatened, Jesus' Galilean contemporaries could well have been ripe for a millenarian movement. It was suggested that Jesus' miracles would have helped him to be seen as an eschatological prophet, and may also have served to symbolize the nature of the kingdom whose coming he was announcing (through the defeat of demonic powers, the overturning of the normal order of things, the inclusion of outcasts in a restored and renewed Israel, and the healing of individuals betokening the healing of society). It is less clear that Jesus' healings and exorcisms caused him to be identified as Messiah in the sense of being seen as a fulfilment of specific messianic prophecies (except perhaps Ezekiel 34), but it is likely that they helped such an identification come about by spreading his fame and enhancing his reputation.

This left one final task: to account for the presence of anomalous (i.e. seemingly impossible) miracles in the Gospels. A plausible explanation was that these were added to the tradition as a result of attributing to Jesus the kind of miraculous deeds associated with prophets such as Elijah, Elisha and Jonah, since Jesus was already perceived to be a miracle-working prophet. A secondary stage then adapted some of these additional stories (in particular the feeding and sea miracle stories) to make them more Moses-like, since Moses was the most significant miracle-working figure in Israelite tradition. Alongside and superimposed on both stages was a Christological interpretation of these stories in the light of post-Easter faith. This symbolic intensification of the Jesus miracle tradition could be seen as a continuation of the politics of symbols Jesus engaged in with his healings and exorcisms.

Historical implications

As Dale Allison wrote, 'however much we better our methods for authenticating the traditions about Jesus, we are never going to produce results that can be confirmed or disconfirmed. Jesus is long gone, and we can never set our pale reconstructions beside the flesh-and-blood original.'[1] This comment applies as much to the present book as to any other work on the historical Jesus, so it may be asked what this study has actually achieved.

---

[1] Dale C. Allison, *Jesus of Nazareth: Millenarian Prophet* (Mnneapolis: Fortress, 1998), 7.

What this study has attempted is not to deduce 'what actually happened' in the ministry of the historical, earthly Jesus (which, by the nature of the evidence, would be an impossible task) but to propose a model of the sort of thing that may have happened and why. The model proposed is far from arbitrary, however; it is a model that appears to fit a number of converging strands of evidence (Israelite beliefs about miracle, the cross-cultural anthropology of healing and spirit possession, the particularities of Jesus' time and place, and the witness of the Gospel texts). To the extent that the model is a good fit, it has a claim on our attention. To the extent that it is a better fit than any other (which is likely to remain a matter of scholarly opinion), it has a claim on our assent. To the extent that this model is plausible it in turn makes plausible the claim that the Gospels preserve a genuine memory of a Jesus who really was a notable healer-exorcist, rather than presenting a tissue of myth, legend and invention. Jesus' healing and exorcizing activity is so central to the presentation of his ministry in the Synoptic Gospels (most of all Mark), that were it not possible to affirm the plausibility of this going back to the historical Jesus, we should have to conclude that the Gospels were too unreliable to give us any information about the historical Jesus at all. The plausibility of the model developed here shows that we are not forced to such a conclusion (though there may be other models that could do this just as well).

A model is an aid to historical understanding, but it is not itself a kind of historical fact, nor can it legitimately be used to generate missing facts, although it can help us evaluate the alleged facts already on offer. Indeed, without some operative model, we could not begin to make any historical evaluations. All work on the historical Jesus inevitably presupposes some model or another (even if the model is implicit and not consciously articulated by the investigator). Trying to make one's working model explicit is therefore a good idea.

The model developed here may seem a little messy, in that it combines a number of disparate elements drawn from a variety of sources; it is more eclectic than neatly systematic. But such messiness and eclecticism may be a positive advantage in enabling us to get a handle on a necessarily messy reality. A model is in any case not a proposed mechanism for how things must have been; it is rather a kind of conceptual framework to help us organize our ideas about how things may have been, and to guide our investigation by suggesting certain kinds of question and ways of providing answers to them. A model is not some kind of Universal Absolute Truth to which all sentient beings in all times and all places must consent; it is rather an aid to understanding for people in our particular time and place. The model suggested here would doubtless have made very little sense to scholars a thousand years ago and may make very little sense to scholars a thousand years hence. One does not have to surrender to cultural relativism to acknowledge that at least some aspects of human understanding are conditioned by the particular circumstances of time, place and culture; indeed, such conditioning forms an integral part of the very model espoused here.

To the extent that the model proposed here makes sense to the readers of this book, or rather, to the extent that it strikes them as persuasive, they will presumably agree that our best guess is that the historical Jesus was a remarkable healer and exorcist, and that his healing and exorcizing activity formed an important part of his ministry, vital if not central to his role, as a symbolic demonstration of the coming of God's rule.

But this is not all there is to be said about the historical Jesus. This book has concentrated on Jesus' miracles to the virtual exclusion of every other aspect of his ministry, apart from a general recognition that he preached the coming of the kingdom of God. A more rounded view of the historical Jesus would have to take every other aspect of his ministry, not least his teaching, fully into account. Such a rounded view might necessitate refinements to the model developed here, and only in the light of such a more rounded view could a fair assessment be made of the importance of Jesus' miracle-working in relation to other aspects of his ministry.

Theological implications

The purpose of this book has been historical, not theological; we have been primarily concerned with what can be said about Jesus' miracle-working activity on the basis of what counts as ordinary, secular historical enquiry in our time and culture. Yet many readers of this book will also be interested in the theological issues it raises, so it would be churlish to end without a brief attempt to address some of them.

Some readers may protest that the conclusion that Jesus did not work any anomalous miracles ('nature miracles' and raising people from the dead) is an assumption brought to our enquiry, not a consequence of the evidence. This is perfectly true, but it rather misses the point, which has been to construct a certain kind of model. Obviously, a model has to incorporate certain assumptions, and the viability of the model is in part a test of the viability of its assumptions. The assumption that anomalies cannot be regarded as historical events was not arbitrary; reasons were given for it (see pp. 145–50); but whether this is a fair assumption to use in relation to the historical Jesus may in part be tested by how well our model works overall. Readers unable to swallow this assumption will inevitably remain unpersuaded, and they and I will have to part company at this point, with the hope that they may nevertheless have found something of value in this book.

Other readers may be wondering whether our model answers the question 'did Jesus actually work miracles?' or whether it simply explains his healings and exorcisms away as non-miraculous. In fact, the model leaves this question open; it leaves it open precisely because it does conclude that Jesus was a remarkable healer and exorcist. The question whether Jesus' healings and exorcisms were really miracles is a theological question, not a historical one. Our model does not deny that Jesus' healings and exorcisms were perceived as remarkable; on the contrary, it supposes that this was the case. The question whether they were miraculous is thus equivalent to the question whether God was at work in Jesus' healings and exorcisms. This question cannot be settled by the means of historical enquiry. It could not be settled by any empirical means; even if we were able to hitch a ride on the Tardis and watch Jesus at work for ourselves, we should not be able to scan him for the emission of divinity particles, and to suppose otherwise is to confuse the kind of truth claim being made in the statement that God was at work in Jesus' healings.

The question may nevertheless be settled quite simply. Christianity asserts that God was especially at work in Jesus. A system of belief that did not assert at least that could hardly be called 'Christian'. It follows that from the perspective of Christian belief, once it is allowed that Jesus did indeed perform remarkable healings and exorcisms, it would be very odd indeed to deny that God was at work in them; thus, on the basis of Christian belief, it can be quite clearly asserted that Jesus did work miracles. Conversely, from an atheistic perspective it would make no sense at all to assert that Jesus really performed miracles, since on this perspective there is no God who could work through Jesus (although on such a perspective it would still make sense to assert that Jesus performed what other people at the time took to be miracles). A theist who is not a Christian believer, a modern Jew or Muslim perhaps, could decide either way, either that Jesus' healings and exorcisms were true miracles authenticating a prophet, or that they were due to sorcery or mere technique, deluding some people into falsely supposing that Jesus was a man of God (as Jesus' contemporary opponents seem to have argued). Thus, how one evaluates Jesus' healings and exorcisms theologically depends almost entirely on one's theological starting point. It is entirely reasonable for a

Christian believer to hold that Jesus really did perform healing miracles, but the miracles cannot be used as an argument for Christian belief, since one first has to be a believer in order to regard them as miracles.

Moreover, the question of Jesus' miracles has less relevance to the question of whether or not he was truly God incarnate than is often supposed. It is most unlikely that any of Jesus' Jewish contemporaries would have regarded the ability to perform miracles (however spectacular) as an indication that God was incarnate in the human being performing them (as opposed to simply empowering the performer), and it would be a theological mistake for us to make belief in the incarnation rest on Jesus' miraculous abilities. The two are strictly speaking quite orthogonal (i.e. not directly related). To put it at its most basic, the incarnation is a theological idea that cannot be proved (or disproved) by empirical evidence. Belief in the incarnation is a decision of faith, not a historical conclusion drawn from historical data. To be sure, the historical data could have considerable bearing on whether Jesus of Nazareth is an *appropriate* object of faith – if we had reason to suppose he was a moral monster then making him the object of faith would surely be inappropriate – but such judgements of appropriateness are quite different from drawing factual conclusions from empirical data, and involve much more than just our intellects. Christian faith is not primarily a matter of assenting to abstract theological propositions about Jesus, it is rather a matter of living one's life in the conviction that God is most fully revealed in Jesus.

A further question concerns the general reliability of the Gospels' portraits of Jesus. It would be possible to argue that this is theologically irrelevant, since it is precisely the Gospel portraits, and not any hypothetical reconstructions of the historical Jesus, that are foundational for Christian faith and preaching. There is some truth in such a response, and yet in practice most Christian believers would feel uncomfortable with the notion that the Gospels were almost total fabrications, religious myth dressed up in the guise of history. It may seem theoretically possible for faith to be adequately nourished on the basis that the Gospels are religiously edifying myths with no historical referent, but it is hard to imagine many actual Christian believers feeling nourished on this basis. This is not purely due to some unreasonable modern prejudice in favour of factual, empirical truth above other forms of truth (though such a prejudice does indeed seem to operate in the modern West); it has more to do with the perception that the Gospels make ostensible historical claims, so that a natural reading of the plain sense of the Gospel texts indicates that they intend to talk about a real person Jesus of Nazareth who actually said and did certain things in and around real places such as Galilee and Jerusalem at the time when real people such as Caiaphas and Pilate were in office. If this ostensible claim is a mistake or a lie, the reason for trusting the religious claims of these texts seems undermined (this may not follow in strict logic, but it is likely to be the psychological consequence for most people).

Whether readers of this book will feel reassured or threatened in this regard probably depends on their starting point. Those whose exposure to New Testament studies in general and historical-Jesus scholarship in particular have led them to despair of ever being able to say anything about the historical Jesus may feel somewhat reassured by an argument that supports the general reliability of one aspect of the Gospels' portrait of Jesus. Those who start from the position that everything stated in the Gospels must be more or less literally true will have gained no such reassurance. But there is clearly a great deal of scope for disagreement over how much historical reliability is sufficient for the Gospels to retain their religious value; in the end it is a matter of subjective judgement. The kind of historical reliability argued for here is of a very general kind, basically arguing that the overall impression of Jesus' healings and exorcisms created by the Synoptic Gospels is broadly correct, without thereby affirming any of the specifics, and explicitly excluding certain classes of miracle. My own instinct is that this is theologically sufficient. A more detailed knowledge of the particularities of Jesus' healing ministry would serve no theological purpose. It might even be theologically counterproductive, tending to emphasize Jesus as a particular person doing particular things in a particular historical context in a manner that might make his relevance outside that context seem questionable.

Indeed, that threat is already present, although it comes not so much from Jesus' healings as from his eschatology, as Albert Schweitzer realized a century ago. If Jesus was indeed an eschatological prophet, as the model I have developed here indicates, then we have to accept that what he prophesied did not come to pass. There was no catastrophic divine intervention, the kingdom of God did not come, and history went on much as before. Of course one can always reinterpret his eschatological prophecies so that they match what happened: Jerusalem did fall, the Roman empire did eventually collapse, and if the kingdom of God was really only the Church then that came too.[2] The problem with such reinterpretations

---

[2] For an example of this kind of interpretation, see Andrew Perriman, *The Coming Son of Man: New Testament Eschatology for an Emerging Church* (Milton Keynes: Paternoster, 2005).

is not that they are impossible, but that they invite the response, 'So what?' If that is all Jesus meant, what was all the fuss about? But if Jesus really did expect the coming of the kingdom of God in which all would be made well, then this scarcely remains credible when two thousand years later we have witnessed two world wars, the Holocaust, the threat of global terrorism, not to speak of ongoing violence, poverty and injustice on a scale not at all diminished from that known in Jesus' day.

The bind the Church finds itself in (at least in the West) is that many of its traditional symbols have lost much of their potency for modern men and women, but the Church can hardly ditch those symbols without abandoning what makes it distinctively Christian. Much of the theological interest in Jesus' miracles lies in their symbolic potency. In Chapter 6 it was argued that this was a large part of how they made an impact at the time. Symbols can still be highly potent today: just try (preferably as a pure thought experiment) burning an American flag outside the White House or turning up to a public event dressed in Nazi regalia. In many circles, religious symbols, including healings regarded as miraculous, continue to exercise a great deal of power. It would be an egregious error of epic proportions to dismiss symbols as 'merely symbolic', not least because symbols can often be the best if not the only way of apprehending any reality beyond the straightforwardly empirical and mundane. But we do not inhabit the same symbolic universe as Jesus' Galilean contemporaries, and so we cannot expect his miracles to have the same direct symbolic resonance for us.

It could be argued that miracle still has a powerful role to play. We have already suggested that miracle can symbolize the overcoming of the apparent natural order of things. To imagine the miraculous is to imagine that things could be radically different from what most people suppose to be inevitable. That does not mean we can achieve the truly impossible, either by sheer force of will or by banging on God's door demanding divine intervention, but it may mean that sometimes what seemed to be impossible turns out to be possible after all, and that amazing results may follow.

Yet if this kind of symbolic appropriation of miracle remains at the purely intellectual level it is unlikely to have much power in practice. Only if it can be imaginatively connected with *our* symbolic universe can full potency be restored. Connection need not imply conformity; connection may also be by way of challenge. In our society we tend to set a high symbolic value on order, as is exemplified by the intellectual dominance of scientific thought. Miracle symbolizes a disruption of the expected order.

Simply by offering a different imaginative point of view, miracle can challenge us to reconsider whether science really has all the answers, no matter what the question. Miracle can be similarly challenging to conventional religion. Religious belief generally becomes most dangerous when it is most sure it has all the answers. Jesus' miracles posed a prophetic challenge to the religious authorities of his day, and such a challenge needs to be heard afresh in every generation if religion is not to turn bad. But perhaps above all, the kind of worldview in which miracles have a role offers an alternative place to stand, a different imaginative perspective from which to view our workaday world. It may be valuable to occupy that different place from time to time, if only to listen to a different story that invites allegiance to a set of symbols not dominated by worldly attachment to greed and power. That, at least, would be consonant with the intention behind Jesus' miracles.

Bibliography

Achtemeier, Paul J., 'The Origin and Function of the Pre-Marcan Miracle Catenae', *JBL* 91 (1972), 198–221.

—— 'Toward the Isolation of Pre-Markan Miracle Catenae', *JBL* 89 (1970), 265–91.

Alexander, Philip S., ' "Wrestling against Wickedness in High Places": Magic in the Worldview of the Qumran Community' in Craig A. Evans and Stanley E. Porter (eds), *The Scrolls and the Scriptures: Qumran Fifty Years After* (JSPSup; Sheffield: Sheffield Academic Press, 1997), 318–37.

Allison, Dale C., *Jesus of Nazareth: Millenarian Prophet* (Minneapolis: Fortress, 1998).

—— *Resurrecting Jesus: The Earliest Christian Tradition and its Interpreters* (New York: T. & T. Clark, 2005).

Anderson, Hugh, *The Gospel of Mark* (softback edn; NCB; London: Marshall, Morgan & Scott, 1981).

Anderson, Øivind, 'Oral Tradition' in Henry Wansbrough (ed.), *Jesus and the Oral Gospel Tradition* (JSNTSup, 64; Sheffield: Sheffield Academic Press, 1991), 17–58.

Anderson, Paul N., *The Fourth Gospel and the Quest for Jesus: Modern Foundations Reconsidered* (London: T. & T. Clark, 2006).

Arnal, William E., *Jesus and the Village Scribes: Galilean Conflicts and the Setting of Q* (Minneapolis: Fortress, 2001).

Barnett, P. W., 'The Jewish Sign Prophets AD 40–70: Their Intentions and Origin', *NTS* 27 (1981), 679–97.

Barton, John, *The Nature of Biblical Criticism* (Louisville: Westminster John Knox, 2007).

Bauckham, Richard, *Jesus and the Eyewitnesses: The Gospels as Eyewitness Testimony* (Grand Rapids: Eerdmans, 2006).

Bell, H. Idriss and Skeat, T. C., *Fragments of an Unknown Gospel and Other Early Christian Papyri* (London: Trustees of the British Museum (Oxford University Press), 1935).

Betz, Otto, 'The Concept of the So-Called "Divine Man" in Mark's Christology' in D. E. Aune (ed.), *Studies in New Testament and Early Christian Literature* (NovTSup; Leiden: Brill, 1972), 229–40.

—— 'Miracles in the Writings of Flavius Josephus' in Louis H. Feldman and Gohai Hata (eds), *Josephus, Judaism and Christianity* (Leiden: Brill, 1987), 212–35.

Blackburn, Barry L., ' "Miracle Working Theioi Andres" in Hellenism (and Hellenistic Judaism)' in David Wenham and Craig Blomberg (eds), *Gospel Perspectives*, vol. 6: *The Miracles of Jesus* (Sheffield: JSOT Press, 1986), 185–218.

—— *Theios Anēr and the Markan Miracle Traditions: A Critique of the Theios Anēr Concept as an Interpretative Background of the Miracle Traditions Used by Mark* (WUNT, 2; Tübingen: Mohr Siebeck, 1991).

Boccaccini, Gabriele, *Beyond the Essene Hypothesis: The Parting of the Ways between Qumran and Enochic Judaism* (Grand Rapids: Eerdmans, 1998).

Boddy, Janice, 'Spirit Possession Revisited: Beyond Instrumentality', *Annual Review of Anthropology* 23 (1994), 407–34.

Bokser, Baruch M., 'Wonder-Working and the Rabbinic Tradition: The Case of Hanina ben Dosa', *JSJ* 16 (1985), 42–92.

Boobyer, G. H., 'The Eucharistic Interpretation of the Miracles of the Loaves in Mark's Gospel', *JTS* 3 (1952), 161–71.

Borg, Marcus J., *Jesus in Contemporary Scholarship* (Valley Forge, PA: Trinity Press International, 1994).

Bornkamm, G., Barth, G. and Held, H. J., *Tradition and Interpretation in Matthew* (London: SCM Press, 1963).

Bourguignon, Erika, *Possession* (San Francisco: Chandler & Sharp, 1976).

Broadhead, Edwin K., *Teaching with Authority: Miracles and Christology in the Gospel of Mark* (Sheffield: JSOT Press, 1992).

Brown, Scott G., 'Reply to Stephen Carlson', *ExpTim* 117 (2006), 144–9.

Burkill, T. Alec, 'The Notion of Miracle with Special Reference to St Mark's Gospel', *ZNW* (1959), 33–48.

Carlson, Stephen C., *The Gospel Hoax: Morton Smith's Invention of Secret Mark* (Waco, TX: Baylor University Press, 2005).

Carnley, Peter, *The Structure of Resurrection Belief* (Oxford: Clarendon Press, 1987).

Chae, Young S., *Jesus as the Eschatological Davidic Shepherd* (WUNT, 2nd series, 216; Tübingen: Mohr Siebeck, 2006).

Chancey, Mark A., *The Myth of a Gentile Galilee* (SNTSMS, 118; Cambridge: Cambridge University Press, 2002).

Cotter, Wendy, *Miracles in Greco-Roman Antiquity: A Sourcebook for the Study of New Testament Miracle Stories* (Abingdon: Routledge, 1999).

Crapanzano, Vincent, 'Introduction' in Vincent Crapanzano and Vivian Garrison (eds), *Case Studies in Spirit Possession* (New York: John Wiley & Sons, 1977), 1–40.

—— 'Mohammed and Dawia: Possession in Morocco' in Vincent Crapanzano and Vivian Garrison (eds), *Case Studies in Spirit Possession* (New York: John Wiley & Sons, 1977), 141–76.

Crossan, John Dominic, *The Birth of Christianity: Discovering What Happened in the Years Immediately After the Execution of Jesus* (San Francisco: Harper, 1998).

—— *Four Other Gospels: Shadows on the Contours of Canon* (Minneapolis: Winston Press, 1985).

—— *The Historical Jesus: The Life of a Mediterranean Jewish Peasant* (San Francisco: HarperCollins, 1992).

Davies, Stevan L., *Jesus the Healer* (London: SCM Press, 1995).

Dionisopoulos-Mass, Regina, 'The Evil Eye and Bewitchment in a Peasant Village' in Clarence Maloney (ed.), *The Evil Eye* (New York: Columbia University Press, 1976), 42–62.

Dodd, C. H., 'A New Gospel', *BJRL* 20 (1956), 56–92, reprinted in C. H. Dodd, *New Testament Studies* (Manchester: Manchester University Press, 1953).

Dodson, Ruth, 'Don Pedrito Jaramillo: The Curandero of Los Olmos' in Wilson M. Hudson (ed.), *The Healer of Los Olmos and Other Mexican Lore* (Dallas: Southern Methodist University Press, 1951), 9–70.

Donahue, John R. and Harrington, Daniel J., *The Gospel of Mark* (Sacra Pagina, 2; Collegeville: Michael Glazier, 2002).

Draper, Jonathan, 'The Jesus Tradition in the Didache' in David Wenham (ed.), *Gospel Perspectives*, vol. 5: *The Jesus Tradition Outside the Gospels* (Sheffield: JSOT Press, 1984), 269–87.

Driver, S. R., *A Critical and Exegetical Commentary on Deuteronomy* (ICC; Edinburgh: T. & T. Clark, 1896).

Duensing, Hugo, 'Epistula Apostolorum' in E. Hennecke et al. (eds), *New Testament Apocrypha* (tr. G. Ogg et al.; London: Lutterworth, 1963), vol. 1, 189–227.

Dunn, James D. G., *Christianity in the Making*, vol. 1: *Jesus Remembered* (Grand Rapids and Cambridge: Eerdmans, 2003).

—— 'Eyewitnesses and the Oral Jesus Tradition', *JSHJ* 6.1 (2008), 85–105.

Dwyer, Timothy, *The Motif of Wonder in the Gospel of Mark* (JSNTSup, 128; Sheffield: Sheffield Academic Press, 1996).

Eisenman, Robert H. and Wise, Michael, *The Dead Sea Scrolls Uncovered: The First Complete Translation and Interpretation of 50 Key Documents Withheld for over 35 Years* (Shaftesbury: Element, 1992).

Elliott, J. K. (ed.), *The Apocryphal New Testament: A Collection of Apocryphal Christian Literature in an English Translation based on M. R. James* (Oxford: Clarendon Press, 1993).

Eve, Eric, *The Jewish Context of Jesus' Miracles* (JSNTSup, 231; Sheffield: Sheffield Academic Press, 2002).

—— 'Meier, Miracle and Multiple Attestation', *JSHJ* 3.1 (2005), 23–45.

—— 'Reconstructing Mark: A Thought Experiment' in Mark S. Goodacre and Nicholas Perrin (eds), *Questioning Q* (London: SPCK, 2004), 89–114.

—— 'Spit in Your Eye: The Blind Man of Bethsaida and the Blind Man of Alexandria', *NTS* 54 (2008), 1–17.

Farrer, A. M., 'On Dispensing with Q' in D. E. Nineham (ed.), *Studies in the Gospels: Essays in Memory of R. H. Lightfoot* (Oxford: Blackwell, 1955), 55–88.

—— *A Study in St Mark* (London: Dacre, 1951).

Flusser, David, 'Healing through the Laying-on of Hands in a Dead Sea Scroll', *IEJ* 7 (1957), 107–8.

Fortna, Robert, *The Fourth Gospel and its Predecessor* (Edinburgh: T. & T. Clark, 1989).

—— *The Gospel of Signs* (Cambridge: Cambridge University Press, 1970).

Fowler, Robert M., *Loaves and Fishes: The Function of the Feeding Stories in the Gospel of Mark* (Chico, CA: Scholars Press, 1981).

Freyne, Sean, *Jesus, a Jewish Galilean: A New Reading of the Jesus-Story* (London: T. & T. Clark, 2004).

Garrett, Susan R., 'Light on a Dark Subject and Vice Versa: Magic and Magicians in the New Testament' in Jacob Neusner, Ernest S. Frerichs and Paul Virgil McCracken Flesher (eds), *Religion, Science, and Magic: In Conflict and in Concert* (New York: Oxford University Press, 1989), 142–65.

Glasswell, M. E., 'The Use of Miracles in the Markan Gospel' in C. F. D. Moule (ed.), *Miracles: Cambridge Studies in their Philosophy and History* (London: Mowbray, 1965), 151–62.

Goodacre, Mark, *The Case Against Q: Studies in Markan Priority and the Synoptic Problem* (Harrisburg, PA: Trinity Press International, 2002).

Goodenough, Erwin R., *An Introduction to Philo Judaeus* (New Haven: Yale University Press, 1940).

Grant, Robert M., *Miracle and Natural Law in Graeco-Roman and Early Christian Thought* (Amsterdam: Noord-hollandsche Uitgevers-Maatschappij, 1952).

Gray, Rebecca, *Prophetic Figures in Late Second Temple Jewish Palestine: The Evidence from Josephus* (Oxford: Oxford University Press, 1993).

Green, W. Scott, 'Palestinian Holy Men: Charismatic Leadership and Rabbinic Tradition' in *ANRW* II.19.2, 619–47.

Guijarro, Santiago, 'The Politics of Exorcism' in Wolfgang Stegemann, Bruce J. Malina and Gerd Theissen (eds), *The Social Setting of Jesus and the Gospels* (Minneapolis: Fortress, 2002), 159–74.

Gundry, Robert H., *Mark: A Commentary on His Apology for the Cross* (Grand Rapids: Eerdmans, 1993).

Hagner, David A., 'The Sayings of Jesus in the Apostolic Fathers and Justin Martyr' in David Wenham (ed.), *Gospel Perspectives*, vol. 5: *The Jesus Tradition Outside the Gospels* (Sheffield: JSOT Press, 1984), 233–68.

Harvey, A. E., *Jesus and the Constraints of History* (London: Duckworth, 1982).

Heil, John Paul, *Jesus Walking on the Sea: Meaning and Gospel Functions of Matt 14:22–33, Mark 6:45–52 and John 6:15b–21* (Analecta Biblica, 87; Rome: Biblical Institute Press, 1981).

Henrichs, Albert, 'Vespasian's Visit to Alexandria', *ZPE* 3 (1968), 51–80.

Holladay, Carl R., *Theios Aner in Hellenistic Judaism: A Critique of the Use of This Category in New Testament Christology* (Missoula, MT: Scholars Press, 1977).

Hollenbach, Paul W., 'Jesus, Demoniacs, and Public Authorities: A Socio-Historical Study', *JAAR* 49 (1981), 567–88.

Hooker, Morna D., *The Gospel According to St Mark* (BNTC; London: A. & C. Black, 1991).

Horsley, Richard A., *Archaeology, History, and Society in Galilee* (Valley Forge: Trinity Press International, 1996).

—— *Jesus and the Spiral of Violence* (Minneapolis: Fortress, 1993).

Horsley, Richard A. and Hanson, John S., *Bandits, Prophets, and Messiahs: Popular Movements in the Time of Jesus* (New Voices in Biblical Studies; Minneapolis: Winston Press, 1985).

Hull, John M., *Hellenistic Magic and the Synoptic Tradition* (SBT, 2nd series, 28; London: SCM Press, 1974).

Jeremias, J., 'An Unknown Gospel with Johannine Elements (Pap. Egerton 2)' in E. Hennecke et al. (eds), *New Testament Apocrypha* (tr. G. Ogg et al.; London: Lutterworth, 1963), vol. 1, 94–7.

Juel, Donald H., *A Master of Surprise: Mark Interpreted* (Minneapolis: Fortress, 1994).

Kahl, Werner, *New Testament Miracle Stories in their Religious-Historical Setting: A Religionsgeschichtliche Comparison from a Structural Perspective* (FRLANT, 163; Göttingen: Vandenhoeck & Ruprecht, 1994).

Kee, Howard C., 'Aretalogy and Gospel', *JBL* 92 (1973), 402–22.

—— *Miracle in the Early Christian World: A Study in Sociohistorical Method* (New Haven: Yale University Press, 1983).

—— 'The Terminology of Mark's Exorcism Stories', *NTS* 14 (1967–8), 232–46.

Kelber, Werner H., *Mark's Story of Jesus* (Philadelphia: Fortress, 1979).

—— *The Oral and the Written Gospel: The Hermeneutics of Speaking and Writing in the Synoptic Tradition, Mark, Paul and Q* (Voices in Performance and Text, Bloomington and Indianapolis: Indiana University Press, 1997).

Keller, E. and Keller, M. L., *Miracles in Dispute* (London: SCM Press, 1969).

Kleinman, Arthur, *The Illness Narratives: Suffering, Healing and the Human Condition* (New York: Basic Books, 1988).

—— *Patients and Healers in the Context of Culture* (Comparative Studies of Health Systems and Medical Care, 3; Berkeley: University of California Press, 1980).

Kloppenborg, John S., *The Formation of Q: Trajectories in Ancient Wisdom Collections* (Studies in Antiquity and Christianity; Harrisburg, PA: Trinity Press International, 1999).

Kloppenborg Verbin, John S., *Excavating Q: The History and Setting of the Sayings Gospel* (Edinburgh: T. & T. Clark, 2000).

Koester, Helmut, *Ancient Christian Gospels: Their History and Development* (London: SCM Press; Philadelphia: Trinity Press International, 1990).

Kvalbein, Hans, 'The Wonders of the End-Time: Metaphoric Language in 4Q521 and the Interpretation of Matthew 11.5 par', *JSP* 18 (1998), 87–110.

Lake, Kirsopp, *The Apostolic Fathers*, vol. 1 (LCL; London: Heinemann, 1912).

—— *Eusebius: The Ecclesiastical History*, vol. 1 (LCL, 2 vols; London: Heinemann, 1926).

Layton, Bentley, *The Gnostic Scriptures: A New Translation with Annotations and Introductions by Bentley Layton* (London: SCM Press, 1987).

Lewis, I. M., *Ecstatic Religion: A Study of Shamanism and Spirit Possession* (2nd edn; London: Routledge, 1989).

McCane, Byron R., *Roll Back the Stone: Death and Burial in the World of Jesus* (Harrisburg: Trinity Press International, 2003).

McCasland, S. V., 'Portents in Josephus and in the Gospels', *JBL* 51 (1932), 323–35.

Machen, Arthur, *The Angels of Mons: The Bowmen and Other Legends of the War* (2nd edn; London: Simpkin, Marshall, Hamilton, Kent & Co., 1915).

Mack, Burton L., *A Myth of Innocence: Mark and Christian Origins* (Philadelphia: Fortress, 1988).

MacRae, G., 'Miracle in the *Antiquities* of Josephus' in C. F. D. Moule (ed.), *Miracles: Cambridge Studies in their Philosophy and History* (London: Mowbray, 1965), 129–47.

Madden, Patrick J., *Jesus' Walking on the Sea: An Investigation of the Origin of the Narrative Account* (BZNW, 81; Berlin: Walter de Gruyter, 1997).

Malina, Bruce J., 'Assessing the Historicity of Jesus' Walking on the Sea: Insights from Cross-Cultural Social Psychology' in Bruce Chilton and Craig A. Evans (eds), *Authenti-cating the Activities of Jesus* (Leiden: Brill, 1999), 351–71.

—— 'Jesus as Charismatic Leader?', *BTB* 14 (1984), 55–62.

—— *The New Testament World: Insights from Cultural Anthropology* (London: SCM Press, 1983).

Marshall, Christopher D., *Faith as a Theme in Mark's Narrative* (Cambridge: Cambridge University Press, 1989).

Meeks, Wayne A., *The Prophet-King: Moses Traditions and the Johannine Christology* (NovTSup, 14; Leiden: Brill, 1967).

Meier, John P., *A Marginal Jew: Rethinking the Historical Jesus*, vol. 1: *The Roots of the Problem and the Person* (New York: Doubleday, 1991).

—— *A Marginal Jew: Rethinking the Historical Jesus*, vol. 2: *Mentor, Message, and Miracles* (New York: Doubleday, 1994).

Micklem, E. R., *Miracles and the New Psychology* (London: Oxford University Press, 1922).

Montefiore, Hugh, *The Miracles of Jesus* (London: SPCK, 2005).

Moule, C. F. D., 'Excursus 1: The Vocabulary of Miracle' in C. F. D. Moule (ed.), *Miracles: Cambridge Studies in their Philosophy and History* (London: Mowbray, 1965), 235–8.

Neirynck, Frans, *Evangelica II 1982–1991: Collected Essays by Frans Neirynck* (BETL, 99; Leuven: Leuven University Press, 1991).

Neusner, Jacob, *Judaism: The Evidence of the Mishnah* (Chicago: University of Chicago Press, 1981).

Neyrey, Jerome H., 'Miracles, in Other Words: Social Science Perspectives on Healings' in John C. Cavadini (ed.), *Miracles in Jewish and Christian Antiquity* (Notre Dame, IN: University of Notre Dame Press, 1999), 19–55.

Nicol, W., *The Sēmeia in the Fourth Gospel: Tradition and Redaction* (NovTSup, 32; Leiden: Brill, 1972).

Nitzan, Bilha, *Qumran Prayer and Religious Poetry* (tr. Jonathan Chipman; STDJ, 12; Leiden: Brill, 1994).

Olson, K. A., 'Eusebius and the Testimonium Flavianum', *CBQ* 61 (1999), 305–22.

Oxford Society of Historical Theology, *The New Testament in the Apostolic Fathers* (Oxford: Clarendon Press, 1905).

Pantuck, Allen J. and Brown, Scott G., 'Morton Smith as M. Madiotes: Stephen Carlson's Attribution of *Secret Mark* to a Bald Swindler', *JSHJ* 6 (2008), 106–25.

Perriman, Andrew, *The Coming Son of Man: New Testament Eschatology for an Emerging Church* (Milton Keynes: Paternoster, 2005).

Perrin, Nicholas, 'The Limits of a Reconstructed Q' in Mark S. Goodacre and Nicholas Perrin (eds), *Questioning Q* (London: SPCK, 2004), 71–88.

Petersen, Norman R., 'The Composition of Mark 4:1—8:26', *HTR* 73 (1980), 185–217.

Pilch, John J., *Healing in the New Testament: Insights from Medical and Mediterranean Anthropology* (Minneapolis: Fortress, 2000).

Prince, Raymond, 'Foreword' in Vincent Crapanzano and Vivian Garrison (eds), *Case Studies in Spirit Possession* (New York: John Wiley & Sons, 1977), xi–xvi.

Pryor, John W., 'Papyrus Egerton 2 and the Fourth Gospel', *Australian Biblical Review* 37 (1989), 1–13.

Puech, E., 'Une apocalypse messianique (4Q521)', *RevQ* 15 (1992), 475–522.

Räisänen, Heikki, *The 'Messianic Secret' in Mark's Gospel* (Edinburgh: T. & T. Clark, 1990).

Reed, Jonathan L., *Archaeology and the Galilean Jesus* (Harrisburg, PA: Trinity Press International, 2000).

Remus, Harold, *Pagan–Christian Conflict over Miracle in the Second Century* (Patristic Monograph Series, 10; Cambridge, MA: Philadelphia Patristic Foundation, 1983).

Rivkin, Ellis, *What Crucified Jesus?* (London: SCM Press, 1984).

Romano, Octavio I., 'Charismatic Medicine, Folk-Healing and Folk-Sainthood', *American Anthropologist* 67 (1965), 1151–73.

Sacchi, Paolo, *Jewish Apocalyptic and its History* (tr. William J. Shortt; JSPSup, 20; Sheffield: Sheffield Academic Press, 1996).

Sanders, E. P., *Jesus and Judaism* (London: SCM Press, 1985).

Saunders, Lucie Wood, 'Variants in Zar Experience in an Egyptian Village' in Vincent Crapanzano and Vivian Garrison (eds), *Case Studies in Spirit Possession* (New York: John Wiley & Sons, 1977), 177–90.

Smith, Morton, *Clement of Alexandria and a Secret Gospel of Mark* (Cambridge, MA: Harvard University Press, 1973).

—— *Jesus the Magician* (London: Victor Gollancz, 1978).

Stemberger, Günter, *Introduction to the Talmud and Midrash* (2nd edn, ed. and tr. Markus Bockmühl; Edinburgh: T. & T. Clark, 1996).

Strauss, David Friedrich, *The Life of Jesus Critically Examined* (4th edn, ed. Peter C. Hodgson, tr. George Eliot; London: SCM Press, 1973).

Strecker, Christian, 'Jesus and the Demoniacs' in Wolfgang Stegemann, Bruce J. Malina and Gerd Theissen (eds), *The Social Setting of Jesus and the Gospels* (Minneapolis: Fortress, 2002), 117–33.

Tabor, James D. and Wise, Michael O., '4Q521 "On Resurrection" and the Synoptic Gospel Tradition: A Preliminary Study', *JSP* 10 (1992), 149–62.

Theissen, Gerd, *The Gospels in Context: Social and Political History in the Synoptic Tradition* (Edinburgh: T. & T. Clark, 1992).

—— *Miracle Stories of the Early Christian Tradition* (ed. John Riches, tr. Francis McDonagh; Studies of the New Testament and Its World; Edinburgh: T. & T. Clark, 1983).

—— 'The Political Dimension of Jesus' Activities' in Wolfgang Stegemann, Bruce J. Malina and Gerd Theissen (eds), *The Social Setting of Jesus and the Gospels* (Minneapolis: Fortress, 2002), 225–50.

Theissen, Gerd and Merz, Annette, *The Historical Jesus: A Comprehensive Guide* (tr. John Bowden; London: SCM Press, 1998).

Tiede, David Lenz, *The Charismatic Figure as Miracle Worker* (SBLDS, 1; Missoula, MT: SBL, 1972).

Tuckett, Christopher M., *Q and the History of Early Christianity* (Edinburgh: T. & T. Clark, 1997).

Twelftree, Graham H., *In the Name of Jesus: Exorcism among Early Christians* (Grand Rapids, MI: Baker Academic, 2007).

—— *Jesus the Exorcist: A Contribution to the Study of the Historical Jesus* (WUNT, 2nd series, 54; Tübingen: Mohr Siebeck, 1993).

—— *Jesus the Miracle Worker: A Historical and Theological Study* (Downers Grove, IL: InterVarsity Press, 1999).

van der Loos, Hendrick, *The Miracles of Jesus* (tr. T. S. Preston; NovTSup, 9; Leiden: Brill, 1965).

van Iersel, Bas M. F., *Mark: A Reader-Response Commentary* (tr. W. H. Bisscheroux; JSNTSup, 164; Sheffield: Sheffield Academic Press, 1998).

—— *Reading Mark* (Collegeville, MN: Liturgical Press, 1988).

Vansina, Jan, *Oral Tradition as History* (London: James Currey, 1985).

Vermes, Geza, *The Complete Dead Sea Scrolls in English* (Harmondsworth: Penguin Books, 1998).

—— *Jesus the Jew* (2nd edn; London: SCM Press, 1983).

Vielhauer, P., 'Jewish-Christian Gospels' in E. Hennecke et al. (eds), *New Testament Apocrypha*, vol. 1 (tr. G. Ogg et al.; London: Lutterworth, 1963), 117–65.

Weatherhead, L., *Psychology, Religion and Healing: A Critical Study of All the Non-Physical Means of Healing, with an Examination of the Principles Underlying Them, together with some Conclusions regarding Further Investigation and Action in this Field* (2nd edn; London: Hodder & Stoughton, 1963).

Wedderburn, A. J. M., *Beyond Resurrection* (London: SCM Press, 1999).

Weeden, Theodore J., 'The Heresy that Necessitated Mark's Gospel', *ZNW* 59 (1968), 145–58.

Wilson, Robert R., 'Prophecy and Ecstasy: A Reexamination', *JBL* 98 (1979), 321–37.

Wise, Michael O. and Tabor, James D., 'The Messiah at Qumran', *Biblical Archaeology Review* 18 (1992), 60–5.

Wolfson, Harry Austryn, *Philo*, vol. 1 (rev. edn; Cambridge, MA: Harvard University Press, 1968).

Wrede, William, *The Messianic Secret* (tr. James C. G. Greig; Cambridge: James Clarke, 1971).

Wright, N. T., *The Resurrection of the Son of God* (London: SPCK, 2003).

Yamauchi, Edwin, 'Magic or Miracle? Diseases, Demons and Exorcisms' in David Wenham and Craig Blomberg (eds), *Gospel Perspectives*, vol. 6: *The Miracles of Jesus* (Sheffield: JSOT Press, 1986), 89–183.

Index of ancient and biblical sources

9.5 12
15.22 10

3 Maccabees
2.21–24 12
5—6 11

Psalms of Solomon
17.40 21

Sibylline Oracles
2.167 12, 21
3.63–70 12, 21
3.741–51 47
8.205–7 47

Sirach
15.3 108 n.24
24.5–6 112
24.19–22 108 n.24
36.1–17 10
38.1–15 8
44—50 9
48.17–22 20
48.21 10
48.23 12

Testament of Levi
18 30

Testament of Naphtali
6 111

Tobit
3.7–8 34
8.1–8 34
14.15 35

Wisdom of Solomon
5.17–23 8, 9
10.6–7 8

11—19 8, 11
16.5–14 7
18.20–25 7
19.6 5
19.18 4
19.22 8

DEAD SEA SCROLLS

1QapGen 7, 33, 68
1QH 11.6 111
1QH 11.12–18 111
1QH 14.23–4 111
1QH 15.4–5 111
1QM 11.10 8
1QS 3.13—4.1 30
4Q185 1.15 9
4Q242 32
4Q510 31
4Q511 31
4Q521 47–9
4Q560 32, 38
11Q5 20, 31–2, 36
11Q5 27.2–4 31
11Q5 27.10 31
11Q11 20, 31–2, 36
CD 12.2–3 30

RABBINIC LITERATURE

Babylonian Talmud
Berakoth 33a 15
Berakoth 34b 16
Me'il 17b 37
Ta'anit 24b–25a 15

Midrash on Ecclesiastes
1.21 21

Mishnah
Berakoth 5.5 14, 16
Sotah 9.15 14
Ta'an 3.8 13

Numbers Rabbah
19.8 37

Tosefta
Berakoth 2.30 14

JOSEPHUS

Against Apion
2.53–4 11

Antiquities
1.14 46
2.284–7 23
2.286 23, 35
5.27 10
5.60 10
5.205 10
5.303 10
6.27 10
6.166–9 7, 36
8.45–9 7, 35
8.319 10
8.322 10
8.346 10
8.349 10
9.48–50 10
9.212–13 10
9.225 11
10.21 10
10.214 11
10.258–62 11
13.318–19 128
14.22–4 14, 72
14.22 10
14.390 10

Index of modern authors

(NB: Only authors whose names appear in the main text are indexed here, not the footnotes.)

Index of subjects